Genesis Chronology and Egyptian King-Lists

VOLUME I: EGYPT'S DYNASTIC PERIOD

Books by Gary Greenberg

❖ The Moses Mystery: The Egyptian Origins of the Jewish People

❖ 101 Myths of the Bible: How Ancient Scribes Invented Biblical History

❖ King David Versus Israel: How a Hebrew Tyrant Hated by the Israelites Became a Biblical Hero

❖ The Judas Brief: A Critical Investigation into the Arrest and Trials of Jesus and the Role of the Jews

❖ Who Wrote the Gospels? Why New Testament Scholars Challenge Church Traditions

❖ Proving Jesus' Authority in Mark and John: Overlooked Evidence of a Synoptic Relationship

❖ Manetho: A Study in Egyptian Chronology

Excerpts from Book Reviews of The Moses Mystery

"seems to delight in a game of scholarly 'gotcha'"—*N.Y. Times*

"insightful and valuable." —*KMT Magazine*

"Fascinating and thought provoking."—*Today's Librarian*

"Guaranteed to raise hackles and lively debate." —*Denver Post*

"A must read for those interested in biblical scholarship."—*Tennessee Tribune*

"An ingenious comparison of biblical and Egyptian history."—*St. Louis Post-Dispatch*

This is an intriguing and controversial book—*MultiCultural Review*

From a review of The Judas Brief

"a keen eye for the ways religious and political motives have shaped the story of Jesus' arrest and execution." —*Catholic Biblical Quarterly*

Genesis Chronology and Egyptian King-Lists

The Egyptian Origins of Genesis History

VOLUME I: EGYPT'S DYNASTIC PERIOD

Gary Greenberg

Pereset Press
NEW YORK, NEW YORK

2019

A Pereset Press Book

Pereset Press
P. O. Box 25
New York, NY 10008
info@peresetpress.com
www.persetpress.com

Book Layout ©2017 BookDesignTemplates.com

Library of Congress Control Number: 2018963629
ISBN 978-0-9814966-5-8

Names: Greenberg, Gary, 1943-, author.
Title: Genesis chronology and Egyptian king-lists : the Egyptian origins of Genesis history , volume 1 , Egypt's dynastic period / Gary Greenberg.
Description: Includes bibliographic references and index. | New York, NY: Pereset Press, 2019.
Identifiers: LCCN 2018963629 | ISBN 978-0-9814966-5-8
Subjects: LCSH Bible--Chronology. | Egypt--History--Chronology. | Egypt--Antiquities. | Egypt in the Bible. | Bible. Old Testament--Criticism, interpretation, etc. | Egypt--Historiography. | Egypt--Kings and rulers. | BISAC RELIGION / Biblical Criticism & Interpretation / Old Testament | HISTORY / Ancient Egypt | RELIGION / Judaism / History
Classification: LCC DT83 .G74 2019 | DDC 932/.01--dc23

Contents

List of Tables

Note on Citations and Terminology

All biblical quotations, unless indicated otherwise, are from the New Revised Standard Version.

All references to Manetho's history of Egypt are from the Loeb Classical Library edition, published by Harvard University Press and translated by W. G. Waddell. Because the Manetho text presents an orderly sequence of Egyptian Dynasties in simple lists (except for the Second Intermediate Period) and are easy to locate, I have omitted citations to the text in such instances. On those occasions where the text cited is not easily located, I include a footnote citing Waddell and the page number.

All references to entries in the Table of Abydos, the Table of Sakkara, and the Royal Canon of Turin king-lists are taken from the chronological appendix to Sir Alan Gardiner's *Egypt of the Pharaohs*.

As to Egyptian names, there is frequent disagreement as to the spelling and, on occasion, the order of syllables. In large part this is due to the lack of vowels in the Egyptian hieroglyphs. As a rule, I follow Gardiner's spelling in *Egypt of the Pharaohs*. However, when quoting from a text, I retain the spelling used by the author I have quoted On some occasions, with a particularly well-known pharaoh, I might default to a popular spelling of that pharaoh's name.

1 The Mystery of the Genesis "Begats"

FULLY CLOAKED AND HEAVILY DISGUISED, THE BOOK OF GENESIS HIDES A deep dark secret about the origins of Genesis history and its influence on Jewish beliefs. The chief clue in Genesis consists of two schematically-connected chronological lists of patriarchal births and deaths that begin with the birth of Adam and conclude with the birth of Abraham. Although scholars obviously know these lists exist, they have no idea that such a hidden mystery stands behind the text.

This lack of knowledge is understandable. To recognize that this secret even exists, let alone that it can be uncovered, a biblical scholar must first become fully familiar with two Egyptian fields of study, chronology and mythology. Few, if any, biblical scholars show any interest in either of these Egyptian disciplines.

If you ever go to a major conference of biblical scholars, with dozens (sometimes hundreds) of panels, and, if by chance they might devote one panel to the subject of Egypt and Israel, the conference usually assigns the event to one of the least desirable spots in the program, possibly in one of the least convenient locations, and it is rarely attended by more than a handful of individuals, most of whom do not yet have a degree in biblical studies. The topics will almost never include Egyptian chronology (too complicated) or Egyptian mythology (too alien.)

The two lists I mentioned above, and several others in Genesis that we will eventually study, are often referred to as the "begats" because the King James translation tells us that each parent in the list "begat" a child. The two lists are constructed so that you know how many years passed before each patriarch had a child and how many years each patriarch lived. With some additional information from later portions of Genesis, we can extend this birth-death list from Abraham through Isaac, Jacob/Israel, and Joseph.

If one knew when to date the birth of Adam, one could establish an exact year for each of the Patriarchal births and deaths listed. But establishing a date for creation is the first problem that needs to be solved before this secret can be exposed and solved. Biblical chronology is loaded with contradictions and inconsistencies, and there is no clear agreed-upon chronological record from Creation to an external anchor date. The bible contains major chronological gaps between Genesis and Exodus and between Exodus and the rise of the Hebrew monarchy. Other archaeological gaps and historical conflicts make it difficult to establish any reliable dates prior than about 900 BCE, and even then, there is much guessing involved.

Orthodox Jews date the Creation, and therefore the birth of Adam, to 3761 BCE, but most scholars consider that date a late artificial creation not originally connected to the list, perhaps originating no earlier than about the third century BCE The Septuagint Greek translation of Genesis contains an altered version of the Jewish text, pushing the date back by a couple of hundred years, often placed at about 4004 BCE, a date which is a late Christian invention of the sixteenth century, calculated by the Archbishop of Armaugh, James Ussher. In Chapter Four, I will demonstrate that the Jewish date of 3761 is almost certainly the intended date of biblical creation, and that is one of the key findings enabling us to unravel the mysterious origin of this Patriarchal Chronology.

The two Genesis lists have several interesting features. The first list, in Genesis 5, gives us a birth-death chronology for dates that fall before the Great Flood. The second list, in Genesis 11, gives us birth and death dates that occur after the Great Flood. Among the lists' many features, two are particularly notable.

First, every one of the patriarchs in this genealogical record, twenty-three in all running from Adam to Joseph, live extraordinarily long lives, with only Joseph's 110-year life span approaching anything resembling a normal human life span. The Genesis 5 patriarchs lived significantly longer than those in Genesis 11. The longest living patriarch was Methuselah at 969 years of age. The second feature of interest is that the list overlaps what would be considered a mythological era (Creation, Flood) and an historical era. I'll provide a more detailed look at the Patriarchal Chronology in Chapter Two.

When faced with such a list, an historian must ask certain questions. Does this list have any sources, and, if so, do we know what they are? Is the list a fictional creation of the author? Does any part of this chronology, even if an author invented the full list, have any relationship to actual historical events? Of course, the religiously orthodox, motivated by theological concerns, would simply say it is an accurate list and should be taken at face value. Other scholars are much more troubled by the nature of these lists.

From an historical perspective, scholars of the ancient near east have pointed out that both ancient Egypt and ancient Sumer (the dominant kingdom of third millennium BCE Mesopotamia) produced major king-lists that, like the Genesis chronology, spanned both a mythological era of god-rulers and an historical era, with many of the king-names from the historical period corroborated from independent archaeological evidence. And, also like the Genesis list, the earlier kings lived much longer lives than the historical kings.

In the Sumerian king-list, for example, the first king ruled for 28,800 years and his successor ruled for 36,000 years.[1] Among the various Egyptian sources, as preserved in ancient Greek texts, we find allegations that a group of 6 deities ruled for 11, 985 years[2] and another king who ruled for 30,000 years.[3]

This has led several scholars to propose that these two Genesis chronologies are fictional, patterned after the Egyptian and Sumerian models, with mythological rulers living longer than the later rulers. Every once in a rare while some scholar comes up with some very contorted effort to twist some data about a king or two in the Sumerian lists and suggests that there might be some sort of possible not far-off parallel with a piece of the Genesis list. But such approaches have not convinced very many scholars of a direct connection between the

Genesis lists and the Sumerian list. The Egyptian lists are completely ignored, even though a great bulk of the Genesis narrative takes place in Egypt.

The analogy to the Egyptian and Sumerian lists has a couple of slight flaws in the pattern analogy, not necessarily fatal but worth pointing out. First, in the foreign king-lists, the persons named are kings. Some are gods and some are humans. There is no indication in the Genesis lists that any of the people mentioned were rulers, or kings, and none are gods.

A second problem is that the number of years associated with each of the foreign rulers signified how many years that king reigned. In the Genesis lists, the number of years assigned signify how long a person lived, not how long he ruled, and how old a person was when he had a child. The nature of the numbers assigned in the Genesis lists are different than the nature of the numbers in the Egyptian and Sumerian lists. Third. the foreign king-lists show some mythological rulers with reigns lasting thousands and tens of thousands of years. In the Genesis list, no Patriarch lives more than 969 years.

These differences suggest that Genesis may be presenting something other than a fictional sequence of king-reigns mimicking that of foreign king-lists. What the Patriarchal Chronology actually represents is the subject of the present study.

The Thesis

I have solved the mystery of the "begats." The solution radically alters our understanding of the origin of the Book of Genesis, and, by implication, the origins of Judaism. The solution is neither obvious nor easy to arrive at. To solve the problem, one needs to do a deep dive into the very problematic study of Egyptian chronology, a subset of Egyptological studies that requires highly specialized attention.

To my knowledge, virtually no biblical scholars have that sort of expertise, and what very few (if any) there are, have no interest in the Patriarchal Chronology. On the other side of the equation, virtually no Egyptologist with a specialty in chronology pays any attention to the Patriarchal Chronology, assuming that at best it is little more than a meaningless fiction. (Kenneth Kitchen, a leading expert on Egyptian chronology, has demonstrated much interest in biblical studies, but to my knowledge has never undertaken a study of the Patriarchal Chronology.)

In this multi-volume work, I will lead you through the evidence step by step and lay it all out in simple easy to follow reviews of the evidence. Let me warn you, though. The breakthrough requires a great deal of simple basic arithmetic, an ability to recognize clear and obvious patterns in numbers, and a good amount of common sense. It will also require a thorough examination of the many problems involved in recovering an accurate chronology of ancient Egyptian kings and dynasties.

Central to this study is the birth-death patriarchal Chronology laid out in Genesis 5 and Genesis 11. When I am done, you will see that it includes (but is not limited to) a record of the starting dates of Egyptian dynasties, that begins in the Egyptian mythological era and continues down to the start of the Eighteenth Dynasty (c. 1576, per this study.) Furthermore, the dates adduced will be consistent with mainstream views of Egyptian chronology (although representing a specific subset of several alternative mainstream views) and the dates provided will signify the exact year (subject to a rounding error of a year or two) that the dynasties began.

When the evidence is fully presented, there should be no reasonable doubt that the Patriarchal Chronology is a document based on Egyptian chronology and that the author must have been working from Egyptian archival records.

I have divided the chronological study of Genesis 5 and 11 into two parts, the historical era, beginning with Egypt's First Dynasty (c. 3000) and Egypt's mythological era king-list preceding the First Dynasty. This volume will deal with the historical era. The second volume will deal with the mythological era. A third volume will deal with related chronological issues in Genesis connecting the biblical Creation and Flood accounts to Egyptian Creation mythology and connecting many human characters in Genesis with Egyptian deities.

To make my case, I need to do much more than show that an occasional birth or death date may be no more than a few years or decades off from some possible dated event in Egyptian history. That would simply be irresponsible cherry-picking that has no academic value. As stated above, I will show that the dates in question are the exact years in which a sequence of Egyptian dynasties began.

Of the 46 birth and death dates in the patriarchal chronology, six (as I will subsequently show) belong to the mythological era and the other forty belong to the historical era. Since there are more Patriarchal dates in the historical era than there are starting dates for the eighteen Egyptian dynasties that we will examine, the birth and death dates will occasionally coincide with the starting dates for certain kings within a couple of dynasties.

The evidence presented herein will show that almost all of the forty historical era dates in Genesis correspond to either the exact starting dates for each of the Egyptian dynasties or the exact starting date for Egyptian kings within a dynasty. These dates will all be consistent with the Egyptological evidence available for these dates.

Having said that I must explain that there is no simple and easy way to show how the Patriarchal Chronology aligns with the Egyptian historical record.

Any Egyptologist reading this is no doubt smirking or outright laughing at what he (erroneously) thinks of as a ridiculous claim. The Egyptologist knows that the many gaps in the archaeological record, the conflicting interpretations of astronomical correlations, the contradictions in the ancient records, the disagreements over what certain terms mean, and the frequently changing perceptions of Egyptologists mean that no agreed upon precise chronology exists.

Therefore, as part of the solution to the biblical mystery, I must also puzzle out a logical and consistent methodology for solving the conflicts over Egyptian chronology. This presents some very serious challenges but a side of effect of solving the mystery behind the biblical chronology also helps resolve many conflicts over Egyptian chronology.

Brief Overview
of Egyptian Chronological Problems

In Chapter Three, I'll present a detailed explanation of the chronological problems faced by Egyptologists in reconstructing Egyptian
king-lists. Here, I present a brief overview of some of the issues.

For the period running from Dynasties 1–20, (c. 3,000–1000
BCE), based on differing interpretations and opinions of archaeological, astronomical, and written evidence, and with frequent gaps in
the record, Egyptologists can be divided into two major chronological camps, High Chronology and Low Chronology. Within each
camp there are further disputes as to how to fill in various gaps due
to a lack of sufficient evidence. So, we have two schools of thought
that present us with multiple chronological solutions.

For most of the twentieth century, the High Chronology had been
preferred. Over the last couple of decades, the Low Chronology has
been ascendant. No smoking gun has resolved this conflict. Some recent carbon-14 tests have indicated a trend towards the High Chronology, but the results are disputed. In a recent complication, another
analysis of carbon-14 testing has suggested the possibility that there is
an error in the underlying data for carbon-14 testing in portions of the
Middle East and that might lead to a lowering of carbon-14 results.
This, too, is contested.

The most important conflict in reconstructing second millennium
Egyptian chronology (Dynasties 11–20) revolves around where certain ancient Egyptians were located when they made some astronomical observations. Different locations lead to different dates for
the astronomical event under observation. While the dispute remains unresolved, the High and Low Chronologies only differ by
about 25–40 years for much of this era.

While that is astonishingly close for such an ancient period, my
thesis requires that I hone in even more closely to get precise dates,
which is the main problem that we will be examining in this study.
Since the astronomical record presents a scientific basis for separating the two schools of thought, any solution to the problem of Egyptian
chronology must be consistent with either one or the other of these

two points of view. I can't just mix and match conclusions from the two schools such that they fit a predetermined outcome. This means eventually aligning my conclusions with either the High Chronology or the Low Chronology.

For the Third Millennium (Dynasties 1–10), the further back you go, the more frequent the archaeological gaps and the fewer the chronological records, making conclusions more uncertain and leading to a wider range of chronological disagreements. One major source of conflict in this period concerns the nature of the "cattle counts." These were censuses of some sort (and not fully understood) and Egyptologists disagree as to whether they were mostly conducted on annual or biennial basis. The reason for conflict is that sometimes cattle counts happened in consecutive years and sometimes they skipped over a year.

The cattle counts play a major role in establishing portions of the third millennium chronology. Whether they were annual, or biennial makes a big difference to the outcome. Did an 18th count of the cattle signify at least an 18-year reign or a 35-year reign (the counts began in Year 1 of a reign)? If you have enough high counts, you can arrive at several decades of difference over the accurate duration of a dynasty and the dates associated with it. Cattle counts, it should be noted, provide only a minimum length of reign, not a maximum. And we don't have enough cattle count data to fill in much of the chronological record.

The cattle count dispute is separate and apart from the High-Low dispute based on astronomical records. Where one stands within the High-Low astronomical dispute is not relevant to where one stands in the High-Low cattle count dispute. As with the High-Low astronomical dispute, any conclusion I reach must also be consistent with either the biennial cattle count theory or the annual cattle count theory. Again, I can't mix and match results based on what works out best for my theory.

Sometime after the start of the Sixth Dynasty and overlapping the start of the Eleventh Dynasty, for a period of one to two hundred years (c. 2300–2100, dates to be more precisely defined in later chapters), Egypt experienced a major period of political disruption known as the First Intermediate Period, with rival claims for the right to rule Egypt. Egyptologists disagree over how long the period lasted. Apparently, ancient Egyptian record keepers felt a keen sense of embarrassment over these events and attempted to whitewash the period out of the country's history. Several king-lists omit that period from the chronological record, jumping from the Sixth Dynasty to the Eleventh Dynasty.

A second, and even more embarrassing political disruption, known as the Second Intermediate Period (c. 1800–1550, dates to be more precisely defined in later chapters,) occurred between the end of the Twelfth Dynasty and the start of the Eighteenth Dynasty, when foreign rulers managed to take military control over portions of Egypt and set up rival dynasties in opposition to the existing line of Egyptian kings. Again, record keepers attempted to whitewash and limit knowledge of this era and much of the chronological record is in a state of disarray.

One other problem that pops up from time to time is that sometimes ancient king-lists or portions of king-lists or inscriptions or writings disagree with each other about how long a king ruled, what sequence kings ruled in, how many kings belonged to a dynasty, and whether a king or group of kings mentioned in a source even existed. Such disputes must be considered in context with other evidence.

As you can see, attempting to establish a precise chronological record of Egypt that can be placed alongside the Patriarchal Chronology for one-to-one comparisons presents more than a simple challenge. If the problems of Egyptian chronology, as outlined above, were solely as I explained them, I would have insufficient data to prove my thesis. There is one more important piece of evidence that affects the study of Egyptian chronology and it causes a lot of grief among Egyptologists trying to resolve chronological issues.

The Manetho Problem

In the third century BCE, an Egyptian priest named Manetho wrote a history of Egypt that began with the Gods, spirits, and humans that ruled in the mythological era and continued down to the human rulers from the First Dynasty and continued further down to his own time. It was replete with king-lists, chronologies, biographical sketches, military conquests, political intrigues, and many other historical elements. Most importantly, for our purposes, it contained a chronological record of rulers that began in the mythological era and continued down to his own time, the end of the dynastic era. From an historical perspective, Manetho probably produced the longest continuous chronological record ever prepared by an ancient writer. But his work presents problems.

The first issue we face is that no original version of Manetho's chronology exists. What we do have are badly redacted, frequently inconsistent, and filled with chronological problems. The evidence suggests that Manetho's history was quite popular and possibly widely-circulated in his time and thereafter. Jews and Christians were especially interested in it because of the chronological listings, which they wanted to compare to the Genesis chronologies and other overlapping portions in other books of the bible. I strongly suspect that the altered form of Genesis chronology in the Septuagint, with a much earlier Creation date, may have been the result of Hellenistic Jewish writers trying to adapt the Genesis chronology to Manetho's historical record.

The second problem we face is the poor quality of the preserved portions of Manetho's history as transmitted by later writers. The Jewish historian Josephus, in the first century, provides our earliest extracts of Manetho's text, but it encompassed only a portion of Egyptian history, running approximately from the Fifteenth through Nineteenth Dynasties (c. 1680–1200).

In the third century, a Christian writer named Africanus provided a chronological record of ancient Egypt that he claimed was based on writings from Manetho, but it focused almost exclusively on what purported to be Manetho's lengths of reign for dynasties and kings. In the fourth century, the church historian Eusebius presented a similar list, also claiming it was based on Manetho, although portions were probably based on Africanus's text. Excerpts from Africanus and Eusebius were transmitted by later writers.

All three versions of the text attributed to Manetho, while appearing to come from a common source, are frequently wildly inconsistent with each other and contradict each other in many places. Nevertheless, for much of post-Eusebius history until about the early twentieth century, the preserved portions of Manetho's history were accepted as the primary reference for the chronology of ancient Egypt. It is these writings that led later Egyptologists to divide Egypt's dynastic period into thirty dynasties.

This leads to the third major problem. As our archaeological record evolved in the twentieth century, and more records were frequently discovered, modern Egyptologists obtained a reasonably good sense of the parameters of Egypt's dynastic history. They began to realize that the purported lengths of reign for many of Manetho's dynasties and kings, in each of the three versions, were much too long to reasonably fit in with the independent archaeological and written evidence.

Given the frequent disagreements within the three Manetho traditions, as well as the conflicts between the alleged Manetho excerpts and the archaeological record, one might think that the Manetho sources should just be discarded as unreliable. But that brings us to the fourth problem. Egyptologists recognize that some of the Manetho source material shows, even in some of the oldest periods of Egyptian history, that Manetho clearly had accurate knowledge of many events that happened long before his time, and many of the data points in the three sources are consistent with the archaeological record. Manetho, himself, would have had direct access to Egyptian archival material.

The consensus seems to hold that Manetho's original history was based in some significant part on reliable sources and that the three Manetho sources preserved badly garbled redactions of the original Manetho text. Egyptologists frequently use some of Manetho's data to fill in gaps in the chronological record or correct data from other chronological sources. This brings us to the fifth problem. How much credible use can we make of Manetho's data?

It will be the argument in this study that Manetho originally had a reasonably accurate chronological history of ancient Egypt that was consistent with (if not always identical to) the archaeological and written evidence from other ancient Egyptian king-lists and chronological sources and that a very large amount of his original chronological data can be recovered through a process of numerical pattern recognition when examined within the context of the archaeological record.

More specifically, I will be able to show that, frequently, what happened to the original Manetho manuscript came about because the redactors did not fully understand the text. Often, I will argue, Manetho's lines of summation for groups of kings were confused with entries for additional kings or additional groups of kings and the summation lines were mistakenly identified as additional groups of kings ruling for the time indicated by the summation line. (I have published a peer-reviewed article introducing this thesis in *The SSEA Journal*.[4]) On other occasions, I will show that summations in the margins by some redactors were later confused by later redactors with additional entries to Manetho's text, who incorporated those comments into the textual transmission as further chronological expansions of what redactors mistakenly thought was Manetho's original text.

My theory, therefore, suggests that if we recognize that the transmitted Manetho sources incorporated summation lines as extra listings of kings, and if we can work out what the actual lengths of reign were from the archaeological and written evidence, then we should be able to show that when Manetho king reigns or dynasty lengths are too long we can back track to show that some of the entries may include summaries of the accurate data that have been added to the text as if they were separate chronological data from what the numbers were summarizing. This will make more sense when we put the practice into play. This thesis will be the lynchpin that brings all the evidence together, showing the Patriarchal Chronology, Egyptian chronology, and Manetho all aligned along the same set of dates.

My Approach to the Chronological Issues

As noted above, there are not only disagreements among modern Egyptologists over the correct chronology, correct sequence of kings, and correct lengths of reign, but such disputes appear in the ancient Egyptian records as well. This means that an ancient Egyptian writer, faced with a conflict in sources or a confused understanding of some terminology might have made a different choice about the correct chronology than one or another of the ancient or modern scholars might have made. In this study, the thesis is that the Genesis author used Egyptian archival records and may have encountered the sort of conflicts and contradictions that modern Egyptologists have dealt with.

It will be the argument set forth in this book that there is a direct alignment, on a precise year-to-year basis between Egyptian dynastic chronology and the Patriarchal Chronology. In other words, I will show that various birth and death dates align with the exact year in which a dynasty or king began to rule. This means, in part, that we will take dates in the Patriarchal Chronology and then look at the Egyptian records and the Manetho texts and see what we might reasonably conclude about the date in question. As we look at more and more dates, patterns in Egyptian chronology will begin to emerge. That said, it is necessary to note that perfect precision may be impossible and that round-off errors of a year or two occasionally come into play.

This round-off error is due to a couple of factors. An Egyptian solar year began during the month of July. So, an Egyptian calendar year overlaps two different modern calendar years, and a modern calendar year overlaps two Egyptian calendar years. There is also an occasional issue as to whether a king's length of reign was calculated from the day he ascended the throne, or from the beginning of the year in which he ascended the throne, or from the first of the year following his ascent to the throne. This means that there may sometimes be disagreements of a year or two between the Genesis chronology and the Egyptian chronology. It is simply an unavoidable problem. However, if we can show that in just about every single case, the error never goes beyond that range of a year or two, then the pattern is fixed, and indicates that those small discrepancies are the result of rounding off partial years. due to minor roundoff errors.

On some occasions we will see that the Genesis chronology aligns with one of the ancient records as opposed to another that some modern Egyptologists think would make a better fit. So, we will encounter an occasional conflict with modern views. But, in resolving that conflict in favor of the Genesis chronology, that resolution must be rooted in actual records that we know about. I can't cite imaginary sources. It won't do for me to say, "Oh well, this difference is explained by some lost record that we have yet to find." To repeat, any conflict between the reconstruction of Egyptian chronology such that it matches Genesis chronology must be based on known records.

It will be the argument that the form of Egyptian chronology that most closely matches that of the Patriarchal Chronology adheres to the following parameters. If there is a dispute over the dating of an astronomical event, the Patriarchal Chronology aligns with the High Chronology. Wherever we find a dispute within the High Chronology between a higher or lower date, the evidence appears to favor the higher date.

As to the problem of the "cattle count" census, there is also a High versus Low chronology issue. The High Chronology view holds that cattle counts should be assumed to be biennial, although on some occasions a count was conducted in a consecutive year. The Low Chronology holds that we should assume the count was conducted annually, although on some occasions a count skipped over a year. The evidence in this study shows that the author of the Patriarchal Chronology worked from a system in which the cattle counts were primarily conducted on a biennial basis, in line with the High Chronology.

This doesn't necessarily mean that the biennial count theory is the correct understanding of the issue, but if someone using ancient Egyptian records understands the counts to be biennial, it is more likely that the ancient source, given his access and intellectual environment, may have had a better understanding of the term than the Low Chronology proponents do. But, even if the ancient source was wrong in assuming the "cattle counts" occurred biennially instead of annually, we find that on all occasions where it is relevant that the Genesis chronology consistently aligns with a biennial cattle count. It is reasonable, therefore, to assume that the author is working from some archival records that included references to the "cattle counts" and simply misinterpreted it. Such an interpretation doesn't undermine the idea that the author is constructing a chronological record based on Egyptian archival records.

To summarize: I will argue that the Patriarchal Chronology aligns precisely, year to year, with an Egyptian dynastic chronology based on the High Chronology for astronomical observations, and with a "biennial" understanding of the term "cattle counts."

Summary

Genesis 5 and 11 each contain a relative chronology of birth and death dates, such that if we had a starting date we could assign a year date to each birth and death. It will be argued in Chapter 4 that the starting date should be 3761. Some of those dates fall into what would be considered a mythical period in Egyptian chronology and some of those dates fall into what would be the historical period of Egyptian chronology. In this volume we will look at the historical period.

Based on different understandings of where certain astronomical events were observed, Egyptologists propose either a High Chronology range or a Low Chronology for the second millennium and portions of the third millennium. Within each grouping there are disputes as to how to fill in the gaps in the record, leading to several slightly different proposed Egyptian chronologies.

For the third millennium, archaeological records show that the Egyptians occasionally made note of how many cattle count censuses occurred during a king's reign. Occasionally, Egyptians dated an event by referencing how many cattle counts had occurred in a king's reign when that event happened. Egyptologists disagree over whether the censuses occurred on a mostly annual basis, occasionally skipping a year, or on a biennial basis, occasionally conducting a census in consecutive years.

The evidence in this study will show that the Patriarchal Chronology constitutes a chronological record of starting dates for Egyptian dynasties from the First through Eighteenth Dynasties, and, on a couple of occasions, gives us the starting dates for specific kings with a dynasty. The evidence will further show that the Patriarchal Chronology aligns precisely, on a year-to-year correspondence, with the High Chronology based on astronomical observances and with the biennial occurrence of cattle count censuses.

A key tool in the analysis will be the attempted reconstruction of Manetho's third century BCE chronology of Egyptian history, in which the wildly large and unacceptable durations assigned to various dynasties or kings were due, per my theory, to redactors confusing summation lines, either in Manetho's original text or in marginal notations made to a Manetho source, with additional groups of kings or as a record for an additional king.

At the end of this study, we will see that the Patriarchal Chronology and the original Manetho closely align with a traditional defensible chronology of Egyptian history as reflected in other Egyptian chronological records.

A second volume of this study will analyze those Genesis dates that fall into the mythical period of Egyptian history. A third volume of this study will deal with chronological issues associated with Creation and the Flood, and the influence of Egyptian creation myths on those stories.

2 Patriarchal Chronology in Genesis

GENESIS 5 AND 11 CONTAIN A BIRTH-DEATH CHRONOLOGY FOR TWENTY generations of patriarchs, from the birth of Adam to the birth of Abraham. The way the lists are set out, we can determine how many years after Creation each of those births and deaths occurred. From other portions of Genesis, we can extend the chronological record of births and death to include the death of Abraham and the birth and death of Isaac, Jacob, and Joseph. We can also determine how many years elapsed from the date of Creation to Noah's flood, which provides an important chronological marker for this study.

If we had a date for Creation, we could establish absolute year dates for each of these births and deaths. For the purposes of this study, I will be using 3761 BCE, the traditional Jewish date of Creation, as the starting point and see what sort of information we can gather about any parallels between this chronological listing and Egyptian king-lists.

Looking more carefully at Genesis 5 and 11 we can see some differences in how the two lists are composed. For one, they have slightly different literary formulas to describe the chronological information. There is also a two-year inconsistency between the end of the Genesis 5 list and the start of the Genesis 11 list. These factors suggest the possibility of different hands in the composition, and/or the existence of separate source lists for the Genesis chronology. As the chronology unfolds, we will also see that all the births and deaths listed in Genesis 5 occur before the Flood and all the Genesis 11 births and deaths occur after the Flood. Additionally. the Genesis 5

Table 2.1: The Birth-Death Chronology in Genesis 5

This table only includes data present in Genesis 5. Dates assume a Creation date of 3761 BCE, per Jewish tradition

Generation	Years After Creation	Age at Son's birth	Life span	Birth year	Death year
Adam	0	130	930	3761	2831
Seth	130	105	912	3631	2719
Enosh	235	90	905	3526	2621
Kenan	325	70	910	3436	2526
Mahalalel	395	65	895	3366	2471
Jared	460	162	962	3301	2339
Enoch	622	65	365	3139	2774
Methuselah	687	187	969	3074	2105
Lamech	874	182	777	2887	2110
Noah	1056	500		2705	
Shem	1556			2205	

patriarchs, except for Enoch, have significantly longer life spans than the Genesis 11 patriarchs.

The Genesis 5 Chronology

The Genesis 5 chronology runs from verses 5:3 through 5:32. In the copy of that text that follows I have omitted the specific verse citations and I have separated passages to reflect the information given for each generation. Table 2.1, *The Birth-Death Chronology in Genesis 5*, summarizes the information provided by Genesis 5 and, counting down from 3761, assigns absolute year-dates for each birth and death mentioned.

- When Adam had lived one hundred thirty years, he became the father of a son in his likeness, according to his image, and named him Seth. The days of Adam after he became the father of Seth were eight hundred years; and he had other sons and daughters. Thus all the days that Adam lived were nine hundred thirty years; and he died.
- When Seth had lived one hundred five years, he became the father of Enosh. Seth lived after the birth of Enosh eight hundred seven

years, and had other sons and daughters. Thus all the days of Seth were nine hundred twelve years; and he died.

- When Enosh had lived ninety years, he became the father of Kenan. Enosh lived after the birth of Kenan eight hundred fifteen years, and had other sons and daughters. Thus all the days of Enosh were nine hundred five years; and he died.

- When Kenan had lived seventy years, he became the father of Mahalalel. Kenan lived after the birth of Mahalalel eight hundred and forty years, and had other sons and daughters. Thus all the days of Kenan were nine hundred and ten years; and he died.

- When Mahalalel had lived sixty-five years, he became the father of Jared. Mahalalel lived after the birth of Jared eight hundred thirty years, and had other sons and daughters. Thus all the days of Mahalalel were eight hundred ninety-five years; and he died.

- When Jared had lived one hundred sixty-two years he became the father of Enoch. Jared lived after the birth of Enoch eight hundred years, and had other sons and daughters. Thus all the days of Jared were nine hundred sixty-two years; and he died.

- When Enoch had lived sixty-five years, he became the father of Methuselah. Enoch walked with God after the birth of Methuselah three hundred years, and had other sons and daughters. Thus all the days of Enoch were three hundred sixty-five years. *Enoch walked with God; then he was no more, because God took him* [emphasis added].

- When Methuselah had lived one hundred eighty-seven years, he became the father of Lamech. Methuselah lived after the birth of Lamech seven hundred eighty-two years, and had other sons and daughters. Thus all the days of Methuselah were nine hundred sixty-nine years; and he died.

- When Lamech had lived one hundred eighty-two years, he became the father of a *son; he named him Noah, saying, "Out of the ground that the* LORD *has cursed this one shall bring us relief from our work and from the toil of our hands."* Lamech lived after the birth of Noah five hundred ninety-five years, and had other sons and daughters.

Thus all the days of Lamech were seven hundred seventy-seven years; and he died [emphasis added].

- After Noah was five hundred years old, Noah became the father of Shem, Ham, and Japheth.

Let me draw your attention to certain features in this passage. First, the text uses a literary formula to describe the chronological information about each of the first several generations. It takes the following form:

> [Name] lived [X] years and became the father of [son's name]. [Name] lived after the birth of [son's name] [Y] years and had other sons and daughters. All the years of [Name] were [X+Y] years, and he died.

For the last three generations, Noah's father, Noah, and Noah's sons, we have some departures from the chronological literary formula, all of which seem related to the fact that that the Flood story bisects the two chronological lists.

For Noah's father, Lamech, the Genesis author (or more likely, a later redactor) inserted a passage explaining how Noah came to be named. This doesn't affect the chronological data. But for Noah and his sons there is a larger problem.

Noah and his sons all died after the Flood. Since either the original author of the Genesis chronology or a later redactor decided to separate the pre-Flood chronology form the post-Flood chronology, the Genesis 5 listing omits the death dates for both Noah and his sons, all of whom survived the Flood.

For Noah, we know from elsewhere in Genesis that he lived 950 years.[5] This dates his death to 1755 according to our chronology. As to Noah's sons, we have a slight chronological problem. For his children, the chronological formula has been abandoned. We are told that Noah had sons *after* he was 500 years old but doesn't say how many years after that any of his three sons were born. The formula suggests that the five hundredth year should be the age of at least one son's birth. Genesis 11 resumes with information about only one of Noah's sons, Shem, and the Genesis 11 chronology gives us Shem's death date.

It is my view that originally, the author of the Genesis chronology dated Shem's birth to the five hundredth year but, at some later point, a change had to be introduced to accommodate the Flood story. Genesis 11, as we shall see, indicates that Shem was born in Noah's 502nd year, introducing a 2-year shift for the subsequent dates. I will argue in either Volume II or III of this study that the Flood story was originally an alternative Creation story and moved out of sequence to create harmony with the current Creation story.

As for the present study, I will continue to use Noah's five hundredth year as Shem's birth year, but should the 2-year shift be valid, it would make no meaningful difference to the chronological comparisons between Genesis and Egyptian chronology. The distortion falls within the margin of error caused by rounding off partial years.

In addition to the breakdowns in the literary formula for Noah and sons, we have another break in the formula for Enoch. In all the completed formulas, except for Enoch, we are told how long the father lived and then we are told when he died. Genesis doesn't say that Enoch died, at least not in the way it's said for the other patriarchs. At the place in the formula where the death notice belongs, it says instead, "Enoch walked with God; then he was no more, because God took him." This notice obviously draws special attention to Enoch, and I will explain why in Chapter Four.

Enoch also has a much shorter life span than everyone else on the Genesis 5 list. He lived for 365 years, over 400 years less than the next shortest life span on the list, Lamech's 777 years. One can't help but notice how nicely Enoch's number of years corresponds to the number of days in the solar calendar. This is particularly interesting since the Hebrews used the 354-day lunar calendar. Enoch's birth-death data will provide an important clue in our later analysis of what lies behind the Genesis patriarchal chronology.

I also want to draw your attention to one other oddity. If we momentarily remove Enoch from the list, all the patriarchs but Lamech die in the same order in which they were born. He is the only patriarch in the list (other than Enoch) who died before his father. Lamech's son, Methuselah, died in the year of the Flood. Of all the patriarchs who were alive during Adam's lifetime, Methuselah was the last to die. It is possible, therefore, given the variation from the formula in which fathers died before their sons, that Lamech's life span was shortened by a later redactor so that he would appear to die before the Flood rather than after. We'll discuss that issue at a later point in this study.

The Genesis 11 Chronology

The Genesis 11 chronology runs from Genesis 11:10 to 11:26, and then inserts some information about Abraham's father, Terah, before concluding. The formulaic conclusion of Terah's chronology appears right after the interruption at 11:32. I will include that verse in the Genesis 11 chronology as it appears to have been separated from the main portion to insert other information about Terah and his family. Table 2.2, *The Birth-Death Chronology in Genesis 11*, summarizes the chronological data from Genesis 11. Again, in setting forth the Genesis 11 text, I omit the specific verse citations and have separated the text according to each generation's description.

- These are the descendants of Shem. When Shem was one hundred years old, he became the father of Arpachshad two years after the flood; and Shem lived after the birth of Arpachshad five hundred years, and had other sons and daughters.
- When Arpachshad had lived thirty-five years, he became the father of Shelah; and Arpachshad lived after the birth of Shelah four hundred three years, and had other sons and daughters.
- When Shelah had lived thirty years, he became the father of Eber; and Shelah lived after the birth of Eber four hundred three years, and had other sons and daughters.
- When Eber had lived thirty-four years, he became the father of Peleg; and Eber lived after the birth of Peleg four hundred thirty years, and had other sons and daughters.

Table 2.2: The Birth-Death Chronology in Genesis 11

Table only includes data from Genesis 11. Dates assume a Creation date of 3761 BCE, per Jewish tradition.

Generation	Years After Creation	Age at Son's birth	Life span	Birth year	Death year
Shem		100	600		1605
Arphaxad	1656	35	438	2105	1667
Shelah	1691	30	433	2070	1637
Eber	1721	34	464	2040	1576
Peleg	1755	30	239	2006	1767
Reu	1785	32	239	1976	1737
Serug	1817	30	230	1944	1714
Nahor	1847	29	148	1914	1766
Terah	1876	70	205	1885	1680
Abraham	1815			1815	

- When Peleg had lived thirty years, he became the father of Reu; and Peleg lived after the birth of Reu two hundred nine years, and had other sons and daughters.
- When Reu had lived thirty-two years, he became the father of Serug; and Reu lived after the birth of Serug two hundred seven years, and had other sons and daughters.
- When Serug had lived thirty years, he became the father of Nahor; and Serug lived after the birth of Nahor two hundred years, and had other sons and daughters.
- When Nahor had lived twenty-nine years, he became the father of Terah; and Nahor lived after the birth of Terah one hundred nineteen years, and had other sons and daughters. When Terah had lived seventy years, he became the father of Abram, Nahor, and Haran . . . The days of Terah were two hundred five years; and Terah died in Haran.

The most problematic feature of the Genesis 11 chronology is that it introduces a small inconsistency in the birth-death data. Genesis 9:28 says the Flood occurred in Noah's six hundredth year, which according to the present dating system falls in 2105, the year of Methuselah's death. Genesis 5:32 implies that the birth of Shem occurred in Noah's five hundredth year, 2205, which makes his one hundredth year 2105, the year of the Flood. But Genesis 11:10 says that Arphaxad was born two years after the Flood, in Shem's one hundredth year. Two years after the Flood should be 2103. So, was Shem's 100th year in 2105 or 2103, and did the Flood occur in Shem's hundredth or ninety-eighth year?

There could be many reasons why the two lists are in conflict, but the size of the error is so small it could be nothing more than the result of rounding off a partial year when constructing the source lists. For now, we can just acknowledge that there is a very slight amount of disagreement between the two chronologies. Nevertheless, we need to decide which chronology to follow for dating purposes. Should the pre-Flood dates be placed two years later; should the post-Flood dates be made two years earlier; or should there be a one-year compromise in both directions?

The present work follows the second course, placing Arphaxad's birth in Shem's one hundredth year, but using the Genesis 5 dating, which places Shem's one hundredth year in 2105, the year of the Flood. Therefore, the dates in Table 2.2 assume that Arphaxad was born in 2105 instead of 2103. In doing so, it must be remembered that all Genesis dates are subject to a two-year margin of error.

Another interesting feature of the Genesis 11 chronology concerns the length of time each patriarch lived. Each of the patriarchs in Genesis 11 lived fewer years than each of the Genesis 5 patriarchs (if we omit Enoch from the Genesis 5 listing).

Genesis 11 also uses a redacted form of the Genesis 5 literary formula, dropping out the ending, which reads, "All the years of [Name] were [X+Y] years, and he died." This leaves us with how many years passed before a son was born and how many years passed after the son was born, but the reader must do the arithmetic to know the total number of years the patriarch lived.

Although Genesis 11 uses a redacted form of the literary formula there is one oddity. Terah, whose formulaic description was separated into two parts,[6] reverts to the original form of the Genesis 5 literary formula. The second part reads "The days of Terah were two hundred five years; and Terah died *in Haran* [emphasis added]." Note that the author tacked on one further piece of information, the city where Terah died. This appears to have been done to connect the end of the Genesis 11 chronology to a specific territorial tradition for Abraham's roots. The very next verse begins the narrative account of Abraham's story, and depicts God telling him to leave his country, presumably Haran.[7]

As in the Genesis 5 listing, we are missing the death data for the last member of the list. In Genesis 11, that is Abram, later called Abraham. We know Abraham lived for 175 years, which places his death in 1640.[8]

Finally, I want to mention one clue that we will make use of later. The Genesis 11 list mentions a patriarch named Peleg. Elsewhere in Genesis, we are told that he was so named because "in his days the earth was divided."[9] Peleg, according to our chronology, lived from 2006–1767. We'll look at the significance of Peleg's name when we consider that period later in our study.

Other Birth and Death Dates

Let me now flesh out the remaining patriarchal birth and death dates in Genesis that are missing from Genesis 5 and 11. I have given Abraham's death date above. We need to complete our chronological sequence with the data for Isaac, son of Abraham; Jacob, the son of Isaac; and Joseph, the son of Jacob, whose death brings Genesis to a close.

Abraham was 100 years old when Isaac was born.[10] Since we dated Abraham's birth to 1815, we can date Isaac's birth to 1715. Isaac lived 180 years.[11] That places his death in 1535. Isaac was 60 years old when Jacob was born.[12] Since Isaac was born in 1715, Jacob must have been born in 1655. He died at the age of 147 years.[13] This dates his death to 1508.

Determining the birth and death dates for Joseph requires a bit more effort. Joseph became Prime Minister of Egypt after interpreting Pharaoh's unusual dream and predicting that there would be seven good harvest years followed by seven years of famine. The seven good years began with his appointment as Prime Minister, in Joseph's thirtieth year.[14]

Jacob came to Egypt in his 130th year,[15] which coincided with the second year of the famine.[16] Because the second year of famine occurred in Joseph's ninth year as Prime Minister, we can place his thirty-ninth year in Jacob's 130th year. Since we have dated Jacob's birth to 1655, his 130th year would be 1525. In that year, Joseph was 39 years old. Therefore, he must have been born in 1564. According to Genesis 50:26, the last verse of the Book of Genesis, Joseph lived 110 years, which dates his death to 1454.[17]

The Sons of God and the Daughters of Men

Before moving on to an overview of Egyptian chronology and sources, I want to introduce one more piece of chronological data. I have pointed out above that the Flood occurred in 2105. According to Genesis, one hundred and twenty years before the Flood, certain events triggered God's decision to wipe out humanity but for Noah and his family.

> When people began to multiply on the face of the ground, and daughters were born to them, the sons of God saw that they were fair; and they took wives for themselves of all that they chose. Then the LORD said, "My spirit shall not abide in mortals forever, for they are flesh; their days shall be one hundred twenty years."[18]

This famous passage about the "sons of God" and the "daughters of men" has long puzzled biblical scholars. Who were these sons of God, and why did their actions trigger God's wish to destroy man kind? The answers will be given in another chapter but they are closely related to the matter of the "one hundred and twenty years" before the Flood. Per our chronology, that would be 2225. We will return to this issue later in this study.

Summary

Using a date of 3761 as the year of Creation, I have established a timeline for the births and deaths of twenty-three generations of patriarchs, beginning with the birth of Adam in 3761 and ending with the death of Joseph in 1454. The chronology also establishes a

Table 2.3: The Patriarchal Birth-Death Chronology in Genesis

Patriarchal Generation	Birth Year	Death Year	Years to son	Years after son	Life Span
Adam	3761	2831	130	800	930
Seth	3631	2719	105	807	912
Enosh	3526	2621	90	815	905
Kenan	3436	2526	70	840	910
Mahalalel	3366	2471	65	830	895
Jared	3301	2339	162	800	962
Enoch	3139	2774	65	300	365
Methuselah	3074	2105	187	782	969
Lamech	2887	2110	182	595	777
Noah	2705	1755	500	450	950
Shem	2205	1605	100	500	600
Arphaxad	2105	1667	35	403	438
Shelah	2070	1637	30	403	433
Eber	2040	1576	34	430	464
Peleg	2006	1767	30	209	239
Reu	1976	1737	32	207	239
Serug	1944	1714	30	200	230
Nahor	1914	1766	29	119	148
Terah	1885	1680	70	135	205
Abraham	1815	1640	100	75	175
Isaac	1715	1535	60	120	180
Jacob	1655	1508	91	56	147
Joseph	1564	1454			110

date of 2105 for the Flood and 2225 as the date of the events that triggered God's desire to punish humanity. Table 2.3, *The Patriarchal Birth-Death Chronology in Genesis*, summarizes all the dates we calculated for each patriarch's date of birth and date of death. I have also referenced several clues that will be used later in our analysis.

- Enoch lived for 365 years (3139–2774) and his chronologic description doesn't follow the literary formula used for the other Genesis 5 patriarchs. We are told that he walked with God. He has obviously been singled out for special attention in this chronological listing.
- Peleg's name comes from the word for "division" and some point in his life span (2106–1776) is associated with the division of lands.
- The Flood occurred in the year 2105, in the same year that Methuselah died.
- God's desire to punish humanity occurred 120 years (2225) before the flood, when the sons of God married the daughters of man.
- There is a two-year inconsistency between the end of the Genesis 5 chronology and the start of the Genesis 11 chronology. This may reflect the use of separate written source texts for the two chronologies.

Before we can make use of any of this chronological information, we must next turn our attention to a general overview of issues in Egyptian chronology. After that, we will spend several chapters focusing in more closely on Egyptian chronology and show how the patriarchal chronology interacts with that data.

3 Egyptian Chronology: An Overview

EGYPT'S DYNASTIC HISTORY BEGINS SOMETIME NEAR 3100 BCE AND ENDS at about 332 BCE, with the conquest of Egypt by Alexander the Great. Creating a chronological history of dynasties and their rulers over almost three thousand years was no easy task, and even today, scholars disagree over many issues. Numerous obstacles had to be overcome. Gardiner, writing just fifty years ago, observed, "What is proudly advertised as Egyptian history is merely a collection of rags and tatters."[19] Since then, we have learned a good deal more.

Ancient Egypt did not date events according to a fixed calendar. Instead they referenced a year in a pharaoh's reign. This meant that if we found some inscription that cited the seventh year of Pharaoh X, unless we had external information, all we could say about that pharaoh was that the king served at least seven years, but we couldn't say when those seven years occurred, or even in what millennium those seven years were served. We needed to build up additional chronological information between that king and other kings so that we could place multiple kings into a sequential relationship. But even with sequential information, we still couldn't establish fixed dates, without some sort of anchor point.

Another difficulty was that between stable periods of rule, there were occasional periods of political disruption that were poorly documented, especially regarding chronological matters, and we had no direct information as to how long these chaotic eras lasted. Again, without chronological anchor points, there was no way to establish how many centuries apart kings on one side of the divide were from kings on the other side.

Egyptian kings also had numerous titles and descriptions appended to their name, some of which they shared with other kings. Consider the following translation of the several names associated with Thutmose III. Those names within the quotation marks are personal names adopted by the pharaoh; the names outside the quotation marks are epithets common to all pharaohs. Imagine the difficulty in trying to identify a pharaoh from an inscription containing only a portion of this full title.

> Life to the Horus 'Strong Bull arisen in Thebes', the Two Ladies 'Enduring of kingship like Re in heaven', the Horus of Gold, 'Powerful of strength, Holy of appearances', the King of Upper and Lower Egypt 'Menkheperre', the Son of Re 'Dhutmose ruler of truth', beloved of Amen-Re who presides in Ipet-eswe, may he live eternally.[20]

The above examples only show some of the problems in trying to reconstruct a dynastic and monarchial chronology for ancient Egypt. Over time, significant chronological data continued to emerge, including some astronomical data that helped fix some anchor points. Despite several disagreements over whether all the referenced dynasties existed, whether some dynasties have been omitted, whether all or part of some dynasties were consecutive to or concurrent with other dynasties, what kings belonged to which dynasty, how long various kings and dynasties reigned, and when certain astronomical phenomena occurred, a mostly consistent chronological model exists.

Nevertheless, the earlier you go in time the more gaps we have in the data. Today, most Egyptologists fall into one of two chronological camps, advocates for a High Chronology or a Low Chronology. The difference often revolves around how certain astronomical data is understood. But even within this framework, the two camps aren't very far apart. Perhaps a couple of decades at most within the second millennium BCE and a little further apart for the third millennium BCE For the first millennium BCE, we have good chronological information from about the seventh century BCE down to the end, with just occasional differences of opinion about small matters in the earlier half of the millennium. Given that we are looking at a period of 3,000 years with frequently poor documentation, that isn't too bad.

During this study we will attempt to home in on many of the still divisive issues and see how precisely we can establish specific time frames. But to discuss Egyptian chronology, one must first understand the political model that frames the issues. Based on the writings of a third century BCE Egyptian priest named Manetho, about whom we will have much to say throughout this work, this dynastic period has been traditionally divided into a group of thirty dynasties. Some Egyptologists add a thirty-first dynasty consisting of three Persian kings who ruled for about a decade before Alexander conquered the country. Despite numerous problems with this Manethonian model (see discussions below and in other chapters) it is almost impossible to talk about Egyptian history and chronology without adhering to this dynastic scheme.

The Dynastic Structure

By modern convention, based on Egypt's historical record, these thirty dynasties have been subdivided into larger political entities according to the following scheme. The dates given in the following list are only estimates, intended to show you the broad time frames involved. Table 3.1, *Some Alternative Chronologies for Egyptian Dynasties 1–20*, shows several alternative chronological schemes for the first twenty dynasties.

Dynastic Breakdown by Eras

Dynasties 1–6	Old Kingdom (c.3000–2100).
Dynasties 7–10	First Intermediate Period (c. 2180–2000)
Dynasties 11–12	Middle Kingdom (c. 2160–1760)
Dynasties 13–17	Second Intermediate Period (c. 1770–1576/1550)
Dynasties 18–20	New Kingdom (c. 1576/1550–1070)
Dynasties 21–25	Third Intermediate Period (c. 1070–656)
Dynasties 26–30	The Late Period (c. 664–343/332)

Table 3.1. Some Alternative Chronologies for Egyptian Dynasties 1–20

Starting dates for the first three dynasties are very speculative and poorly documented.

Period	Gardiner[a] (1961)	CAH[b] (1971–75)	Kitchen[c] (1996)	Beckerath[d] (1997)	Shaw[e] (2000)	Krauss/ Warburton[f] (2006)
Old Kingdom	**3100–?**	**3100–2181**	**3100–2176**	**3032–2216**	**3000–2181**	**2900–2120**
1st Dynasty	3100–?	3100–2890	3100–2900	3032–2853	3000–?	2900–2730
2nd Dynasty	?–2700	2890–2686	2900–2700	2853–2707	?–2686	2730–2590
3rd Dynasty	2700–2620	2686–2613	2691–2617	2707–2639	2686–2613	2592–2544
4th Dynasty	2620–2480	2613–2498	2617–2515	2639–2504	2613–2494	2543–2436
5th Dynasty	2480–2340	2494–2345	2515–2362	2504–2347	2494–2345	2435–2306
6th Dynasty	2340–?	2345–2181	2362–2176	2347–2216	2345–2181	2305–2118
First Intermediate[g]	**?**	**2181–2040**	**2136–2023**	**2216–2025**	**2181–2025**	**2118–1980**
7th Dynasty	?	2181–2173	2176–?	?	2181–?	
8th Dynasty	?	2173–2160	?–2136	2216–2170	?–2160	2150–2118
9th Dynasty	?	2160–2130	2136–?	2170–?	2160–?	2118–?
10th Dynasty	?	2130–2040	?–2023	?–2025	?–2025	?–1980
Middle Kingdom	**2134–1786**	**2133–1786**	**2116–1795**	**2119–1794**	**2125–1773**	**1980–1760**
11th Dynasty	2134–1991	2133–1991	2116–1973	2119–1976	2125–1985	2080–1940
12th Dynasty	1991–1786	1991–1786	1973–1795	1976–1794	1985–1773	1939–1760
Second Intermediate	**?**	**1786–1570**	**1795–1540**	**1794–1550**	**1773–1550**	**1759–1539**
13th Dynasty	?	1786–1633	1795–1627	1794–1648	1773–1650	1759–1630

14th Dynasty	?	1786–1603	?	?–1648	1773–1650	?–?
15th Dynasty	?	1674–1567	1638–1540	1648–1539	1650–1550	?–1530
16th Dynasty	?	?	?	?	1650–1580	?–?
17th Dynasty	?–1575	1650–1570	1638–1540	1645–1550	1580–1550	?–1540
New Kingdom	**1575–1087**	**1570–1085**	**1540–1070**	**1550–1070**	**1550–1069**	**1539–1077**
18th Dynasty	1575–1308	1570–1320	1540–1295	1550–1292	1550–1295	1539–1292
19th Dynasty	1308–1194	1320–1200	1295–1186	1292–1186	1295–1186	1292–1191
20th Dynasty	1184–1087	1200–1085	1186–1070	1186–1070	1186–1069	1190–1071

a(Gardiner 1961), 430–453. Gardiner's 1st Dynasty starting date is 3100 +/- 150 years. Based on the Turin Canon of Kings. Gardener estimates the Old Kingdom endured for about 955 years, but he has no specific starting date or ending date.

b Cambridge Ancient History, Vol. 1, Part 2B, 994–96; Vol. II, Part 1, 44–64; Vol. II, Part 2B, 1038–1039.

c(Kitchen 1996), 11–12. Kitchen starts the First Intermediate Period with the 9th Dynasty.

d(Beckerath 1997), 187–90. Beckerath has two sets of dates for the Old Kingdom, one 50 years higher than the other. I list the higher numbers here.

e(Shaw 2000), 485–87.

f(Hornung, Krauss and Warburton 2006), 490–93.

g Shaw and Hornung begin the First Intermediate Period with Dynasty IX and place Dynasties 7–8 with the Old Kingdom.

As you can see from Table 3.1, the death of Joseph in 1454, the last of the patriarchs in our chronological scheme, falls somewhere into the transition from the Second Intermediate Period to the New Kingdom, depending upon which chronological scheme you follow. Let me briefly explain the reason for these groupings, the broad chronological issues involved, and a few of the issues that divide the authors of the respective chronologies in Table 3.1.

The Old Kingdom and First Intermediate Period

At sometime around 3100–3000 BCE, the founder of the First Dynasty united Egypt for the first time. Tradition identifies him as Menes but we have no such name in our archaeological records. He is almost certainly one of three monarchs, Scorpion, Narmer, or Hor-Aha, known from the archeological record and who ruled in succession. This first king ruled from Memphis and that city served as the capitol of a united Egypt throughout the first six dynasties. The continuity of rule in Memphis is one of the chief reasons for incorporating the six dynasties into a single political unit.

Because of the substantial lack of information about the first two dynasties, most Egyptologists now separate them from the Old Kingdom and refer to them as the Archaic Period. Some Egyptologists have taken to including the Third Dynasty within the Archaic Period. This subdivision into two political units has no bearing on the chronological issues.

Sometime during or after the Sixth Dynasty an era of political chaos erupted and Memphis lost full control over a united Egypt. Once again, the country was divided. This era of conflict has been called the First Intermediate Period and it appears to have been highly embarrassing to the ancient compilers of Egyptian king-lists, who tended to omit Memphis's rivals from their listings. Because of the poor quality of the records, Egyptologists incorporate The Seventh through Tenth Dynasties into this era.

We have no clear evidence from the archaeological and written records for the existence of a Seventh and Eight Dynasty and some Egyptologists question the existence of one or both. What ancient records we do have, as we shall eventually see, disagree on how many kings there were in the Memphite Sixth Dynasty. This has led to the idea that the extra kings in the longer lists might correspond to the Seventh and/or Eighth Dynasties as a continuation of Memphite rule, possibly corresponding to those Memphite kings that remained in power over at least parts of Egypt after the rebellions broke out.

During this period of chaos, we have some poorly documented evidence for the rise of a House of Akhtoy in the city of Heracleopolis, and Egyptologists identify its rulers as the kings of the Ninth and/or Tenth Dynasties. The record is unclear if there were one or two Heracleopolitan dynasties and how long they lasted. The evidence does show that the last few Heracleopolitan rulers served concurrently with, and in opposition to, the first few rulers of the Eleventh Dynasty, assuming you identify the start of the Eleventh Dynasty with the beginning of the ruling family as opposed to the year in which the ruling family reunited Egypt.

One important chronological issue is that we don't have any clear evidence for when the Sixth Dynasty ended and how long the chaotic period lasted. This creates a chronological gap between the end of the Sixth Dynasty and the start of the Eleventh Dynasty, and Egyptologists rely on educated guesses to resolve the chronological issues.

The Middle Kingdom

The Middle Kingdom began with the second unification of Egypt under Theban rule, sometime during the Eleventh Dynasty, establishing Thebes as the nation's capital. The Middle Kingdom usually refers to Dynasties 11–12, but some Egyptologists would include all or part of the Thirteenth Dynasty in the definition. This is because the earlier portion of the Theban Thirteenth Dynasty appears to have continued without disruption to rule over all of Egypt.

We have very good chronological information for the Twelfth Dynasty and some good information for the Eleventh. More importantly, we have an important piece of astronomical data that helps establish an absolute anchor date for the Twelfth Dynasty chronology.

This astronomical information, based on the sighting of the star Sothis under special circumstances, can be closely tied to a very narrow range of dates. However, Egyptologists disagree over which dates to use and that is one of the major factors separating the High Chronology from the Low Chronology. We'll take a closer detailed look at the Sothis issue in the next chapter.

The Second Intermediate Period

The Second Intermediate Period is another era of great chaos and conflict. It marks the first time that part (or perhaps all) of Egypt had been conquered by a foreign power and, as with the First Intermediate Period, ancient Egyptian compilers were reluctant to include information about this era in their king-lists and other records. Even today, the chronology is poorly documented, and Egyptologists mostly speculate about dynastic dates within that era.

Within this framework, Dynasties 13, 16, and 17 are identified with Thebes, but there is some question as to whether the Sixteenth Dynasty existed. There are also issues as to when the Thirteenth Dynasty ended and when the Seventeenth Dynasty started, and whether there was a chronological gap between them (perhaps filled by the Sixteenth Dynasty.)

Dynasty 15 is known as the Great Hyksos Dynasty. The Hyksos were the foreigners who somehow came to power in Egypt and established themselves in the Egyptian Delta. Records suggest they ruled for perhaps a century or so. While they clearly ruled for some period of time from the delta area (Lower Egypt) it is not clear if they ever ruled over all of Egypt for some portion of that time.

Dynasty 14 is poorly documented and it is not clear what sort of power it had. Some consider it a separate Hyksos dynasty, concurrent in part with the Great Hyksos Dynasty. Others think it may have been a minor group of princes who took advantage of the chaos to establish a local stronghold.

The war to evict the Hyksos started with the last rulers of the Seventeenth Dynasty and the last of these, Ahmose, successfully expelled them during his reign. Because of his success, he is considered the founder of the New Kingdom's Eighteenth Dynasty.

Dating within the Second Intermediate Period is at least partly dependent upon how one resolves various chronological issues for the Twelfth and Eighteenth Dynasties.

The New Kingdom

Our chronological investigation won't reach much further than the early part of the Eighteenth Dynasty. I'll only note for now that we have a great deal of very good but incomplete information from the Eighteenth Dynasty, but a precise chronology depends upon how one resolves certain astronomical issues involving lunar calendars and additional issues related to the sighting of the star Sothis. Disagreement over how to use this data is the primary cause of the disagreement between the advocates of High Chronology and the Low Chronology. The astronomical issues will be discussed in the next chapter.

Manetho

Prior to the advent of modern archaeology, the chief source of information about Egyptian kings and Egyptian chronology came from the writings of a third century BCE Egyptian priest named Manetho, who had written a history of Egypt that included a chronological record of all Egyptian rulers, beginning with the reigns of various gods, demigods, spirits, and mythical kings, and continuing down into the historical period through the conquest of Egypt by Alexander the Great in 332 BCE

Unfortunately, we have no extant copy of his original writing. Instead, we have three ancient texts written in Greek—one from the first century Jewish historian Josephus, one from the third century Christian chronographer Africanus, and one from the fourth century Christian historian Eusebius, all writing several hundred years after Manetho's time—that claim to be based on Manetho's history, but they are frequently and substantially in many respects inconsistent with each other and all three are often at great odds with the known Egyptian record as uncovered through modern archaeology. Manetho, himself, probably also wrote in Greek to suit the Greek-speaking Ptolemaic rulers of Egypt.

That three such sources, writing several hundred years after Manetho himself wrote his history, suggests that the priest's work was quite popular and widely circulated. The present practice of dividing Egyptian history into a period of thirty dynasties derives from the Africanus and Eusebius texts and is known as the Manetho or Manethonian model.

Among the problems found in these three accounts, we find many of the king names are unrecognizable, often due to the transformation of Egyptian names into Greek; many king-reigns are too long; several dynasties have too many kings; some dynasties have no king names at all; some king names appear out of order; many dynasties are far too long; and some dynasties may be spurious. Nevertheless, detailed studies of Manetho's texts indicate that the original source must have been based on genuine Egyptian records, some going back all the way to the earliest years of Egypt's dynastic history. Kenneth Kitchen, for example, has written of the Twenty-first Dynasty, "Here the sequence of 7 kings found in Manetho is fully substantiated by the first-hand monumental evidence . . . Their regnal years can be closely determined from original documents, almost totally agreed to by Manetho's text (well preserved at this point)."[21]

Many of the problems in the Manetho texts can probably be traced to significant errors in transmission, and in some instances the underlying text can be recovered. I have separately published a study of the transmission errors in Manetho that show a much more accurate underlying chronological source than we now have.[22]

Manetho's history also had a strong influence on biblical studies. His long chronological record, probably the only known such extensive history in the ancient world, provided some anchor points to which biblical dates could be connected, and some are referenced in the Manetho sources. Josephus's identification of the biblical Exodus with Manetho's account of the expulsion of the Hyksos at the beginning of the Eighteenth Dynasty, for example, has been highly influential throughout the centuries and several scholars still adhere to the Josephus model.

On the other hand, it is not clear that Manetho himself adhered to this thirty-dynasty structure. He does seem on occasion to have summarized the reigns of groups of kings from time to time, based on some sort of political context, but may have done so on many more than thirty occasions and not necessarily in line with the divisions in the Manetho model. Josephus, in his version of Manetho, covering Dynasties 15–19, has lists of kings but shows no dynastic breaks as he moves from one dynasty to another within the same list. The present arrangement is more a product of the subsequent transmissions of Manetho than of Manetho himself.

Manetho's history began with a mythical period ruled by various gods, demigods, spirits, and mythical kings, and continued through an Egyptian historical period beginning with what we now refer to as the First Dynasty and ending with the conquest of Egypt by Alexander the Great. It is the only known ancient document to have covered such a vast period of continuous history, with both historical commentary and chronological detail about the various rulers of that nation.

Josephus

The Josephus account, which appears in his book *Against Apion*, covers only a portion of Manetho's history, spanning approximately from the Fifteenth through the Nineteenth Dynasties. His account appears in narrative form and, despite listing a sequence of kings spanning several dynasties, contains no reference to numbered dynasties or any direct reference to dynastic divisions, although he does describe shifts in control from one political faction to another that is somewhat consistent with the corresponding dynastic divisions. It also includes some sequences of named Egyptian rulers along with lengths of reign and some collective durations for groups of kings. His recitation of the named kings, number of kings, and their lengths of reign frequently disagree with what we know from the archaeological record.

He appears to have had at least two versions of Manetho's history to work from and these earlier copies of Manetho already exhibit evidence of inconsistencies in transmission. For example, referring to Manetho's account of the group of kings known as the Hyksos, Josephus says that in one account the definition of Hyksos means "king-shepherds" but that in another version it means "captive shepherds."[23] In another instance, in one place he gives one set of personal names to the Egyptian kings who defeated the Hyksos and elsewhere he gives another set of personal names to these same kings.[24]

Some of the inconsistencies in the Manetho texts seem to have led Josephus to believe that the conflicting accounts described two separate events rather than differing accounts of the same event. As a result, his narrative appears to include both accounts, treating them as if they were part of a single Manetho narrative, but he doesn't tell us that the combined accounts come from separate sources. In one instance, for example, he tells us about a rebellious group of priests and on two separate occasions in the narrative, he tells us that the priest's followers called him Osarseph, but on the second occasion he tells us this as if he had never previously told us what the priest's followers called him.[25]

Africanus and Eusebius

The two later accounts by Africanus and Eusebius are similar to each other in that they both take the form of tabular accounts of the various dynasties in sequential order along with, in most cases, a list of kings within each dynasty and their lengths of reign. And, in most instances, they parallel each other closely as to the sequence of dynasties and kings contained within. Neither contains much narrative material about the rulers although a few very short anecdotes are preserved.

While both seem to draw on similar source materials (Eusebius may have partially drawn on Africanus) and follow the same sequential structure, there are several points where the two lists diverge with respect to the chronological information about kings and dynasties. Scholars generally consider Africanus more accurate than Eusebius regarding the transmission of the Manetho texts, and it is clear that on occasion Eusebius has a more garbled source than does Africanus. Consider, for example, a comparison of the Fifth and Sixth Dynasties in the two works.

Where Africanus lists nine kings (although alleging that there were only eight kings) for the Fifth Dynasty and lists six more kings for the Sixth Dynasty, Eusebius says that the Fifth Dynasty had 31 kings but names only one, a king who served in the Sixth Dynasty. And then, for the Sixth Dynasty he lists only the last ruler. It is obvious, in retrospect, that Eusebius relied on a confused or confusing transmission of the Fifth and Sixth Dynasties that concatenated them into a single continuum. On the other hand, our examination of Manetho's history will show that sometimes Eusebius preserves traces of a better account than does Africanus.

It should be noted here that both the Africanus and Eusebius lists are preserved only in copies written down in later times by other writers, allowing additional opportunities for error in the copying and interpreting process.

The Africanus material comes chiefly from a work by George the Monk, also known as Syncellus, who wrote it down at about the end of the eighth century.[26] For Eusebius, we have extracts preserved by Syncellus, but we also have an Armenian translation of the whole work made between 500 and 800, and a Latin version made by Jerome toward the end of the fourth century.[27] There are some differences among these various copies of Eusebius. In Eusebius's Fourteenth Dynasty, for example, Syncellus preserves a duration of 184 years (the same as in Africanus) while the Armenian version has 484 years.

The Africanus and Eusebius lists divided the king-list into a sequence of thirty dynasties down to the conquest of Egypt by Alexander the Great. In modern times, Egyptologists have taken to identifying the last couple of Persian rulers in Egypt as a thirty-first dynasty.

Other Syncellus Accounts

Syncellus also preserves some material that he attributes to Manetho as independent of and different from Africanus and Eusebius. One such work is *The Book of Sothis*. Although purportedly written by

Manetho, some scholars believe it was a later work attributed to Manetho by the author. [28] It is a clumsy redaction listing several kings, some out of sequential order, without dynastic divisions and with many kings missing from the sequence of rulers.

Syncellus also preserves another document called *The Old Chronicle*, which he believes to have influenced Manetho and led him into error.[29] That document, however, is probably post-Manetho but may have in fact been a fourth independent preservation of Manetho's account. It was concerned primarily with the reigns of the gods and we need not concern ourselves with it at this point. We will look at it more closely when we examine the pre-dynastic portion of the king-lists in Volume II of this study.

Some Chronological Concerns

According to the Africanus and Eusebius texts, Manetho's chronology from the First Dynasty to the last encompassed just under 5,500 years, dating the onset to sometime prior to 5000 B.C. The presently accepted view of Egyptologists is that the First Dynasty began no earlier than about 3100 B.C., give or take 150 years,[30] approximately two millennia shorter than that established by the Manetho sources.

A good deal of this excess can be confined to the Second Intermediate Period, the chaotic era that lasted approximately two hundred years. In Africanus, for example, Dynasties 13–17 lasted over 1600 years while Eusebius gives them a duration of almost 1200 years. Josephus doesn't include the entire Second Intermediate Period in his account, but what durations he does give are on the same order of error as in the other two lists. Even if we allow for the now-accepted idea of concurrent dynasties within the Second Intermediate Period, the three sets of Manetho figures are still highly excessive.

Another large erroneous time span can be confined to Manetho's First Intermediate Period, which, in its preserved form, has hundreds of years too many for the Ninth and Tenth Dynasties. Furthermore, the Manetho texts present these two dynasties in sequential order, falling between the Sixth and Eleventh Dynasties, when, in fact, the Ninth and Tenth Dynasties were mostly concurrent with those other dynasties.

It is common among Egyptologists to dismiss Manetho's error-laden First and Second Intermediate Periods as the result of poor documentation for these eras, a problem which afflicts even modern Egyptologists trying to get an accurate account of these times. The ancient Egyptians were highly embarrassed by the First and Second Intermediate Periods, especially the latter, which resulted in foreign rulers taking control of Egypt for the first time. Some ancient Egyptian records pass over these eras as if they never existed. Much of the rest of Manetho, they believe, comes closer to the mark.

Even allowing for the poor state of his First and Second Intermediate Periods, several other dynasties also present chronological problems. The 277 years assigned by Africanus to the Fourth Dynasty and the 248 years assigned by him to the Fifth Dynasty are each more than a century more than the accepted parameters. Eusebius is in even worse shape when it comes to these two dynasties. Manetho's Third Dynasty lasts more than twice as long as any accepted durations.

Within that framework it is generally accepted that while there are many errors in Manetho's preserved chronology and often major inconsistencies with other more reliable evidence, the original Manetho chronology does appear to have been based, at least in part, on authentic and reliable source materials. As discoveries emerge and debates proceed, there is still a tendency to compare the conclusions with what appears in Manetho, and in some instances, Egyptologists use Manetho as a default chronological datum.

Other Egyptian King-lists

A most important key to unraveling the puzzle of Egyptian chronology comes from a series of king-lists that give us a significant amount of information about the sequence of kings in several dynasties, and in one case, a chronological history of these kings. None of these lists, however, continues past the Nineteenth Dynasty. The king-lists include the following items:

- The Table of Abydos
- The Table of Sakkara
- The Table of Karnak
- The Palermo Stone
- The Turin Canon of Kings.

The Table of Abydos

The Table of Abydos can be found on the wall of the Temple of Sethos I, at Abydos. It lists a series of seventy-six kings in chronological order, starting with the first ruler of the First Dynasty and ending with Sethos I of the Nineteenth Dynasty.[31] A mutilated copy of this list was also found in the Temple of Ramesses II. The more complete list arranges the kings in two rows, the lesser list in three rows.[32]

Signifying the great turmoil occurring in the Second Intermediate Period, it omits the kings of Dynasties 13–17.[33] In the same manner, the rebellious rulers of the Ninth and Tenth Dynasties in the First Intermediate Period are also left out. The Abydos list, however, has a significantly longer list of Memphite rulers beginning with the Sixth Dynasty than do any of the other king-lists.[34] This lengthy list of rulers has no indicated break for a Seventh and Eighth Dynasty ruling in Memphis, and several Egyptologists would treat the later portion of this long list as corresponding to the Seventh and/or Eighth Dynasties.

The Table of Sakkara

Beginning with the sixth king of the First Dynasty, the Table of Sakkara preserves the cartouches of forty-seven (originally fifty-eight) kings, the last of the listed kings being Ramesses II of the Nineteenth Dynasty.[35] It, too, omits the rulers of Dynasties 13–17, further evidence of the discord aroused by the Second Intermediate Period.[36] And it, too, omits the kings associated with Ninth and Tenth Dynasties. But it also omits the latter portion of the Sixth Dynasty found on other lists, having only four kings, the fewest number of rulers in this dynasty of all the available listings.

The Table of Karnak

The Table of Karnak lists several kings, beginning with the first king of Dynasty 1 and continuing to Thutmose III of the Eighteenth Dynasty.[37] It originally had sixty-one names, forty-eight of which are legible in whole or part, but the names are not in chronological order.[38] The display also names several kings not included in the other lists, but the lack of a chronological order limits the usefulness of those entries.[39]

The Palermo Stone

Inscribed during the Fifth Dynasty, the Palermo Stone presents one of the most interesting of ancient documents. In its original form, it contained a year by year record of the first five dynasties.[40] Once a large slab of black diorite, about seven feet long and two feet wide, only fragments remain. The portions we do have show one set of marks recording significant events for certain years, and another set referring to the levels of the Nile. There are also occasional markings signifying the change of reign.[41]

The Turin Canon of Kings

Also known as the Royal Canon of Kings and the Turin Papyrus, the Turin Canon of Kings is one of our most important sources for information about the chronology of Egyptian kings. It comes to us on a papyrus prepared during the reign of Ramesses II, of the Nineteenth Dynasty. As in Manetho, the roster begins with a series of mythological rulers and follows them with the names of the historical rulers of Egypt. It once contained a sequential list of over three hundred kings along with their lengths of reign.[42]

Unfortunately, the original papyrus is in numerous fragments and badly mutilated. Only portions of the list are readable, and not all its chronological data is consistent with the archaeological record.[43]

Unlike the Abydos and Sakkara lists, the Turin Canon includes a list of all the kings (known to the compiler) of the Second Intermediate Period.[44] It also includes a list of kings associated with the Ninth and/or Tenth Dynasties, but where it listed eighteen kings for this sequence, Manetho had two groups of nineteen kings each.[45] It also shows more Memphite kings in the Sixth Dynasty than the Sakkara list but fewer than the Abydos list.[46]

The document was written on the back of what appears to be a discarded fiscal record, and, as Redford warns, "can scarcely qualify as an 'official' record."[47] Still, Egyptologists generally accept the Turin Canon entries, where readable, as a default value for the duration of a particular king or dynasty, subject to revision when other evidence comes along. On the other hand, if this list only existed as less than an official record, it speaks to the fact that the Egyptians of the New Kingdom had records of all the earlier kings who ruled in the earlier dynasties.

Other Sources

In addition to the various king-lists we have many chronological inscriptions for individual kings and data that links groups of kings together through short lists or family relationships. These continue to refine our chronological reconstructions. In addition, modern scientific techniques such as carbon[14] dating as well as the recovery of potentially datable artifacts based on archaeological contexts, also give us new insights. But some developing conflicts are beginning to appear. Some carbon[14] studies are starting to support the High Chronology while some archaeologists are arguing that their finds support the Low Chronology.

As noted above, the use of astronomical data helped play a role in establishing some anchor points for fixed dates in Egyptian chronology, particularly sightings of the star Sothis, and references to the lunar calendar. The Sothic dating system plays an important role in this study and in the following chapter we look at what is involved.

4 Enoch and Sothis: A Smoking Gun?

IF YOU TAKE ANOTHER LOOK AT TABLE 3.1 YOU WILL SEE THAT, DESPITE some differences in the precise dating of events, Egyptologists are in broad agreement on the approximate time frames for each of the dynasties within each of the major political eras. Except for the earliest dynasties the disagreements are usually less than fifty years apart for most of this almost three-thousand-year long period of time. This is true even for the First and Second Intermediate Periods.

That's pretty good. But, you might ask, if we have very little solid chronological data for the First and Second Intermediate Periods, and the Manetho king-list shows a Second Intermediate Period of five consecutive dynasties well over one thousand years longer than current Egyptological estimates and a First Intermediate Period of four consecutive dynasties running a couple of hundred years longer than present estimates, how did we get to the point where we could shrink the First and Second Intermediate Periods so substantially that we can have so much relative agreement on the framework for absolute dates for all Old, Middle, and New Kingdoms dynasties?

Of course, since the earlier days of Egyptology, we have discovered numerous pieces of sequential and chronological data about individual kings, and short sequences of kings, and family relationships that enable us to provide a more detailed sequential and chronological record. But despite all the available material there were still some difficult problems. We needed some way to chronologically connect the Old, Middle and New Kingdoms to each other and to establish approximate time frames for each of the eras and dynasties. We needed fixed dates linked to the king-lists. Then, building up from our knowledge of surrounding kings, we could connect dates for one group of rulers to other groups of rulers. How did Egyptologists solve this problem?

The answer consists of a combination of Egyptian agricultural needs and a quirk in the Egyptian civil calendar. From the agricultural standpoint, Egypt's most important event each year was the annual flooding of the Nile River, which created the rich soil needed for growing food. This occurred at about the same time each year and the Egyptians needed to know approximately when that would occur. Ideally, they should get this information from their civil calendar, but there was a major problem.

The Egyptian civil calendar was a solar calendar consisting of 365 days. (The Egyptians may have been the first culture in history to have invented the solar calendar.) The year was broken into twelve months, each lasting thirty days, with five days added to the end of the twelve months, which days they associated with the births of specific gods. The twelve months were divided into three seasons of four months each. Egyptians named the seasons *Inundation* (i.e., referring to the flooding of the Nile), *Emergence* (the growth of the crops), and *Harvest*, reflecting the agricultural nature of the Egyptian year. But the calendar had a flaw.

While the calendar had a 365-day year, the solar year is 365 1/4 days long. The Egyptians, however, did not make allowance for the extra quarter day as we do with the quadrennial leap year. Every year, the civil calendar would fall another 1/4 day out of phase with the true solar year, one full day every four years, one full month every 120 years. As a result, the civil calendar could not indicate when the seasons began, or when the Nile flood would begin its annual inundation. An old papyrus states the problem quite poetically. "Winter is come in the summer, the months are reversed, the hours in confusion."[48]

The Egyptians were keen observers of the stars and the star that we now call Sirius was one of the brightest. The Egyptians called it *Sopdet*, and the Greeks transliterated it as *Sothis*, the latter being the name that Egyptologists currently use when referring to that star's calendrical role. The Egyptian astrologers noticed something interesting about Sothis.

Every year the star disappeared for seventy days. Very close in time to when it re-appeared for the first time, the Nile overflowed its banks. Astronomers call the annual re-appearance of a star after its disappearance, the *heliacal* rising. This heliacal rising of Sothis signaled the onset of the Nile flooding.

This sighting depended upon both the height of the star above the horizon and the latitude of the observer, and in different areas of Egypt sightings could be as much as a day apart. Still, this was close enough to permit farmers to make the appropriate arrangements and the heliacal rising of Sothis came to be celebrated as New Year's Day. This Sothic New Year, separate from the civil New Year, fell on what we would date to July 19th. Because the Egyptian solar year ran from July to July instead of January to January, we have a minor round-off error when converting ancient Egyptian year-dates into our modern year-dates.

While this solved the immediate problem for the Egyptians, their interest in natural patterns and cycles led them to take one additional step, the one that provided the key to the chronological puzzle. The Egyptians thought it important that there be harmony between the solar cycle and the Nile flood. Because the civil calendar fell out of alignment with the solar year by 1/4 of a day every year, they realized that it should take 1460 solar years for the civil calendar to lose 365 days. Since 1460 solar years equaled 1461 civil years, the annual Sothic New Year (July 19th), when the Nile flooded, would coincide with the New Year date on the civil calendar every 1461 civil years

This New Year's coincidence was a matter of great religious moment. The Egyptian treated the 1460-year solar period as a "Sothic Year" and divided it up in the same way they did the civil calendar, the Sothic calendar mimicking the civil calendar. Four solar years equaled one Sothic day; the civil month had thirty days, so a Sothic month equaled 120 solar years; the civil year had three seasons of four months each, so each Sothic season had three seasons of four months each, a total of 480 solar years per Sothic season.

Fortunately, as we will see shortly, ancient Egyptians on occasion marked the occurrence of an event by citing both the month and date on the Sothic calendar (enabling an absolute date by calculating how much time passed from the start of a dated Sothic cycle) and the civil calendar.

This Sothic practice offered Egyptologists the opportunity to build a skeletal structure for Egyptian chronology. If Egyptologists could locate such dual dates, Sothic and Civil, they could establish some fixed anchor dates. They just needed to determine on what date a Sothic cycle started and then find some archaeological records linking one or more pharaohs to specific years within the Sothic cycle. That was not so easy.

To begin with, history knows of only one reference to the start of a Sothic cycle. The Roman historian Censorinus noted the coincidence of a Sothic New Year and a civil New Year in AD 139, during the reign of the Roman emperor Antoninus Pius, a claim that is corroborated by the issuance in Alexandria of a coin commemorating the event.[49]

Although the evidence for Censorinus's dating is sparse, Egyptologists have seized upon it as the foundation from which they could establish not only the chronology of ancient Egypt but, by cross reference to the extensive Egyptian records of Mediterranean and Middle Eastern contacts, much of the chronology of those other areas as well. By counting backwards in 1460-year cycles, starting with AD 139, it was initially determined that Sothic cycles would have started in 2781 and 1321 BC.[50] These dates, however, were based on the erroneous assumption that the length of a Sothic cycle was constant, always 1460 solar years.

The time between consecutive heliacal risings of Sothis depends on the length of time in which the center of the sun passes from the elliptic meridian of Sothis and returns to that position. If Sothis were fixed in position this event would take 365.25636 days, what is known as a sidereal year, and the Sothic cycle would be 1460 years long. But Sothis is not fixed in position. It has its own period of motion. This means that a Sothic cycle could vary from 1460 years by as much as ten years.[51]

The length of the Sothic cycle was first calculated in 1884 by Theodor Oppolzer and, in 1904, Eduard Meyer used those numbers for the first time to obtain starting dates for the Sothic cycles before AD 139.[52] From these new calculations, it was determined that Sothic cycles began in 2773 and 1317.[53] A more recent set of studies, conducted in 1969, has determined that the cycle preceding AD 139 lasted 1453 years and the one before that 1456 years, providing alternative starting dates of 1314 and 2770.[54] The chief chronological difference between the two studies is that the later study proposes a slight shorter Sothic cycle for the period ending in 139 A.D.

Which study is more accurate is hard to say, but since the various dates proposed for the start of the Sothic cycle differ by only a few years over several millennia, the overall impact on the chronological framework is not significant.[55] The more difficult problem was obtaining archaeological links between Egyptian kings and the Sothic cycle.

The recognition of slightly different lengths for a Sothic cycle introduced a separate problem. Did the Egyptians, on seeing an unexpected heliacal rising on the Civil New Year calendar adjust the starting date of the next Sothic cycle, or did they continue to leave the Sothic calendar in place without modification? What that means practically is this. The Sothic Calendar used by the Egyptians may have varied slightly from the actual astronomically determined Sothic cycle.

Assume for the sake of argument that Sothic cycle started on 2773, as indicated above, but that the Egyptians did not make an adjustment to their Sothic calendar to account for the subsequent shorter cycles. On the astronomical level, the Sothic cycle ended in 1317, but the Sothic calendar continued until the calendar cycle ended in 1313. If an astronomical Sothic cycle were used, Year 1 of the next cycle would begin on 1317. But, if the calendar-based Sothic cycle were used, Year 1 of the next cycle would begin on 1313. So, if we found a Sothic date, say for Year 100 of the next Sothic cycle, would that refer to 1217 or 1213? We don't know how Egyptian resolved this issue. Whichever method Egyptians used, they were not concerned with fixed dates but with relative dates within the Sothic cycles.

After much searching, Egyptologists found three important inscriptions connecting three separate kings to a Sothic cycle. One was to year 1469, falling in an unspecified year of the reign of Thutmose III, another to the ninth year of Amenhotep I, and the last to the seventh year of Senwosre III. The first two kings ruled during the Eighteenth Dynasty; the third ruled during the Twelfth Dynasty. This gave us links to the New and Middle Kingdoms and provided a potential for calculating how long the Second Intermediate Period lasted.

The Twelfth and Eighteenth Dynasties bracket the Second Intermediate Period and we have good records for the sequence and chronology of the kings in these two dynasties, with full and partial lengths of reign for all of them. Now, with the ability to attach the relative chronologies for both dynasties to approximate anchor dates, we can establish chronological boundaries for the beginning and end of the Second Intermediate Period. Working back to the earlier dynasties before the Twelfth, we can also establish some reasonable boundaries for the First Intermediate Period, but the duration is less certain than it is for the Second Intermediate Period.

Sothic Dating for the Eighteenth Dynasty

The next issue to consider was how many Sothic cycles intervened between 139 CE and the Eighteenth Dynasty. If only one complete cycle elapsed between the Eighteenth Dynasty and 139 CE, then the dynasty came to power sometime in the sixteenth century. If two cycles occurred, then the Eighteenth Dynasty began about 3000 BCE There was too much historical and contextual data inconsistent with the earlier date and it was obvious that the Eighteenth Dynasty must have started sometime in the sixteenth century.

The Sothic boundaries established, a date for the ninth year of Amenhotep I could be determined. But first, another matter had to be resolved, one which is still the subject of much debate. Did the observation of the heliacal rising of Sothis occur in Thebes or Memphis?

If the sighting took place in Memphis, the ninth year of Amenhotep I would have to have fallen between 1544–1537, with proponents of this view congregating around a proposed date between 1544–1542.[56] If the sighting occurred in Thebes, the ninth year fell between 1525–1517, with proponents of this view congregating around the low end of the range.[57]

This is one of the unresolved issues that separates advocates of the High Chronology from the Low Chronology. The Memphis dates lead to the High Chronology; the Theban dates to the Low Chronology. The difference, however amounts to no more than about thirty years, depending upon which year in the two cycles you choose as your preferred date.

It is my view that the issue over where the sighting took place may be moot. The issue, as I see it, is not where the sighting occurred, but what Sothic calendar was in play. If the sighting happened in Thebes, the scribes should have dated the event according to whatever that date was on the contemporaneous Sothic calendar. Since the Sothic cycle under consideration began in the Old Kingdom, under Memphis rule, then the dates on the Sothic calendar would have originated with an initial Memphis sighting.

It is highly unlikely that there would be separate Sothic calendars in Thebes and Memphis conflicting with each other. That would lead to chaos and conflict in Egyptian affairs. The Theban government would have continued to use the Sothic calendar that was in use at the time they came to power in the Eleventh Dynasty. If I am right, this suggests that the Sothic date reflects a Memphite perspective and that the High Chronology is preferable to the Low Chronology.

The Sothic reference to an unspecified year in the reign of Thutmose III presented a different problem. The Sothic date, itself, was to 1469, but it didn't indicate what year of the monarch's reign that was. In addition to the Sothic date, the text also incorporated references to the lunar calendar, a different Egyptian calendar than the solar-based civil calendar. The lunar data suggested three possible dates for the ascension of Thutmose III to the throne, 1504, 1490 or 1479.

Since Thutmose III ruled for fifty-four years, and the Sothic date of 1469 was not connected to any specific year within his reign, all three dates allowed for plausible solutions. Each of these dates has its advocates and Egyptologists remain divided over which one is correct. The choice usually reflects whether one accepts the High Chronology or the Low Chronology and how one fills in various gaps in the chronological record.

So, while we don't have perfect agreement among Egyptologists regarding the precise boundaries for an absolute chronology of the Eighteenth Dynasty, the range of disagreement falls within about 35 years. There are also a couple of disputes about how long some Eighteenth Dynasty kings ruled and questions about the existence and duration of coregencies. Within the current framework, most Egyptologists date the start of the Eighteenth Dynasty to somewhere between about 1575 and 1540, and end it somewhere between about 1319 and 1292.

Sothic Dating for the Twelfth Dynasty

While the chronological gap between the Eighteenth Dynasty and its successors was easily resolved, that between the Twelfth and Eighteenth Dynasties presented more of a problem. In between was the Second Intermediate Period, that poorly documented era of political and social chaos. If no Sothic cycle intervened between these two dynasties then the seventh year of Senwosre III probably occurred between 1876 and 1864.[58]

One group of scholars, following Parker, tends to accept 1872 as the likely date.[59] Another group follows Beckerath, who advocates a date of 1866. [60] A small minority agree with Krauss, who proposes a date of 1830, but his theory is based on a Sothic sighting at the extreme southern location of Elephantine. This chronological dispute is another factor in the dispute over High Chronology versus Low Chronology.

If, on the other hand, there were an intervening cycle, then the date in question had to be around 3300 BC. Such an early date seemed unlikely, but the historical record wasn't as forcefully dispositive as it was for the Eighteenth Dynasty.

The king-lists were of little help. Three lacked any references to Dynasties 13–17. One, the Table of Karnak, had only a partial list and it wasn't in chronological order. The Turin Canon and Manetho both had chronological information, but, as noted above, they do not provide sufficient reliable information for the Second Intermediate Period. Further, despite the conflicts in the Manetho numbers, both Africanus and Eusebius (and implicitly Josephus) indicate that the Second Intermediate Period lasted over 1,200 years, which, if even close to correct, would put the Middle and New Kingdoms in separate Sothic cycles.

Flinders Petrie, one of the earliest and greatest of Egyptologists, thought, at least in part based on the Manetho numbers, that the Twelfth Dynasty must have occurred in the previous Sothic cycle, creating an approximate break of 1,800 years between the Twelfth and Eighteenth Dynasties.[61]

But such a long interval has no support in the archaeological record, and the absence of such evidence is a chief argument against the claim. Today, as we keep learning more about the Second Intermediate Period, almost all Egyptologists accept an approximate length of no more than about two hundred years for its duration, placing the Twelfth Dynasty in the same Sothic cycle as the Eighteenth, and yielding a Sothic date of somewhere between 1877 and 1864 for the seventh year of Senwosre III. Other data for this dynasty enables us to set up a reasonably accurate absolute chronology for the Twelfth Dynasty, although here, too, there are some disagreements as to the correct interpretation of the data.

Most Egyptologists place the starting date of the Twelfth Dynasty somewhere between 1991 and 1976 and end the dynasty somewhere between 1794 and 1786.

Although we have some chronological data for the kings of the Eleventh Dynasty, it is not complete. As a result, most Egyptologists accept the Turin Canon entry of 143 years as the dynastic duration and date the start of the Eleventh Dynasty 143 years earlier than whatever date they accept as starting date for the Twelfth Dynasty. Prior to the Eleventh Dynasty we have the First

Intermediate Period, about which we know less than we do for the Second Intermediate Period.

The Old Kingdom

Although the Sothic dates give us chronological anchors for the Middle and New Kingdoms, we lack any Sothic evidence for the Old Kingdom. The First Intermediate Period creates a chronological break between the end of the Memphite Sixth Dynasty and the start of the Theban Eleventh. Here we work mostly with relative chronology, with various theories as to how many years separate the Sixth and Eleventh Dynasties. Most Egyptologists would probably consider the gap to be less than a century long.

As to the first three dynasties we lack significant chronological data. For the first two dynasties, proposed estimates can differ by as much as two centuries.[62] The Palermo Stone indicates that the first two dynasties lasted 455 years and Manetho has over 550 years for the two, but Gardiner warns that neither claim can be trusted and both are much too long.[63]

For the Third Dynasty, we rely mostly on the Turin Canon entries.[64] For the Fourth through Sixth Dynasties we have a substantial amount of evidence as to the relative chronology of the kings, but we don't have a complete record and there is room for a considerable amount of disagreement as to time frames.

Gardiner determined that the Turin Canon had 955 years from the beginning of the First Dynasty to the end of the Sixth Dynasty.[65] Estimates in Table 3.1 range from about 800 years to 925 years. These differences revolve around how many years to assign to the poorly documented Dynasties 1 and 2, and how Egyptologists fill in various gaps for the remaining dynasties.

The Birth and Death Dates for Enoch

Let us now turn our attention to Enoch in the Patriarchal chronology. Enoch lived for 365 years, a possible solar year reference. Since the Hebrews used a lunar calendar, such a reference would be unusual, and biblical scholars have no satisfactory answer for why the Hebrews might use a solar reference in constructing the patriarchal chronology. It could be just a coincidence of course, but other factors suggest otherwise.

For one, this 365-year life span is hundreds of years shorter than those of all the other Genesis 5 patriarchs. This suggests a carefully drafted construct to signal that Enoch is somehow to be understood differently than the other patriarchs. Such an indication is reinforced by the break in the genealogical formula announcing the births and deaths of each patriarch. There is no statement that Enoch died. Instead, we are told that "Enoch walked with God, to which the author appends "he was not, because God took him." There is no direct reference to Enoch dying. Clearly, he was singled out for special notice.

According to our calculations, Enoch died in the year 2774. In the two studies of the Sothic cycle starting dates cited above, one determination placed the start of a Sothic cycle at 2773 and the other at 2770. These two dates are one Sothic Calendar Day (4 years) apart. Enoch's death year would be consistent with the end of one cycle and the start of the next one.

If an ancient writer were using a traditional Egyptian method of anchoring a long period of time to a specific date, that person would establish a dating system in which events were recorded relevant to when a Sothic Cycle started. The author would be using the Sothic Calendar year of 1460 solar years (1461 civil years) as a method for indicating when events happened according to a Sothic Calendar system.

I suggest that Enoch points to either the beginning of the next Sothic Cycle or the end (a death date, consistent with his end date of 2774) for the previous cycle of a Sothic Calendar Year and the dates in the Patriarchal Chronology are entered relevant to the Sothic dating system. The start of a Sothic cycle signified the first appearance of Sothis after its seventy-day disappearance, after which it began to rise through the heavens and cross over the sky. The indication that Enoch walked with God suggests a similar pattern. Enoch appeared in the heavens and walked along with God.

The first appearance of Sothis was celebrated as New Year's Day. They called that day *wp rnpt*, meaning "opening of the Year."[66] The name Enoch, according to the Anchor Bible Dictionary, "may be derived from the West Semitic root *ḥnk*, to introduce, initiate."[67] There is some debate among scholars as to why Enoch was so named but it is striking that the name signifies the same role that Sothis played as the "initiator" of a New Year.

In looking at the relationship between Enoch and Sothis we have identified the following links.

- The Genesis author has clearly singled out Enoch from the other patriarchs with special notices.
- Enoch's 365-day life span suggests a solar year signal, even though Hebrews used a lunar calendar.
- Enoch's "end" date of 2774 suggests a marker for the end of a Sothic cycle. This would signify a start of a Sothic cycle in 2773. One study places the start of a Sothic cycle at 2773; the other places it at 2770.
- The appearance of Sothis marked the movement of the star through the heavens. The "end" date for Enoch suggests the movement of the patriarch across the heavens (as he walked with God.)
- Egyptians celebrated the annual re-appearance of Sothis as opening (initiating) a New Year. The name "Enoch" derived from a Semitic word meaning "introduce" or "initiate."

These coincidences strongly suggest that the author of the Genesis chronology used Enoch as a pointer to the start of a Sothic cycle. Yet, on this evidence, some might still reasonably remain skeptical of such a conclusion. To make a solid case that Enoch represents a Sothic cycle marker, we need to show that the Patriarchal chronology, built around Enoch's "end" date, constitutes an important record of verifiable dates for key events in Egyptian history, events that cannot be based on cherry-picking odd and unusual matters that have no meaningful pattern. In the following chapters, I expect to show that the Genesis chronology serves as an accurate chronological record, consistent with the archaeological and historical evidence, for Egyptian dynastic history from Dynasty 1 through Dynasty 18.

5 Methuselah and Memphis

THE UNIFICATION OF UPPER AND LOWER EGYPT BY THE FOUNDERS OF THE First Dynasty established the city of Memphis as Egypt's political capitol. An unbroken line of kings ruled from Memphis for almost one thousand years. Based on the writings of Manetho, modern Egyptologists divide the Memphite line of kings into eight consecutive dynasties.

The ancient Egyptians believed that each legitimate ruler of Egypt was an aspect of the god Horus. So, despite the succession of one legitimate king after another, Horus continued to rule. To the Egyptians, this meant that all was right with the world and that Horus would bring peace and tranquility.

Sometime either during or just after the last century of Memphite rule chaos broke out in Egypt and questions were raised about who legitimately ruled Egypt. In Heracleopolis and Thebes native families seized local power. Egyptians wondered if Horus had abandoned Egypt? A contemporaneous text gives an account of the corruption.

> The bowman is ready. The wrongdoer is everywhere. There is no man of yesterday. A man goes out to plough with his shield. A man smites his brother, his mother's son. Men sit in the bushes until the benighted traveler comes, in order to plunder his load. The robber is a possessor of riches. Boxes of ebony are broken up. Precious acacia-wood is cleft asunder.[68]

As Memphis receded from the political scene, Heracleopolis and Thebes remained in contention for about a century. At some point midway through the Theban-based Eleventh Dynasty, king Menthotpe II defeated his Heracleopolitan rivals and reunited Egypt under Theban rule. Horus had returned to the throne, and Egypt had its first legitimate ruler since the collapse of Memphis's authority. The old order had been swept away and a new order arose out of the destruction.

Egyptologist's identify this poorly-documented chaotic era as the First Intermediate Period and they disagree as to how long it lasted, with one faction arguing for about a century and another suggesting about two centuries. The era left a deep scar on the Egyptian psyche. Almost a thousand years after the collapse of Memphis, the authors of the Tables of Sakkara and Abydos omitted from their king-lists all non-Memphite rulers prior to Menthotpe II, even omitting Menthotpe II's predecessors on the Theban throne. The two compilers, however, disagreed with each other as to how many of the last Memphite rulers could be considered legitimate.

Gardiner dates the beginning of the First Dynasty somewhere between 2950 and 3250.[69] These aren't necessarily fixed boundaries. They are estimates intended to accommodate a wide range of disagreements over the correct chronological data for Dynasties 1–11. If you glance back at Table 3.1, you will note that everyone cited, except for Krauss/Warburton, adheres to Gardiner's First Dynasty parameters, and that one departure is only off by about fifty years.

A related problem concerns how long the Old Kingdom lasted. We have no fixed anchor date tying the Memphite Kingdom to a specific year and very little reliable chronological data for Dynasties 1–3. The differing chronological estimates in Table 3.1 reflect diverse combinations of educated guesses rather than a collection of precise conclusions. How each Egyptologist resolves numerous difficulties and gaps in the record determines how each outlines the dates and lengths of Dynasties 1–8.

Turn now to Table 2.1, the list of birth and death dates in Genesis 5. Even allowing for the later Krauss/Warburton starting date, only two Genesis dates fall within Gardiner's wide range of tentative starting dates for the First Dynasty, the birth dates for Enoch (3139) and Methuselah (3074). If Enoch serves as a pointer to the start of a Sothic cycle, then any connection between his birth date and the start of the First Dynasty would have to be a coincidence. That leaves Methuselah, and, in this study, I will take his birth date as the Patriarchal Chronology date for the start of the First Dynasty.

Methuselah has several interesting characteristics. He is the son of Enoch, whom we have identified as a symbolic pointer to the start of the Sothic Cycle, and he lived longer than any other human in the bible, 969 years. He is also the last patriarch born while Adam still lived. His date of death, 2105, coincides with the onset of the biblical Flood, a marker signifying something tragic happened to the known world, and that a new order arose out of the chaos.

In biblical studies, many scholars see some sort of theological significance in the fact that the death of the last patriarch alive during Adam's life time brings on the flood that wiped out a sinful earth. However, God's reason for wiping out humanity has nothing to do with Adam's sin and this theological connection seems somewhat strained.

In the present study I will identify Methuselah's death date, 2105, as the year in which the nearly millennium-long Memphite dynasty collapsed, a terrible tragic event to the ancient Egyptians that we see reflected in various king-lists composed almost a thousand years later. Biblical authors, I will suggest, dated the Flood to coincide with the collapse of the Memphite Kingdom, as a literary parallel to the political chaos surrounding the kingdom's collapse.

Methuselah's name is also of symbolic interest. Strong's Enhanced Lexicon translates it as "Man of the dart."[70] Others have suggested alternatives to "dart," such as "weapon," "canal," or a deity's name.[71] If his name does signify some sort of warrior, it adds another potential clue for his identification with the First Dynasty. One of the three kings thought to be the possible founder of the First Dynasty through military conquest has the name "Hor-Aha", which means "Horus the Fighter."[72] The militaristic name parallel between Methuselah and Horus-Aha certainly intrigues.

Excluding Enoch, Methuselah has six ancestors, Adam, Seth, Enosh, Kenan, Mahalalel, and Jared. Their birth dates all fall into the predynastic period, and both Manetho and the Turin Canon of Kings identify the period before the First Dynasty with what we would consider a mythical era of rule by deities, spirits, and humans. The birth dates of these six Patriarchs will be identified with this same mythical era in Volume II of this study.

Table 5.1: Proposed Genesis Chronology of Memphite Dynasties		
Dynasty[a]	Patriarch[b]	Dates
Dynasty 1	Methuselah	Born 3074
Dynasty 2	Adam	Died 2831
Dynasty 3	Seth	Died 2719
Dynasty 4A	Enosh	Died 2621
Dynasty 4B	Kenan	Died 2526
Dynasty 5	Mahalalel	Died 2471
Dynasty 6	Jared	Died 2339
End of Memphite Kingdom	Methuselah	Died 2105

[a]In the proposed Genesis alignment, Dynasty 4 is divided into two parts, 4A and 4B. The two parts taken together equal the traditional Dynasty 4. See text for further explanation.
[b]The Patriarchal list includes everyone born before Methuselah except for Enoch.

More importantly, for now, the death dates for these same six Patriarchs, will each be identified with the starting dates for Dynasties 2–6 in the Memphite Kingdom. Methuselah stands as a pivot point, his birth simultaneously marking the end of the mythical era and the start of the First Dynasty. Table 5.1, *Proposed Genesis Chronology of Memphite Dynasties*, outlines the structure. I need to explain a couple of features.

First, you will notice that I have identified Methuselah's 969-year life span as the duration of the Memphite Kingdom. This identification incorporates the Sixth, Seventh and Eighth Dynasties as a single entity encompassing all the Memphite kings that ruled after the end of the Fifth Dynasty. This 969-year duration runs longer than most Egyptologists accept but it is not out of line, with Kitchen's 964 years (3100–2136) and the CAH's 940 years (3100–2160) for Dynasties 1–8 coming quite close.

Furthermore, according to Gardiner's reconstruction of the Turin Canon, that document covered a period of 955 years down to the end of the Sixth Dynasty.[73] The Table of Abydos, however, extends the TC's Sixth Dynasty by another 10 kings, all of whom are thought to have ruled very briefly. From the perspective of ancient Egyptian scribes, therefore, 969 years for the Memphite kingdom is quite reasonable. Whether the evidence supports such a duration remains to be seen in this chapter.

True, we will find conflicts among the various ancient sources and between them and some of the archaeological evidence, as well as conflicts among the Egyptologists trying to interpret the available evidence. And we will address those issues as they arise. I need to remind the reader, though, that we must look at the Patriarchal Chronology not only based on the modern archaeological record, but also from the perspective of how ancient Egyptian scribes understood their own even earlier records.

Second, you will notice I have omitted the Seventh and Eighth Dynasties from the list of Memphite Dynasties. Our only evidence for the existence of these two dynasties comes from the Manetho sources, Africanus and Eusebius, and many Egyptologists question their identification of these dynasties as separate from the Sixth Dynasty. I will argue below that these two dynasties never existed, and that the information preserved in Africanus and Eusebius constitutes a garbled transmission of summation lines having to do with the first six dynasties and that redactors misread them as two additional dynasties.

Third, you will notice that Dynasty 4 is divided into two parts, 4A and 4B, each aligned with a different patriarch. This is not an attempt to introduce a new dynasty into the structure. Both parts belong to the Fourth Dynasty. It is my view that this partition had to do with a need for symmetry in the Patriarchal Chronology.

The Genesis author had assigned the seven birth dates from Adam to Methuselah to predynastic chronological markers and wanted to use the death dates of these same Patriarchs as the chronological markers for the Memphite dynasties, but the Memphite sequence was one dynasty short (if we combine Dynasties 6–8 as a single political entity) and the compiler needed to create a division in one of the dynasties to accommodate the literary scheme of parallel births and deaths.

Table 5.2: The Eight Memphis Dynasties: Date Comparisons to Genesis 5 Patriarch Death Dates[a]

Memphis Dynasties Date Range	Gardiner (1961)	CAH (1971–75)	Kitchen (1996)	Beckareth (1997)	Shaw (2000)	Krauss/War-burton (2006)	Genesis 5 Death Dates
	3100–?	3100–2160	3100–2136	3100–2160	3000–2160	2900–2120	3074–2105 Life span of Methuselah
1st Dynasty	3100–?	3100–2890	3100–2900	3032–2853	3000–?	2900–2730	3074–2831
2nd Dynasty	?–2700	2890–2686	2900–2700	2853–2707	?–2686	2730–2590	2831–2719
3rd Dynasty	2700–2620	2686–2613	2691–2617	2707–2639	2686–2613	2730–2590	2719–2621
4A Dynasty	2620–2480	2613–2498	2617–2515	2639–2504	2613–2494	2592–2544	2719–2621
4B Dynasty	NA	NA	NA	NA	NA	2543–2436	2621–2526
5th Dynasty	2480–2340	2494–2345	2515–2362	2504–2347	2494–2345	NA	2526–2471
6th Dynasty	2340–?	2345–2181	2362–2176	2347–2216	2345–2181	2435–2306	2471–2339
7th Dynasty	?	2181–2173	2176–?	NA	2181–?	2305–2152	2339–2105
8th Dynasty	?	2173–2160	?–2136	2216–2170	?–2160	NA	NA
						2150–2118	NA

[a] Egyptological dates taken from Table 3.1. Dynasties 1–6 correspond to the Old Kingdom. Dynasties 7–8 continue the Memphite line of kings but have been traditionally grouped with the First Intermediate Period.

The Fourth Dynasty presented such an opportunity. Egyptologists disagree over the length, nature, and number of kings that belong to the Fourth Dynasty. This proposed Patriarchal division focuses in on the area of contention, and the below analysis of the data will show that this break occurs at just the point where the conflict arises.

Table 5.2, *The Eight Memphite Dynasties: Date Comparisons to Genesis 5 Patriarch Death Dates*, combines data from Table 5.1 and Table 3.1 to display an array of some alternative proposals by Egyptologists for the dating of the eight Memphite Dynasties, and compares them to the proposed dates from the Patriarchal Chronology. Allowing for the fact that several of the Egyptologists disagree with each other on many of the specific starting and ending dates, as well as the durations, each of the proposed Patriarchal Chronology dynastic time frames falls approximately within the same chronological frame-work of the several Egyptological chronologies in Table 5.2. We will look at many of the details later.

Because of the uncertainty over fixed dates for each of the dynasties, I also converted the absolute dates in Table 5.2 into relative time-spans, not anchored to a specific date. By looking at how long each of the dynasties lasted according to the various theories, we have another way to compare the Patriarchal dates with the other arrangements. I present that information in Table 5.3, *The Eight Memphis Dynasties: Duration Comparisons of Egyptian Dynastic Durations and the Sequence of Genesis 5 Patriarch Death Dates*. For additional comparisons, I have added to Table 5.3 a few summary totals for different groups of dynasties.

Here again, given the many variations and sometimes wide disagreements, the pattern of durations for the Genesis time-spans parallels the Egyptological date ranges. Longer dynasties in the Egyptian record are longer in the Genesis record, and shorter dynastic durations in the Egyptian record are shorter in the Genesis record.

Table 5.3: The Eight Memphis Dynasties: Duration Comparisons of Egyptian Dynastic durations and the sequence of Genesis 5 Patriarch Death Dates

Memphis Dynasties	Gardiner (1961)	CAH (1971–5)	Kitchen (1996)	Beckareth (1997)	Shaw (2000)	Krauss/War-Burton (2006)	Gen. 5 Dates
Duration Range		940	964ª	862	840	781	969
1st Dynasty		210	200	179		170	243
2nd Dynasty/Seth		205	200	146		140	112
Sum Dyn. 1–2	400	415	400	325	314	310	355
3rd Dynasty	80	73	74	68	73	48	98
4A Dynasty	140	115	102	135	119	107	95
4B Dynasty	0	0	0	0	0	0	55
Sum Dyn. 4A–4B	140	115	102	135	119	107	150
5th Dynasty	140	149	153	157	149	129	132
6th Dynasty		164	186	131	164	154	234
7th Dynasty		8					0
8th Dynasty		14	40	46	21	32	0
Sum Dyn. 6-8		186	226	177	185	186	234
Sum Dyn. 1–6		843	915	816	819	781	969
Sum Dyn. 1–8		938	955	862	840	813	969

ªKitchen gives a span of 964 years by dates, but his individual dynastic sums only add up to 955 years. He has placed a 9-year gap between the end of his Second Dynasty and the start of his Third Dynasty, which does not show up in the individual dynastic totals.

For Dynasties 1–2, which Egyptologists usually take as a unit and for which we have very poor information, the Patriarchal Chronology duration falls in the middle of the various estimated ranges in Table 5.3. For Dynasty 3, the Patriarchal Chronology, like the others, has less than a hundred years, but is a little longer than the estimated durations in the other proposals. But, as we shall see, several Egyptologists believe that 100 years is just about right for the Third Dynasty. Reconstructing Third Dynasty chronology runs into several problems, and I'll address those issues when we come to them.

The Patriarchal Chronology divides the Fourth Dynasty into two portions, 4A and 4B, for a total of 150 years. From Table 5.3 we see estimates ranging from Kitchen's 102 years to Gardiner's 140 years. Such disparities indicate a wide range of chronological disagreements, and we will address them at the proper time. Although the Patriarchal duration is a little longer than indicated at the high end of range, my analysis will show that it is consistent with the ancient sources.

The Patriarchal Chronology's Fifth Dynasty of 132 years closely aligns with Krauss/Warburton's 129 years, but is somewhat shorter than most of the other proposals. Again, when we address the many issues involved in reconstructing this dynasty's chronology, we will see that the Patriarchal duration is right on target.

For the Sixth Dynasty, the proposed Patriarchal Chronology dates incorporate Dynasties 6–8 and has a longer time span for these three dynasties, 234 years, than most other estimates, but close to Kitchen 226 years. A key problem here is that most Egyptologists tend to use the Turin Canon as a template for the Sixth Dynasty, but, as we shall see, the Turin Canon is off by about 30 years on one of its reigns, and when we make that adjustment Manetho's longer Sixth Dynasty appears to be the better fit with the archaeological record.

In what follows, we will look take a close look at each of the Memphite dynasties, examining the archaeological evidence, the king-lists, what issues are in dispute, and what proposals have been made to resolve the issues. In each instance we will see how this affects the validity of the data. A very important factor in this study will be to take a closer look at Manetho's frequently questionable chronology as preserved by his redactors, and try to logically understand how Manetho's redactors misunderstood his text and what sort of errors they made. The nature of my reconstructions of Manetho's chronology is, for the most part, original with me.

The Chronology of Dynasties 1-2

Of all our ancient chronological sources, only Manetho indicates a dynastic division between the string of rulers making up the first two Egyptian dynasties. Outside of Manetho, we have very little data about how long any these monarchs served. Compounding the problem, the two Manetho sources, Africanus and Eusebius, disagree with each other about various lengths of reign, and Egyptologists consider the Manetho numbers to be highly inflated.

Surveying the data, Krauss/Warburton write, "The contemporaneous dates available today do not suffice to establish a coherent chronology for Dynasties 1–3. Furthermore, the history of the second half of Dynasty 2 is unclear, insofar as kings might have ruled simultaneously and not successively."[74] That Egyptologists continue to indicate the existence of a break between the two groups of kings is a testament to the power of the Manethonian model of Egypt's dynastic history. Nevertheless, where Egyptologists draw the line is highly speculative, basically educated guesses for the sake of argument.

In the analysis below, it will be argued that Manetho's original chronological data for Dynasties 1 and 2 have been badly garbled in transmission but that through numerical pattern analysis we can logically reconstruct what errors occurred, how they came about, and what Manetho originally indicated for the chronology of these two dynasties. The evidence will show that the original Manetho text had the same dynastic durations for these two dynasties as indicated by the proposed Patriarchal Chronology. I will also offer some evidence from the Turin Canon providing some partial corroboration for this chronological thesis.

I think it appropriate to remind you that the Genesis author wrote well before Manetho composed his text and couldn't have used Manetho as a source. If my thesis is correct, we will have two independent sources (Manetho reconstructed and Genesis) agreeing on the duration of both dynasties, an indication that at least some ancient scribes, looking at earlier Egyptian source data, believed this information to be accurate. Whether there might have been errors in the original source data is a different issue and doesn't undermine the idea that the Genesis author worked from Egyptian sources to compile a Genesis chronology based on ancient Egyptian dynastic records.

The Archaeological Evidence

Our only direct archaeological evidence for the total duration of the first two dynasties comes from the Palermo Stone. Although badly damaged, it indicates a total of 450 years for both, but few, if any, current Egyptologists consider that figure reliable.[75] The Palermo Stone is not actually a king-list, but it does reference occasional events during a king's reign. Gardiner warns, "we must again stress the improbable nature of the 450 years which the Palermo Stone seems to demand for the two dynasties combined."[76]

Table 5.3 shows some estimates for the combined number of years for both dynasties, 400 (Gardiner), 415 (CAH/Hayes), 400 (Kitchen), 325 (Beckareth), 314 (Shaw), and 310 (Krauss/Warburton), all of which depart significantly from the indicated Palermo Stone total. Back in the 1960s, Hayes surveyed what various Egyptologists up to that time had come up with for the duration. The data showed a wide range of differences, to wit, 544 years (Borchardt, 1917 and 1935), 520–543 (Sethe, 1905), 519 (Weigall, 1925), 453 (Meyer, 1904), 444 (Parker, 1957), 420 (Breasted, 1921), 419 (Meyer, 1925), 400 (Frankfurt, 1948), 373 (Sewell, 1942), 310 (Hall, 1924), and 295 (Helck, 1956).[77] Hayes's own estimate of 415 years (cited in Table 5.3) is offered as a compromise figure.[78] The two dates coming closest to the Palermo Stone estimate are Meyer, in 1904, and Parker in 1957.

Turning from the Palermo Stone to the king-lists and inscriptions on monuments, we have the following information.

- *The Turin Canon* appears to have about sixteen to eighteen kings assigned to this period, but the lengths of reign for all but the last four are lost.[79] These last four have a total of 65 years (8, 11, 27, 19.) There is also an issue as to whether the last king in that list, Nebka, was the last king of the Second Dynasty, the first king of the Third Dynasty, or a later king in the Third Dynasty. We'll review that issue in more detail below.

- *The Table of Abydos*, which has no lengths of reign, assigns fourteen or fifteen kings to these two dynasties, again depending upon whether the last king in that sequence, Nebka, belongs to the Second or Third Dynasty.[80]

- *The Table of Sakkara* lists only eleven kings, also without lengths of reign.[81] This low number is due to the scribe omitting the first five kings of the First Dynasty.[82] He probably did so because his list represents the traditions of Lower Egypt, which didn't recognize the legitimacy of the first five kings.[83] Adding in the five missing kings, the Table of Sakkara indicates sixteen kings ruled from Memphis.

- *From inscriptions on the monuments* we find fourteen identifiable kings down to Nebka, many of which bear similarities to the names in Manetho and/or the other king-lists.[84] Four to six of these additional king names do not match any of the names on the king-lists.[85] These unmatched names may identify additional kings or they may be alternative names for those kings already present in the king-lists.

From this data, we can set some boundaries for the number of kings who ruled in the first two dynasties. The Table of Abydos sets a low end of 14 kings and the Turin Canon sets a high end of 16–18 kings. To the high end we may have to add up to six additional kings, whose names do not appear on the king-lists. Most (and perhaps all) of these additional names may be alternative names for kings already listed.

Into this mix, we can now look at the Patriarchal data, which proposes a First Dynasty of 243 years in length and a Second Dynasty of 112 years in length, for a total of 355 years. This falls in the middle to lower end of the spectrum offered above, not too far off from several of the estimates in Table 5.3. These durations will be proposed as fixed durations and it will be argued herein that when we unscramble the garbled Manetho data, it will show that these are the exact durations Manetho originally set down. Therefore, we need to begin by looking at the Manetho king-list.

Manetho's First Dynasty

Africanus and Eusebius each have accounts of Manetho's First and Second Dynasty and both indicate that there were eight kings in the First Dynasty and nine kings in the Second Dynasty, but there are some disagreements between them as to how many years certain kings ruled, and Eusebius has omitted the names and lengths of reign for almost all the Second Dynasty kings. The total of 17 kings is consistent with the number of rulers set forth in the king-lists, which indicate a range of at least 14–18 kings, suggesting that there are some legitimate underlying sources behind Manetho's original history of these two dynasties. Additionally, the Manetho lists preserve a few anecdotal comments about some of the kings, suggesting that some of his historical accounts (accurate or not) have been preserved.

Table 5.4, *Manetho's First Dynasty*, sets out both the Africanus and Eusebius versions of Manetho's First Dynasty. Some observations are in order.

To begin with, Africanus and Eusebius each include a line of summation indicating how long the dynasty lasted. Africanus says 253 years, Eusebius 252 years. But, if you add up the individual lengths of reign set out in both lists, the total durations exceed the number of years in the summation lines. The total number of years for the individual lengths of reign in the Africanus list add up to 263 years, ten years longer than that indicated in his summation line. In Eusebius's list, the individual lengths of reign add up to 258 years, six years longer than indicated in his summation line.

Another difficulty is that there are some significant disagreements between Africanus and Eusebius concerning the lengths of reign attributed to several kings. While both lists agree on the lengths of reign for the last four kings and vary only slightly for the length of the first reign, they disagree substantially with each other

Table 5.4: Manetho's First Dynasty[a]		
King Name	Africanus Durations	Eusebius Durations
1. Menes	62	60[b]
2. Athothis	57	27
3. Kenkenes	31	39
4. Uenephes	23	42
5. Usaphaidos(A) Usaphais (E)	20	20
6. Miebidos (A) Niebais (E)	26	26
7. Semempses	18	18
8. Bieneches (A) Ubienthes (E)	26	26
Total: Claimed	253	252
Total: Actual	263	258

[a](Waddell 1940; reprint 1980), 27–33.
[b]The Armenian version of Eusebius gives Menes
  30 years.

about the lengths of reign for the second, third, and fourth kings in the list, Africanus has 57, 31, and 23 years, while Eusebius has 27, 39, and 42. Despite these wide variations in these lengths of reign, if you sum up each set of three reigns the totals are only three years apart.

That there could be such a large diversion in so many lengths of reign yet have totals that are nearly identical suggests that redactors reading copies of Manetho's manuscript over the centuries leading up to Africanus and Eusebius, had a lot of trouble figuring out how many years each king ruled, where partial reigns might have been described for the purpose of indicating how many years of a king's reign passed when an important event occurred, and which partial reigns belonged to which king.

Despite the large variation in lengths of reign, both lists converge to nearly identical lines of summation, 253 years for Africanus and 252 years for Eusebius. At the same time, though, the individual lengths of reign add up to more than the number of years given in the summation line. Clearly, something has gone wrong in transmission of the data, with different lines of transmission departing from other lines of transmission.

The Patriarchal Chronology dates indicate a First Dynasty duration of 243 years, about ten years short of what the Africanus and Eusebius lists claim for the First Dynasty. Ordinarily, one might be inclined to say that, given that the events happened over two thousand years earlier than the Genesis author's time, this is a reasonably close match and good enough to suggest a close agreement. But, I think I can demonstrate that Manetho originally had a total of 243 years and, on a later occasion, ten years originally belonging to the Second Dynasty were mistakenly transferred to the First Dynasty.

The several differences between the Africanus and Eusebius lists concerning the lengths of reign for the first four kings of the First Dynasty show that scribes in the process of transmission did in fact, on several occasions, mistakenly transfer some years from one king in a sequence to another. In this dynasty alone, we see four consecutive instances where this occurred. The problem we need to solve is how to prove that happened with regard to the difference between the Genesis numbers and the Manetho numbers as preserved in the sources.

More specifically, I want to show that there are two separate errors in both Africanus and Eusebius. For Africanus I need to show that during transmission from Manetho to Africanus, the summation line changed from 243 years to 253, ten years too high, and that Africanus also had an additional ten-year error in his indicated lengths of reign, which add up to 263 years rather than the proposed 243 years. For Eusebius, I need to show a nine-year error in the summation line, giving 252 years instead of 243 years. and an additional six-year error in his indicated lengths of reign that increase the total duration from Eusebius' 252 years to 258 years. To make the case, we need to look at Manetho's Second Dynasty data.

Table 5.5: Manetho's Second Dynasty[a]			
Africanus Version		**Eusebius Version**	
King Name	**Reign**	**King Name**	**Reign**
1. Boethos	38	Bochos	
2. Kaiechos	39	Kaichoos	
3. Binothris	47	Biophis	
4. Tlas	17		
5. Sethenes	41		
6. Chaires	17		
7. Nephercheres	25	Name omitted	
8. Sesochris	48	Sesochris	48
9. Cheneres	30	Name omitted	
Total: Claimed	302		297
Total: Actual	302		?
Total for Dynasty 1-2[b]	555		549

[a] (Waddell 1940; reprint 1980), 35–41.
[b] This summation line is by Greenberg, not Manetho.

Manetho's Second Dynasty

Table 5.5, *Manetho's Second Dynasty*, compares the Africanus and Eusebius versions of Manetho for the Second Dynasty. The most obvious differences are that Eusebius has omitted all lengths of reign but one and some king names are missing. Eusebius indicates that there were nine kings but has omitted any entries where kings 4–6 belong and has omitted the names for the kings referenced in reigns 7 and 9. The one length of reign given by Eusebius, Sesochris ruling for 48 years, corresponds to the length of reign for the same king in the Africanus list.

Africanus has a summation line of 302 years, which matches the total lengths for individual reigns, and Eusebius has 297 years for the dynasty but lacks the individual lengths of reign necessary to double-check against his summation line. Eusebius' summation total for the Second Dynasty is five years lower than what Africanus sets forth. These Manetho figures for the duration of the Second

Dynasty are widely rejected as too high. The proposed Patriarchal Chronology duration for this dynasty is 112 years, approximately two hundred years less than what Africanus and Eusebius indicate.

If we add up the Africanus summation lines for Dynasties 1 and 2 (253 + 302), the total would be 555 years for the first two dynasties. If we add up the same summation lines for Eusebius (252 + 297), the total would be 549 years, six years less than the Africanus total. Interestingly, though, if we add Eusebius's Second Dynasty total (297) to the sum of his individual lengths of reign in the First Dynasty (258), the total would be 555 years, the same as Africanus. This suggests that somewhere along the line of transmission six years from one dynasty may have been added to or subtracted from the other dynasty. Later, we'll identify where those six years belong.

The Africanus and Eusebius totals for the two dynasties combined are more than a century longer than all of the more recent estimated durations listed earlier in this chapter. The Patriarchal Chronology duration for both dynasties should be 355 years. The Africanus total of 555 years for the first two dynasties is exactly 200 years higher. I will attempt to demonstrate that the original Manetho figure for the Second Dynasty should have been 112 years, the same as in the Patriarchal Chronology and I will identify the source of the two-hundred-year error.

Something Odd about the Africanus Numbers

There is something curious about Africanus's individual lengths of reign. They not only seem inordinately large, but the numbers seem to be almost repetitive. Notice the pattern of the figures. There is a "47", a "48", and a "41". There is also a "38", a "39", and a "30". Lastly, there are two "17"s and an isolated "25". That six out of nine pharaohs have reigns longer than thirty years is highly suspect, and the addition of a twenty-five-year reign among one of the remaining three reinforces this suspicion.

Table 5.6, *Numerical Patterns in Africanus's Second Dynasty*, takes the pattern of repetitive duration lengths and separates them into

Table 5.6: Numerical Patterns in Africanus's Second Dynasty

Numbers below in parentheses indicate the sequential position in the order of the king-reigns.

Set 1	Set 2	Set 3
(1) 38 Years	(2) 39 years	(9) 30 years
(3) 47 years	(5) 41 years	(8) 48 years
(4) 17 Years	(6) 17 years	(7) 25 years
Total = 102 years	Total = 97 years	Total =103 years

three groups of figures, Set 1, Set 2, and Set 3, each Set consisting of one high length of reign (47, 41, 48), one middle length of reign (38, 39, 30), and one low length of reign (17, 17, 25). Set 1 contains the first high, middle, and low lengths of reign to appear in the Africanus list; Set 2 the second high, middle, and low lengths of reign to appear in the Africanus list; and Set 3 the third high, middle, and low lengths of reign to appear in the Africanus list.

This arrangement, following Africanus's numerical distribution, eliminates any opportunity to play around with the numbers and cherry-pick which reign should go into which Set to produce desired results. The numbers in parenthesis show the sequential position in Africanus's sequence of reigns.

When we arrange the numbers as indicated, something very interesting occurs. As I point out several unusual coincidences, keep in mind that the Patriarchal figures should be 243 for the First Dynasty and 112 for the Second Dynasty, with a combined total of 355 for both.

- If you replace **Africanus's** summation line for the Second Dynasty (302) with the **Set 1** summation line figure (102) and add it to **Africanus's** First Dynasty summation line (253), the total is **355** years, exactly 200 years less than the Africanus total for Dynasty 1 (253) and Dynasty 2 (302) and precisely equal to the proposed **Patriarchal Chronology** sum of 355 years for the two dynasties.
- If you replace **Eusebius's** summation line for the Second Dynasty (297) with the **Set 2** summation line figure (97) and add it to **Eusebius's** total for the individual lengths of reign in his First

Dynasty (258), the total is also **355** years, and exactly 200 years less than the Eusebius total for Dynasty 1 (258) and Dynasty 2 (297), and, again, precisely equal to the proposed **Patriarchal Chronology** sum of 355 years for the two dynasties.

- If you replace **Eusebius's** summation line for the Second Dynasty (297) with the **Set 3** summation line figure (103) and add it to **Eusebius's** First Dynasty summation line (252), the total is again **355** years, and again the same total as the proposed **Patriarchal Chronology** duration of **355** years.

- If you sum up the totals for **Set 2 and Set 3**, the sum is 200 years. This last figure gives us an important key to restoring Manetho's original chronology for the Second Dynasty.

Each set of three numbers, when combined with one of the preserved versions of Manetho's duration for the First Dynasty (i.e., the Africanus summation line, the Eusebius total for individual reigns, and the Eusebius summation line,) yields a sum of 355 years, the same number of years suggested as the total for both dynasties in the Patriarchal Chronology. In two instances, the Set totals are exactly two hundred years less then set forth in Africanus and Eusebius summation lines for the Second Dynasty. We also see that the sum of the Set 2 and Set 3 totals is exactly 200 years.

That the sum of each Set when added to one of the indicated durations for the First Dynasty generates the same sum, 355 years, and also equals the combined duration of 355 years proposed for the Patriarchal total for both dynasties, seems to be a remarkable set of correlations that can't be simply explained by random coincidence. This suggests that the Set 1, Set 2, and Set 3 totals may represent three independent sets of Dynasty 2 subtotals generated in transmission by Manetho redactors, which in turn were confused with different lengths of reigns for various kings.

Furthermore, despite the lack of any data for the length of reign for eight out of nine kings in the Eusebius list for the Second Dynasty, we find that Sets 2 and 3 each play a role relating to Eusebius's summary data for the two dynasties. Why is the chronological data behind those two sets of Eusebius summations missing in Eusebius but present in the Africanus list of reign lengths?

The most sensible answer, it seems to me, is that the Africanus figures represent an end process in which multiple redactors at different stages of transmission placed partial summaries in the margins of the manuscripts and identified those marginal partial totals by referencing a king, probably in a form that said something like, "to King X" or "From King X" or "After King X" or "Through King X." These marginal totals, as they were passed along, came to be confused by later redactors with corrected totals for individual kings.

Some variations of the Africanus figures followed a line of transmission to Eusebius (see below) and others followed a line of transmission to Africanus. Both chroniclers worked just with the end product of the transmission, unfamiliar with what happened before they received their copies of the heavily redacted manuscripts.

Let's look at the three data sets and note some additional coincidences.

- The Set 1 total (102) for Africanus's reconstructed Second Dynasty duration is ten years less than the Patriarchal Chronology duration of 112 years for the Second Dynasty, and the Africanus summation line for the First Dynasty is ten years higher than the proposed Patriarchal figure of 243 years for the First Dynasty. If the Patriarchal data reflects Egyptian chronology for the duration of the first two dynasties, then either the Genesis author or Manetho (or one of his later redactors) moved ten years from one dynasty to the other.
- This means that the total duration of the First Dynasty must fall between 243 years and 253 years, depending upon who moved the ten years. Consequently, the 263-year sum for the individual reigns of Africanus's First Dynasty must be at least 10 years too high and must be the result of an independent error that occurred after the Africanus source had already integrated the three Sets of data into the Manetho text.

- The Set 3 total (103) for Eusebius's reconstructed Second Dynasty duration (which connects with his summation line for the First Dynasty) is nine years less than the Patriarchal Chronology duration of 112 years, and the Eusebius First Dynasty summation line (252 years) is nine years more than the Patriarchal Chronology duration of 243 years for the First Dynasty. Again, if the Patriarchal Chronology reflects Egyptian data for the duration of the first two dynasties, then either the Genesis author or Manetho (or one of his later redactors) moved nine years from one dynasty to the other.
- Since the numbers don't allow for the Genesis author to have moved both nine years and ten years from one dynasty to the other, there is an error in at least one Manetho source for how many years must be moved to account for the difference. Africanus says ten years and Eusebius says nine years. This still leaves open whether the Genesis author or the Manetho source moved the ten years or nine years.
- If you add the 200 years from the sum of Set 2 and Set 3 to Set 2, (double counting Set 2) the total is 297 years, the number of years Eusebius claimed for the Second Dynasty.

Since the Eusebius First Dynasty summation line (252) is nine years higher than the Patriarchal Chronology duration of 243 years and Eusebius's sum of individual reigns (258) is fifteen years too high, and if we assume (for the sake of argument) that the Patriarchal Chronology is correct, logic suggests that there should be at least two errors in the Eusebius data stream, one associated with the addition of nine years to both the sum line and the individual reigns, and another error in which an additional six years is added to the individual reigns.

If we can find evidence that such errors were present in the Eusebius data stream, then the movement of years from one dynasty to another must have come from the Eusebius line of transmission and not the Genesis author. If such an error is present in the Eusebius trail, then it must also, of necessity, be present in the Africanus data stream. A look at Sets 1, 2, and 3 suggests just such a set of errors in Eusebius's data.

- Africanus's Dynasty 2 duration consists of the sum of Set 1 (102) + Set 2 (97) + Set 3 (103), for a total of 302 years.
- The Eusebius Dynasty 2 duration, however, consists of Set 2 (97) + Set 2 (97) + Set 3 (103), for a total of 297 years, five years fewer then Africanus. The Eusebius data stream, somewhere along the line, replaced Set 1 with a repeat of Set 2.

A closer look at the three figures that make up each set shows where the errors are buried.

- Set 1 and Set 3 show, respectively, high reigns of 47 years and 48 years. Set 2, however, has a reign of only 41 years. The Set 2 figure appears to be an outlier and it is six years shorter than the Set 1 figure and seven years shorter than the Set 3 figure. Since Set 2 (97) replaced Set 1 (103) in the transmission of the Manetho data to Eusebius, then we have a 6-year reduction in the Eusebius data stream when compared to the Africanus data stream. This error was partially offset by 1 year in that the Set 2 data has a 38-year length of reign versus the Set 1 figure of 37 years. As a result, the Eusebius Dynasty 2 summation line (297) is 5 years lower than the corresponding Africanus summation line (302).
- Set 1 and Set 2 show, respectively, midsize reigns of 38 years and 39 years. Set 3, however, shows a reign of 30 years. This reign is nine years less than the corresponding Set 2 figure and eight years fewer than the Set 1 figure.
- Since the Eusebius Second Dynasty duration (297) consists of Set 2 (97) + Set 2 (97) + Set 3 (103), we find within Set 2 and Set 3, a six-year reduction in Set 2 from the corresponding Set 1 figure, and a nine-year reduction in Set 3 from the corresponding Set 2 figure. *These are the two errors we are looking for.*
- Because the Africanus total for Dynasty 2 also includes the Set 3 numbers, his 302-year summation line incorporates that nine-year error.

- Because Africanus also includes the Set 2 numbers in his total for Dynasty 2, his 302 years also includes the six-year error.
- Because the Eusebius data stream replaced the Set 1 numbers with a second copy of the Set 2 numbers, the Eusebius total for the Second Dynasty (297) incorporates a second missing six-year total. Eusebius's extra six First Dynasty years are the six years that have been moved out of the Second Dynasty and into the First. That is why the sum of Set 2 (97) and the total of the individual lengths of reign in Eusebius's First Dynasty (258), which is six years higher than the Eusebius summation line (252), adds up to the same total as the Set 3 total (103) and the Africanus summation line (252) for the First Dynasty.

Our goal in this analysis was to show that somewhere during the transmission of Manetho's data, there were two occasions in which years were moved from the Second Dynasty to the First Dynasty, one involving six years and one involving 9 years.

First, we wanted to reduce the Manetho First Dynasty from either Africanus's 253 years or Eusebius's 252 years to a revised total of 243 years. The analysis above showed that someone during the transmission of Manetho's data appears to have assigned nine years from the Second Dynasty to the First Dynasty. Subtracting nine years from Eusebius's First Dynasty summation line (252) gives a revised figure of 243 years, aligning with the proposed figure of 243 years for the Patriarchal Chronology First Dynasty. Adding those nine years back to Eusebius's Set 3 figure (103) for the Second Dynasty gives a sum of 112 years, the precise number we were looking for to match the proposed Genesis figure of 112 years for the Second Dynasty.

Second, we were looking for evidence that an additional six years had been moved from the Second Dynasty to the First Dynasty. We found that evidence in Set 2 when compared to the other two Sets. That error was incorporated into the Second Dynasty summation lines for both Africanus and Eusebius.

Careful study of the three sets of Manetho figures for the Second Dynasty shows that we have one more data discrepancy to be explained. The low figure in Set 1 and Set 2 is "17." The corresponding figure in Set 3 is 25 years. A look at the limited data in the Turin Canon, immediately following, suggests that the 17-year figures should have been 27 years and the difference between the two corresponds to the ten years moved from Dynasty 2 to Dynasty 1.[86] Let's take a closer look.

Manetho and the Turin Canon

The above analysis seems to support the proposed Patriarchal Chronology durations for the first two dynasties, but it would be helpful if we could find some independent evidence that the Manetho numbers derive from legitimate ancient sources. Unfortunately, the chronological evidence for that period, outside of Manetho, is almost nonexistent. Nevertheless, there are a few entries preserved in the Turin Canon, that, although not disposing of the question with authority, do corroborate the proposed reconstruction of Manetho's Second Dynasty figures.

Counting Nebka as the last king of the Second Dynasty, the Turin Canon preserves the lengths of reign for the last four kings of the Second Dynasty. They are, respectively, 8, 11, 27, and 19 years. By way of contrast, the last four reigns in Africanus's Second Dynasty are 17, 25, 48, and 30, clearly a higher order of numbers, and clearly inconsistent with the much shorter reigns recorded in the Turin Canon.

Since the Turin Canon is probably less subject to gross error than the multi-redacted editions of Manetho, it is a safe bet that the Turin Canon is closer to the truth regarding these Second Dynasty reigns than are the much lengthier ones in the Africanus and Eusebius manuscripts. Either the Manetho figures are wildly inaccurate, or, as suggested by our analysis above of Sets 1, 2, and 3, the Manetho figures are subtotals for multiple reigns.

The four Turin Canon reigns have a collective sum of 65 years. Assuming for the moment that 112 years is the correct total for the Second Dynasty, the missing Turin Canon reigns would be expected to have a collective sum of 47 years. Interestingly, Manetho's figures include reigns of 48 years, 47 years, and 41 years, with the last one being upped to 47 years to account for Eusebius's six-year error.

Furthermore, if you take the 8, 11, and 19-year reigns from the Turin Canon, you have a total of 38 years, coinciding with the Manetho reigns of 38, 39 and 30 years, the last one being upped to 39 to account for Eusebius's nine-year error. Where the correspondences seem to fall off is with the remaining figure.

The proposed original Turin Canon summation sequence would be 47 (theoretical), 38 (sum of 8+11+19) and 27, whereas the Set 1 sequence has 47, 38, 17, (the order of the subtotals isn't relevant). The remaining Turin Canon figure of 27 years should correspond to the Manetho figure of 17 years, but the Turin Canon number is ten years higher. However, as you will recall from above, I pointed that either nine (Eusebius) or ten (Africanus) years belonging to Manetho's Second Dynasty were transferred to the First Dynasty. Since we are comparing the Turin Canon to the Set 1 Africanus figures, we will use the ten-year error for this reconstruction.

This allows us to add the ten years to the remaining 17-year reign, giving us a total of 27 years, exactly the total we would expect. Adding 10 years to the Set 1 sum of 102 years gives us 112 years, exactly what the Patriarchal Chronology indicates. This indicates that the 17-year figure in Set 1 and Set 2 should have originally been 27 years in Manetho but that the extra ten years had been moved into Manetho's First Dynasty.

If the Patriarchal Chronology thesis is correct, then the missing Turin Canon Second Dynasty reigns would probably have lasted 47 years (112 - 65 = 47), three of the reigns (8, 11, 19) add up to 38 years, and the one reign for the next to the last king in the dynasty would be 27 years.

The one problem that keeps the Turin Canon from being fully convincing as corroboration of the Manetho-Genesis figurers is that we don't know how long the missing Turin Canon Second Dynasty reigns lasted. If the duration lasted 47 years, then everything is perfect, but we don't have that figure available. But there is good evidence that two of the three subtotals in the Turin Canon match the proposed Set 1 numbers (after the missing ten years in Africanus are restored.)

A Possible Late Typo in Africanus

Africanus's First Dynasty had a summation line of 253 years and a sum for the individual reigns of 263 years. I suggested above that this additional ten-year difference was a late-stage typo that did not come from Manetho. Eliminating those ten years brought Africanus's summation line into harmony with the individual lengths of reign, both indicating 253 years. Although I don't need to trace the origin of this error to sustain my underlying thesis, I would like to suggest how this typo may have come about.

If you look at the names of the fifth king in Table 5.4, you will see that Africanus names the king as "Miebidos" and Eusebius lists the name as "Niebais." Manetho wrote in Greek and the first letter in the Africanus name is Greek "mu" and the first letter in the Eusebius name is the Greek "nu." These letters, when hand written look a lot like the letters "U" and "V", and, as you may recognize from English handwriting, it is often difficult to determine if a letter is a U or a V and you need context to figure it out.

With numbers, however, context is rarely available to help you correctly figure out an ambiguously written number. The ancient Greeks, like the Romans, used letters to represent numbers. The letters "mu" and "nu" signified, respectively, "40" and "50." Because of the similarity of the shapes and possible ambiguity in the handwriting, the two letters can be confused for each other, as they are in the name of King Miebidos/Niebais.

In Africanus, King Athothis has a reign of 57 years and no other king in the Africanus First Dynasty list has a reign of 50-plus or 40-plus years. I strongly suspect that somewhere in the transmission process to Africanus, an editor misread a "mu" for a "nu" and changed what was supposed to be a 47-year reign into a 57-year reign, creating a ten-year disparity between the lengths of the individual reigns and the summation line.

Conclusions

The archaeological record provides few guidelines to the chronology of the First and Second Dynasties. Opinion as to the true length of the two dynasties differ by as much as 250 years, from as high as 544 years to as low as 295 years. One of the most explicit ancient claims is that of the Palermo Stone, which was compiled more than five hundred years after Menes came to the throne. It seems to indicate a period of 450 years for this era, but most Egyptologists do not find this claim convincing. Of the other great ancient chronology, the Turin Canon, only the last four reigns are preserved, having a total of only 65 years.

Manetho's redactors have concocted a chronology that assigns the First Dynasty approximately 252/253 years, and even without adjustment, that figure coincides quite well with the Patriarchal Chronology claim of 243 years, especially given how difficult it must have been for Manetho to recreate the chronology of the First Dynasty.

For the Second Dynasty, Manetho and the Patriarchal Chronology appear to part company, Genesis requiring a total of 112 years, where Manetho's redactors claim approximately 300 years. But the Manetho Second Dynasty figures seem wide of the mark. The combined total for both dynasties exceeds 550 years, over a hundred years higher than the unaccepted claim of the Palermo Stone. Furthermore, the few preserved figures from the Turin Canon are significantly lower than the corresponding figures in Manetho, and lead to the conclusion that the Manetho figures for the Second Dynasty are greatly inflated.

The Patriarchal Chronology has a combined total of 355 years for the first two dynasties, placing at the lower end of the spectrum of Egyptological opinion, but still within acceptable parameters. Additionally, the First Dynasty coincides quite well with Manetho's unadjusted figures. The 112 years required for the Second Dynasty are probably thought of as low by most Egyptologists, but there is not much evidence against which to measure it.

Still, our goal was to conform Genesis not only to the archaeological record but also to show what the ancient Egyptian scribes would have believed. In that regard, an attempt was made to reconcile the Patriarchal Chronology with Manetho. The primary argument offered on this issue showed that during transmission, multiple redactors of Manetho's Second Dynasty text had mistakenly conflated and triple-counted the lengths of reign for the Second Dynasty. The analysis above disentangled the three sets of figures and restored the original Manetho chronology for the First and Second Dynasties. Through a study of numerical patterns, I showed that virtually all the discrepancies between the Africanus and Eusebius manuscripts can be accounted for by this interpretation, and that the original Manetho appears to have supported the argument that the first two dynasties had respective durations of 243 years and 112 years for a combined sum of 355 years.

Finally, the argument in favor of the triple-count theory received some modest corroboration from the Turin Canon, whose own numerical patterns seemed to corroborate the proposed Manetho reconstruction and included the 10 years that appear to have been moved from the Second Dynasty to the First Dynasty. However, due to the incomplete nature of the Turin Canon's Second Dynasty an authoritative corroboration is not possible.

The Patriarchal chronology shows a proposed duration of 243 years for the First Dynasty and 112 years for the Second Dynasty. The evidence cited above shows that there is a reasonably good probability that these figures coincide precisely with what Manetho originally set forth and that conclusion receives some corroboration from the Turin Canon. The Patriarchal chronology also indicates fixed dates for these reigns, with the First Dynasty beginning in 3074 and the Second Dynasty beginning in 2831.

The Cattle Count Problem

Before we move on to the remaining dynasties in the Memphite Kingdom, we need to briefly address an important chronological issue related to the matter of cattle-count censuses. During the Old Kingdom (Dynasties 3–6), Egyptians conducted a cattle census known as the "Occasion of the Count." They frequently left inscriptions indicating that an event occurred in relation to the number of cattle counts that had occurred in a king's reign prior to the event in question. In addition to enumerating how many cattle counts had occurred, the inscriptions said the event in question occurred either in the "year of" the indicated cattle count or in the "year after" the indicated cattle count. Miroslav Verner says, "Specialists have acknowledged that this census formed the basis for counting regnal years during the OK."[87]

The first cattle count in a king's reign occurred in his first year. Because of references to a "Year after the Occasion of the Count" Egyptologists, early on, had assumed that the cattle counts happened on a biennial basis in the odd years of each king's reign.[88] For a long time, Egyptologists had accepted Gardiner's thesis that the census was regularly conducted on a biennial basis throughout the Old Kingdom.[89] But there were a couple of chinks in the argument.

On some occasions, the census had been conducted in consecutive years. The Seventh and Eighth Counts for King Snofru, for example, occurred in consecutive years.[90] Similar examples have occurred on other occasions.[91] Several Egyptologists began to raise questions as to how regular the biennial cattle counts were.

Verner observed that references to the "Year of the Occasion of the Count" far outnumber references to the "Year *After* the Occasion of the Count." If the discovery of "cattle count" inscriptions were random, and the census was routinely conducted on a biennial basis, he argues, shouldn't we expect that the number of references to "Year of" and "Year After" be more evenly distributed.[92] This imbalance, along with examples of counts in consecutive years led Verner to argue that the system is far more complex than previously acknowledged and we don't really know how the system of cattle counts were utilized in dating a year within a king's reign.[93]

To address this problem, Verner has suggested we utilize the cattle counts differently. He says we should assume, for the sake of argument, that cattle counts occurred annually and take that as a base minimum figure, to which one should add the number of references to a "Year After the Occasion of the Count." He would use that calculation for establishing the minimum length of reign for a king.[94]

Summarizing the current state of opinion on the cattle count problem, Verner provides the following overview.

> Nowadays, some Egyptologists maintain that the census was biennial during Snofru's reign with the sole exception of the seventh and eighth counts which were conducted in successive years. Others are of the opinion that a biennial system was not employed under Snofru, while yet others equivocate. For subsequent reigns, opinions fluctuate from the presumption of a biennial system to the assumption that on certain occasions an "odd" count could have been ignored. Finally, there is also the theory that annual cattle counts became more and more frequent during the OK until they became the rule by the end of Dynasty 6.[95]

It's important to understand that the highest known cattle count number for a king establishes only a minimum length of reign for a king, not a maximum. We don't have full cattle count records for the various kings. We have only occasional references in an inscription to some Occasions of the Count within the reign of some kings.

The cattle count problem leaves us with dueling options for calculating a king's minimal length of reign, a High Minimum and a Low Minimum. For a king's High Minimum, one would assume a biennial count and subtract from that number all documented occasions in which the cattle count was done in consecutive years. For a king's Low Minimum, one assumes an annual cattle count and adds to the highest-numbered cattle count the number of documented "Year after the Count" inscriptions.

By way of illustration, let's say that a king's highest known cattle count is the "Year *After* the Seventh Occasion" and there is also one reference to a "Year *After* the Third Occasion of the Count." If the counts were biennial, then the High Minimum would be 14 Years, (= 13 years for the Seventh Occasion + 1 year for the "Year After the Seventh Occasion.") If the counts were annual, the Low Minimum would be 9 years, (= 7 years for the Seventh Occasion + 2 years for the two "Year After" references.)

In the following study of Old Kingdom Chronology, where necessary, we will look at both High and Low Minimums. The evidence will show that the Patriarchal Chronology coincides with the evidence for the High Minimums.

The Chronology of Dynasty 3

The proposed Patriarchal Chronology dates the Third Dynasty to 2719 and ends with the death of Enosh in 2621, indicating a duration of 98 years give or take a year or two due to rounding off partial years at the beginning and/or ending of a dynasty. Summarizing the Third Dynasty data in Tables 5.2 and 5.3, we have a variety of suggested starting dates and durations.

- 2700–2620, 80 years (Gardiner)
- 2686–2613, 73 years (CAH)
- 2691–2617, 74 years, (Kitchen)
- 2707–2639, 68 years, (Beckerath)
- 2686–2613, 73 years, (Shaw)
- 2592–2544, 48 years (Krauss/Warburton)

Except for the very short Krauss/Warburton Third Dynasty, the proposed Patriarchal Chronology overlaps large portions of the chronological timeframe proposed by the other Egyptologists. Differences amongst the starting dates depend on a variety of issues throughout the Old Kingdom. In each of the above chronologies, the Third Dynasty is the shortest of Dynasties 1–6. The same is true for the proposed Patriarchal chronology (counting 4Aand 4B as a single dynasty.) These parallels place the Patriarchal data within an acceptable chronological framework for the Third Dynasty.

The chief objection might be that the Patriarchal dates show a longer Third Dynasty than do the others. The Turin Canon indicates a duration of no more than 74 years and the other chronologies are largely based on the data in the Turin Canon. But the Turin Canon data for the Third Dynasty isn't universally trusted and there are several issues in play that need to be resolved before we can say how long the dynasty lasted.

W. Stevenson Smith, for example, writing in the CAH, says,

There is far from complete agreement concerning the length of this dynasty. In spite of the fact already mentioned that the lengths of the five kings listed in the Turin Canon add up to seventy-four years, *it is difficult not to believe that at least a hundred years should be allowed* for a period so important for the political and cultural experimentation which reached its culmination in the Fourth Dynasty [emphasis added].[96]

Smith's "hundred years" estimate precisely coincides with the 98 years set forth by the Patriarchal chronology.

In reconstructing the chronology of this dynasty, Egyptologists need to resolve several problematic issues, including: Did King Nebka belong to the Second Dynasty or the Third? How long did King Nebka rule? How long did King Djoser rule? The answers aren't self-evident.

Gardiner, for instance, places Nebka in the Second Dynasty, but, if the Turin Canon's 19 years for Nebka are attached instead to the balance of Gardiner's Third Dynasty, where many Egyptologists place it, his suggested starting date would be 2719, and his duration would be 99 years, both figures identical with the dates and duration indicated by the Patriarchal Chronology.[97]

We will look at these questions further below. We will also need to look at Manetho's chronology, and, once, again, unravel some scrambled transmissions. Then we will look at how Manetho and the Turin Canon interact.

The Archaeological Record

Egyptologists rely primarily, but not exclusively, on the Turin Canon as a guideline for Third Dynasty chronology, tinkering here and there when they think the archaeological evidence suggests an adjustment.

The Turin Canon places King Nebka immediately before Djoser, attributing to each a reign of 19 years, but nowhere does it explicitly state where the Third Dynasty begins.[98] It does, however, draw special attention to Djoser's name by the unusual use of red ink, suggesting that this pharaoh was highly respected among later Egyptians.[99] His grandest achievement was the construction of the Step Pyramid of Sakkara, Egypt's first monumental tomb.

Because of the attention drawn to Djoser's name, many Egyptologists would identify him as the founder of the Third Dynasty, but no similar markings identify the start of any other dynasty elsewhere in the Turin Canon, so it is not necessarily a dynastic anchor point. Djoser may have been important and highly thought of, but he may not have been the dynasty's founder.

The Turin Canon gives Djoser a duration of 19 years but some Egyptologists are skeptical. Gardiner writes,

> *The nineteen years allotted to Djoser seem an absurdly short time* for the completion of so stupendous a monument as his. The twenty-nine years given by Manetho might be accepted the more readily were it not that his Dynasty 3 counts nine kings, all of them except Tosorthros [=Djoser] with unidentifiable names and having 214 years as the total of their reigns [emphasis added].[100]

Smith also thinks Djoser had a longer reign. He argues,

> If Sanakhte is really the Horus-name of Nebka, and if he was also the king who began the construction of the building later incorporated into the Step Pyramid of his younger brother Djoser, it is difficult not to doubt the figure of 19 years given to each in the Turin Canon. The remarkable architectural achievement of Djoser and Imhotep, as well as the lasting memory which they left in the minds of later Egyptians, would seem to imply a longer reign for Djoser than Sanakhte, at least in the present state of our knowledge of the latter's monuments which seem very scanty.

In my reconstruction of the Second Dynasty chronology I made some use of the Turin Canon data for possible corroboration. That data included the Turin Canon entry for King Nebka. This raises an issue of whether I am erroneously double-counting Nebka in order to resolve the Second and Third Dynasty chronologies. To address the problem, I will offer evidence below suggesting that the Turin Canon scribe erroneously assigned these 19 years to Nebka, and that the 19-year reign belonged, not to Nebka, but to the last king of the Second Dynasty, Khasekhemwy, whose name is missing from the Turin Canon king-list.

After Djoser, the Turin Canon enumerates three more rulers before reaching the Fourth Dynasty, and assigns them respective reigns of 6, 6, and 24 years.[101] Djoser's successor was named Djoser-teti, a name so like his predecessor that it might have been a source of confusion in the transmission of Manetho's chronology and other ancient king-lists.[102]

For reference, here is the sequence of kings in the Turin Canon, along with their lengths of reign.[103] I am labeling each of the kings with a TC number and will use them as an abbreviation for the indicated Turin Canon king.

- TC1 = Nebka, 19 years
- TC2 = Djoser, 19 years
- TC3 = Djoser-teti, 6 years
- TC4 = (?), 6 years
- TC5 = Huny, 24 years

Per the Turin Canon, counting from Nebka, the dynasty reigned for 74 years; counting from Djoser, it lasted 55 years. Other than Gardiner, the Egyptologists in Table 5.3, include Nebka in their Third Dynasty totals. Gardiner's longer duration excludes Nebka but significantly increases Djoser's length of reign.[104] Krauss/Warburton include Nebka but place him in the fourth position.[105] They don't say how long Nebka ruled but they give him and his successor a combined duration of about 15 years.[106]

Counting Nebka, the Turin Canon has five kings. The Abydos list, which has no reign lengths, also places Nebka before Djoser, and has three rulers after Djoser, but there are some differences between the Abydos list and the Turin Canon as to the names of the kings.[107] The Sakkara list omits Nebka altogether, but does have three kings listed after Djoser.[108] Here, too, we find discrepancies between the Sakkara list and the Turin Canon.[109]

Another document, the Westcar Papyrus, reverses the order and places Djoser before Nebka.[110] The Palermo Stone is so damaged in the area accounting for the Third Dynasty that it is of little help in resolving the puzzle of Nebka's relationship to the Third Dynasty. There is also some evidence from a quarry marking that the Third Dynasty had a sixth king, Sanakhte, whose name does not appear in any of the lists.[111] As mentioned above, this is the king Smith suggests may be the same as Nebka. Shaw includes both Nebka and Sanakhte in his Third Dynasty but places a question mark after the latter's listing.[112]

Together, the Turin Canon, Table of Abydos, and the Table of Sakkara indicate that Djoser was followed by three more kings in the Third Dynasty before reaching the Fourth Dynasty, but there is disagreement on the names of some of Djoser's successors. There is also disagreement among the sources as to the placement of Nebka. Nevertheless, we will count Nebka as part of the Third Dynasty. Therefore, we should expect there to be five kings in the dynasty.

This brings us to the problems with Manetho. If Manetho's predecessors, more than a thousand years earlier, had so much difficulty sorting out the Third Dynasty's "Who's Who," one should imagine that it would be much harder for Manetho's later reactors to do better.

Manetho's' Third Dynasty

The Africanus version of Manetho's Third Dynasty has nine kings ruling 214 years. His dynastic summation line corresponds to the sum of the individual lengths of reign. His first two kings are Necherophes (who may correspond to Nebka), ruling 28 years, and Tosorthros, whom Egyptologists routinely equate with Djoser, ruling 29 years. Manetho's figures for the Third Dynasty are considered highly unreliable, but, as Gardiner indicated above, some Egyptologists agree that his higher figure for Djoser may be closer to the truth than the Turin Canon's.

Eusebius says the Third Dynasty had eight kings (versus Africanus's nine) but lists only the first two, who have the same names as in the Africanus list. Contra Africanus, though, he says the dynasty lasted for 197 years, 17 years fewer, but preserves no lengths of reign. The Armenian version of Eusebius says the dynasty lasted 198 years. Since Eusebius omitted all the individual lengths of reign, we have no way to cross-check against Africanus to see whom he may have omitted, or whom Africanus may have added.

Obviously the two Manetho sources are out of line with the other king-lists regarding the number of kings in the dynasty and they indicate a duration at least a century longer than the experts would allow. These sorts of departures from traditional sources usually suggest to me that the Manetho sources may have been badly garbled in transmission, with marginal subtotals being confused with corrected lengths of reign for either existing kings or imagined additional kings.

Here is the Africanus Third Dynasty king-list. I am labeling each king with an M number for use in the analysis below.

- M1 = Necherophes, 28 years
- M2 = Tosorthros, 29 years
- M3 = Tyreis, 7 years
- M4 = Mesochris, 17 years
- M5 = Soyphis, 16 years
- M6 = Tosertasis, 19 years
- M7 = Aches, 42 years
- M8 = Sephuris, 30 years
- M9 = Kerpheres, 26 years

Analyzing Manetho and the Turin Canon

As we begin our analysis of the Manetho and Turin Canon figures, keep in mind 1) the proposed Genesis duration of 98 years, and 2) our observation of the conflict between Africanus and Eusebius regarding how long several kings ruled, even though they were both passing on what should have been data from the same original source.

It remains my suggestion that the earlier portions of the Manetho king-list were not necessarily based on direct statements of how long each king ruled but on narratives that referenced events according to what year in a king's reign such incidents occurred. This required redactors to try to extract multiple pieces of data for different kings and interpret what may have been ambiguous references to strange names and titles for Egyptian kings that were transliterated into

Greek formats. As we saw in the review of Dynasties 1 and 2, different redactors looked at the same data and came up with different conclusions about how long some kings ruled.

Since the king-lists suggest that there should be five kings in the dynasty, let's begin with an experiment by summing up the lengths of reign for the first five kings in the list. The sum for M1–M5 is 97 years. This is virtually equivalent to the Genesis figure of 98 years and consistent with Smith's estimate that this dynasty should have lasted about a hundred years and Gardiner's belief that the period from Nebka to the end of the Third Dynasty lasted 99 years.

If, for the sake of argument, the Patriarchal data reflects Egyptian chronology, then these five Manetho kings should correspond to the five kings who ruled the dynasty, and the sum of their lengths of reign agrees with what the Patriarchal data indicates. Therefore, the remaining reigns must signify something other than a continuous list of additional kings for the Third Dynasty. Let's take a closer look.

Moving from the first five kings, focus now on Manetho's last three kings' reigns. The sum of those three durations equals 98 years, one year off from the sum of M1–M5. This seems like a strong clue that the last three lengths of reign constituted subtotals for the first five reigns and that they came to be confused with actual lengths of reign for other kings. This leaves us with one additional king to account for, M6, which we will do below.

If we treat the last three Manetho reigns as summation lines, then the last two, M8 (30 years) and M9 (26 years), add up to 56 years. The Turin Canon total, beginning with Djoser, adds up to 55 years. This suggests that M7 (42) years,) includes Nebka's reign plus any additional years not accounted for by the Turin Canon. Implicitly, if the Manetho total is correct, then it corroborates the Patriarchal Chronology duration, at least as far as it coincides with Manetho.

Counting Nebka's 19 years in the Turin Canon, bringing the total to 74 years, there is a discrepancy of about 23 or 24 years between Manetho and the Turin Canon, depending whether the original Manetho duration was 97 years (M1–M5) or 98 years (M7–M9). Almost all of that discrepancy can be traced back to disagreements over the lengths of Djoser's reign. In its present form, Manetho has 29 years for Djoser and the Turn Canon has 19 years. Some Egyptologists, however, as we shall see below, believe Djoser served much longer, possibly over 40 years.

Tosorthros and Tosertasis

In the arrangement above, I have aligned the first five Manetho reigns (M1–M5) with the five kings that belonged to the Third Dynasty, and the last three kings (M7–M9) with separately arrived at lines of summation that came to be confused with additional lengths of reign for additional kings. This leaves one Manetho king unaccounted for, Tosertasis (M6), with a reign of 19 years. Both the name and the number of years are curious.

The name Tosertasis looks very much like the name Tosorthros (M2), Manetho's second king and the one who is identified with Djoser (TC2). Tosertasis ruled for 19 years, the same number of years ruled by Djoser in the Turin Canon. It is my suggestion that Tosertasis represents a 19-year subset of Djoser's larger reign of at least 29 years, as indicated by Manetho's Tosorthros. In other words, Manetho's Djoser ruled at least 29 years and 19 of those years are assigned to Tosertasis. The Turin Canon assigned the same 19 years to Djoser.

In the Turin Canon, Djoser is followed by Djoser-teti, who is assigned a reign of 6 years. In Manetho, the king following after Tosorthros is Tyreis, ruling for 7 years. In the Turin Canon, Djoser and Djoser-teti had a combined reign of 25 years. In Manetho, Tosertasis (M6) and Tyreis (M3) have a combined reign of 26 years. M9, one of the proposed summation lines, has a duration of 26 years, the sum of M3 and M6. M9, therefore, appears to be a summation line for the 19-year portion of Djoser's reign (M6, TC2) and the 6 or 7 years for Djoser's successor (M3, TC3).

It is my proposal therefore that Djoser had at least a 29-year reign and within that duration there was a 19-year period that was singled out for special attention. The Turin Canon preserved only the 19-year part, and Manetho preserved the 19-year segment with the reign of Tosertasis (M6) and a combined 29-year portion with the reign of Tosorthros.

Manetho's 30-year Reign for Sephuris.

Let me turn now from the M9 summation for Djoser and his successor to the proposed M8 summation line, Sephuris's 30-year reign. We don't have an obvious match in the Manetho data but we do in the Turin Cannon. TC4 (6 years) and TC5 (24 years) have a combined duration of 30 years, an exact match for the number of years ruled by Manetho's eighth king. I suggest that the 30-year reign assigned to Sephuris is a summation line for the last two kings in the Third Dynasty.

While Manetho's M8 summation line corresponds to the total number of years in the Turin Canon for TC4 and TC5, his individual lengths of reign for his own fourth and fifth kings (M4, M5) differ from those in the Turin Canon. His M4 (17 years) and M5 (16 years) add up to 33 years, close to the Turin Canon's 30-year total for the same two kings, but his individual lengths of reign for M4 (17 years) and M5 (16 years) differ significantly from TC4 (6 years) and TC5 (24 years). The fact that M8 coincides precisely with the sum for TC 4 and TC5 but differs slightly from the sum of M4 and M5 suggests that Manetho's original entries for those reigns were garbled in transmission, with 8 years from M5 transferred to M4, and an additional 3 years added to M4.

The Manetho-Turin Canon Alignment

We have now established the following relationships between Manetho and the Turin Canon.

- Manetho assigned M9, proposed as a line of summation, a span of 26 years. TC2 (19 years) and TC3 (6 years), representing the sequence of Djoser and Djoser-teti, have a combined total of 25 years. M6 (19 years), representing the 19-year portion of Manetho's Djoser (M2), and M3 (7 years) for Manetho's successor to Djoser, have a combined reign of 26 years. Not only are the totals virtually identical, the two numbers in each set are of the same order, 19/19 and 6/7. Manetho appears to have incorporated the equivalent of those two consecutive Turin Canon reigns for Djoser and Djoser-teti, and either Manetho or his redactors added a summation line. But Manetho has a separate entry indicating a longer length of reign for Djoser than the Turin Canon indicates.

- M8, also proposed as a line of summation, is assigned a duration of 30 years. This corresponds precisely with the next two lengths of reign in the Turin Canon, TC4 (6 years) and TC5 (24 years.) This gives us two consecutive reigns in Manetho (M8 and M9) that each equal the total number of years ruled by two consecutive sets of two kings in the Turin Canon. Additionally, Manetho's individual reigns, M4 (17 years) and M5 (16 years), add up to just three years more than TC4 (6 years) and TC5 (24 years). Unfortunately, the M4 and M5 lines appear to have been garbled in transmission.

- M8 (30 years) and M9 (26 Years) add up to 56 years. TC2 (19 years) + TC3 (6 years) + TC4 (6 years) + TC5 (24 years) add up to 55 years. In both cases, the two sets of sums add up to the number of years in the Third Dynasty from the start of the 19-year portion of Djoser's reign to the end of the Third Dynasty.

- M7 (42 years), the third proposed Manetho summation line, should correspond to the number of years belonging to Nebka plus all the unaccounted-for years missing in the Turin Canon but present in Manetho, which additional years presumably belong to Djoser.

The coincidences between Manetho's lengths of reign for his eighth and ninth kings, which I suggested were summation lines, and the lengths of reign for the four consecutive kings in the Turin Canon beginning with Djoser, strike me as remarkable and highly unlikely to be the product of happenstance. Therefore, it is not unlikely that the third summation line M7, the 42 years assigned to a king Aches, reflects whatever preceded the final 19 years of Djoser's reign.

The Problems of Nebka's Reign

In my reconstruction of the Second Dynasty chronology, I used the Turin Canon's 19-year entry for Nebka in reconstructing the Second Dynasty chronology and used the Turin Canon as a possible corroboration for the Manetho-Genesis correlation. In the Turin Canon, Nebka is Djoser's predecessor. But it is not clear that Nebka belongs to the Second Dynasty or that he preceded Djoser. The Turin Canon scribe may have made an error in assigning that 19-year reign to Nebka. Alternatively, the Turin Canon doesn't fully corroborate the Genesis-Manetho correlation for the Second Dynasty.

The Turin Canon and the Abydos list both place Nebka immediately preceding Djoser but the Sakkara list omits him altogether. Another document, the Westcar Papyrus, reverses the order and places Djoser before Nebka.[113] Hornung, together with his co-editors, Krauss and Warburton, in their survey of the chronological evidence say that, "It has recently been confirmed that Kha-sekhemwy's successor was Netjery-khet (Djoser), not Nebka. The sequence Khasekhemwy: Djoser is recorded in row 5 of the Palermo stone."[114] Khasekhemwy, who is well attested from inscriptions on monuments, is missing from all the main king-lists.[115] The ancient Egyptian sources are obviously confused about the transition between the Second and Third Dynasties.

Gardiner places Nebka at the end of the Second Dynasty.[116] Krauss/Warburton list him in the fourth place of the Third Dynasty and make Djoser the founder of the Dynasty.[117] Most of the other chroniclers place Nebka ahead of Djoser.

The two Manetho sources both also place a Third Dynasty king in front of Djoser. This strongly suggests that Manetho is following the Turin Canon tradition with respect to Nebka appearing before Djoser. In this arrangement, then, we have Khasekhemwy, who is missing from the Turin Canon, as the last king of the Second Dynasty, followed by Nebka as the first king of the Third Dynasty, followed by Djoser.

Since the sources are confused as to whether Nebka preceded Djoser, and since the Turin Canon omits Khasekhemwy from the king-list, there is a possibility that the assignment of 19 years to

Nebka was a mistake and that those years should have been assigned to Khasekhemwy at the end of the Second Dynasty. There is some evidence in support of this thesis.

One very likely possibility is that Nebka and Khasekhemwy ruled simultaneously, in conflict with each other for at least portions of their reigns. As you may recall from above, Krauss/Warburton advise us, "the history of the second half of Dynasty 2 is unclear, insofar as kings might have ruled simultaneously and not successively." Gardiner notes:

> More problematic are some broken pieces from the tomb of a prophet of that King Nebka whom the Turin Canon and the Abydos king-list place immediately before Djoser; this king is also named in the story of the Magicians . . . where, however, it seems to be implied that his reign fell between those of King Djoser and Snofru. From what has already been said *Nebka could not have been the predecessor of Djoser unless he were a successful rival of Khasekhemui; the nineteen years assigned to him remain a problem* [emphasis added].[118]

We do know that political conflict rived the latter part of the Second Dynasty, with one group of kings identifying themselves with the god Set in conflict with political opponents who supported the traditional identification of the king with the god Horus.[119] Khasekhemwy's support for the Seth faction may have rendered him illegitimate in the eyes of later Horus kings, and that may account for his being removed from the king-lists. This would be especially true if Nebka, a Horus-king, ruled simultaneously over parts of Egypt not under Khasekhemwy's control. From the Egyptian perspective, there can only be one legitimate king on the throne at any particular time and that king was Horus, not Set.

The competing kings thesis suggests the possibility that the latter part of the Second Dynasty overlapped the first part of the Third Dynasty. If there was a split in rule after Khasekhemwy's predecessor died, and Nebka and Khasekhemwy both ruled from approximately the same starting point, and Djoser later unified the kingdom under his single rule, then both

Khasekhemwy and Nebka would have the same or similar lengths of reign, so the 19 years assigned in the Turin Canon could also apply to a 19-year period of rule for Khasekhemwy, eliminating the problem of double-counting Nebka's reign. In this scenario, Djoser may have been the unifying ruler who brought both factions together under a single administration, and possibly accounting for why his name was singled out for special attention in the Turin Canon.

If there were an overlap between Khasekhemwy and Nebka then we might have to reduce the Genesis starting dates for Dynasties 1–2 by the number of years in which the two kings ruled simultaneously. But that doesn't shorten the duration of any of the first three dynasties.

Gardiner, however, has raised doubts about whether Nebka could have served for 19 years.[120] Smith raised a similar concern. He notes that Nebka's predecessor, Khasekhemwy, and Djoser had a close association with each other through Queen Nymaathap, who was the wife of Khasekhemwy and the mother of Djoser.[121] (Smith is working from the sequence in which Nebka's reign fell between Khasekhemwy and Djoser.) Under such circumstances, he suggests, 19 years is too long a gap between Khasekhemwy and Djoser.[122]

We also have some archaeological evidence that Nebka may have had a shorter reign. According to Smith, the Palermo stone connects the year after an "eighth biennial count" with the last year of Nebka's reign.[123] As to the cattle count census, a "year after the Eighth Occasion" would indicate a High Minimum reign of 16 years and a Low Minimum reign of 8 Years. However, we also have an indication that the first two cattle counts occurred in the first two years of Nebka's reign.[124]

That would reduce the High Minimum to 15 years although the Low Minimum would remain unchanged. Given the presence of consecutive counts in the first two years of the reign, we must be at least suspicious as to whether other counts were also in consecutive years. In any event, assuming the otherwise regularity of biennial counts for Nebka's reign, he may have served for at least 15 years, but we can't be certain how much longer he served. If the biennial counts were less regular, the minimum length of reign would be even shorter.

However long Nebka served, we still must deal with the fact that the last king of the Second Dynasty was Khasekhemwy and he was succeeded by Djoser. How log Nebka ruled remains up in the air as are the questions of how long he served contemporaneously with Khasekhemwy and how much time he may have ruled in between that king and Djoser.

My suggestion that the Turin Canon's 19-year reign for Nebka might have belonged instead to Khasekhemwy or that both Khasekhemwy and Nebka both served for 19 years seems plausible. On the other hand, it may simply be that, at worst, we cannot fully corroborate the Manetho-Patriarchal alignment for the Second Dynasty by using the Turin Canon. This doesn't mean that Manetho and the Patriarchal Chronology had different durations, but it does mean we have slightly less proof than we would like.

Manetho's 42-year reign for Aches

If M8 and M9 sum up the reigns of Djoser and his three successors, as a comparison between Manetho and Turin Canon seem to suggest, then the 42 years assigned to M7 would represent a third portion of the proposed 98-year dynastic duration. Unfortunately, except for Nebka, the Turin Canon has no additional evidence to assist us for the purpose of corroboration, and the Manetho data isn't as obvious as we would like.

I begin by reminding you that Smith argued that the Third Dynasty should have lasted about one hundred years to accomplish its notable achievements. Additionally, Gardiner assigned 80 years to the Third Dynasty but did not include Nebka in the total. If he had, the dynasty would have had a duration of 99 years. In both cases, the higher number of years must come primarily from Djoser, whose reign they consider far too short. For Gardiner to have reached 80 years without Nebka, and assuming the extra years belonged to Djoser, then Gardiner assigned Djoser a reign of 44 years.[125]

Assuming for the sake of argument that Djoser ruled for Gardiner's 44 years, 19 of those years were already accounted for in the

M9 summation line for Djoser and Djoser-teti. That would leave an additional 25 years for Djoser. Subtracting those 25 years from the 42 years for M7 leaves 17 years for Nebka, a very good fit with the archaeological data. If we adjust Nebka up a couple of years because of the Turin Canon's 19 years for this reign, we would reduce Djoser's reign by an equivalent amount.

In the Manetho data, the first two kings, corresponding to Nebka and Djoser, have respective reigns of 28 years and 29 years, for a combined duration of 57 years. But 19 of those years are already accounted for by M6, ruling 19 years. This leaves us with 38 years for Nebka and the balance of Djoser's reign, 4 years short of the 42-year M7 summation line. However, if you recall, 3 extra years seem to have been added to Manetho's fourth king, who served 17 years. The only place those 3 years could have come from, given the M8 and M9 summation lines, is from the reigns of either Nebka or the additional years assigned to Djoser. If we move that 3 years back to one of those kings, the combined total would be 41 years, one year short of the 42-year M7. This one-year difference is reflected in the 97-year sum for M1–M5 and the 98-year sum for M7–M9. We have a one-year difference between the two summations.

The Manetho data, when properly examined, clearly shows that he worked from a source indicating that the Third Dynasty lasted just short of 100 years, consistent with the estimates of Smith and Gardiner and identical to that of the Patriarchal Chronology. How long Djoser ruled remains a mystery. The tendency is to pick a number somewhere between what the Turin Canon has and what Manetho appears to have for his second king, who corresponded to Djoser. A duration of 42 to 47 years, however, closely tracks Gardiner's speculative 44 years and allows the dynasty to meet Smith's estimated length of one hundred years.

So, while it is possible that Djoser served a significantly shorter reign than 40–44 years (depending on the length of Nebka's reign), Manetho's data shows that some ancient sources thought Djoser did serve such a long term. It may be that tradition to which the Patriarchal Chronology is heir.

Conclusions

The Patriarchal Chronology indicates a starting date of 2719 for the Third Dynasty and gives it a duration of 98 years. The Turin Canon shows only 74 years (counting Nebka.) Smith, however, says the dynasty required about one hundred years to account for its accomplishments, and Gardiner, if we reinstate Nebka to the Third Dynasty, has a conjectured duration of 99 years starting in the same year indicated by the Patriarchal data. Admittedly, if we are going to expand the Third Dynasty from the Turin Canon's 74 years to a period close to one hundred years, most of that difference will have to depend on extensions to the reign of Djoser, for which we have no direct evidence.

The Third Dynasty had five kings (although a sixth king was possible.) Turning to Manetho, the Africanus version had a dynastic duration of 214 years and numbered nine kings, too many kings and too many years. This suggested that there may have been a good deal of double-counting and mistaken use of marginal summation data that came to be misidentified as the reigns of additional kings.

Our review of Manetho showed that matching the first five kings with the five kings making up the Turin Canon's Third Dynasty, gave us a total duration of 97 years, a virtual match to the proposed 98 years in the Genesis chronology. Additionally, we saw that the last three reigns in Manetho added up to 98 years, again a perfect match with the Patriarchal data and a strong indication that these last three reigns may originally have been summation lines that were confused with individual lengths of reign for other kings.

Manetho's second king, Tosorthros, identified by Egyptologists with Djoser, the second king in the Turin Canon list, had a reign of 29 years, but the Turin Canon only assigned 19 years. It is my argument that Manetho's sixth king, Tosertasis, who falls in between the first five kings and the three prosed lines of summation, corresponded to the Turin Canon's 19-year reign for Djoser but that it was only a portion of Manetho's 29-year Djoser reign.

To test out these relationships I examined the proposed summation lines and looked at the data in Manetho and Turin Canon. This produced very useful results.

In the Turin Canon, the second king, Djoser, had a reign of 19 years, and the third king, Djoser-teti, had a reign of 6 years, giving the two kings a duration of 25 years. If we substituted Tosertasis (M6) for Tosorthos (M2), Manetho's second king, then Manetho's Djoser substitute (M6) and Manetho's Djoser successor (M3) with 7 years, had a combined the total of 26 years. The two kings in Manetho matched the corresponding two kings in the Turin Canon, both as to total duration and as to the individual lengths of reign for each of the kings. Additionally, the proposed Manetho summation line for the ninth king also equaled 26 years. So, the Djoser-Successor sequence in Manetho and the Turin Canon were virtually identical.

I then looked at the third and fourth kings in both lists. In the Turin Canon, they had a total duration of 30 years. Manetho's eighth king, another proposed summation line, also equaled 30 years, another very good correlation. Unfortunately, the Manetho figures for the two individual reigns may have been garbled. The total, 33 years, was quite close to the Turin Canon/M8 totals of 30 years, but the sum of Manetho's individual lengths of reign exceeded the corresponding portion of the Turin Canon by three years, suggesting some garbling in the transmission of those two Manetho reigns.

This brought us to the third and final Manetho summation line, M7 ruling 42 years. Regrettably, the only remaining data in the Turin Canon, Nebka's reign of 19 years, together with the ten extra years for Manetho's Djoser equivalent (M2), we couldn't fill out the total of 42 years. We had to arbitrarily assign the balance to Djoser. Unfortunately, outside of Manetho and the Turin Canon, we have no evidence for how long Djoser ruled. But several Egyptologists are convinced that the 19 years assigned to him are too few.

Nevertheless, based on the good correspondences between M8 and M9 with the Turin Canon, Manetho appears to be based on legitimate original resources, and M7–M9 appear to be summation lines confirming that at least some ancient Egyptian sources assigned 98 years to the Third Dynasty.

Additionally, we looked at some evidence indicating that Nebka and the last king of the Second Dynasty, Khasekhemwy, may have been political rivals and ruling concurrently in different parts of Egypt, and possibly ruling for about the same number of years. It is my suggestion that Djoser was responsible for reuniting Egypt under a single king and that may be, in part, why he appears to have been so highly revered by later Egyptians.

The Chronology of Dynasty 4

The Fourth Dynasty became famous through its three great pyramid builders, Khufwey, Khafre, and Menkaure (whom Herodotus referred to as Cheops, Chephren and Mycerinus,) who built the three pyramids at Giza. The founder of the dynasty, Snofru, also erected pyramids, the two less famous but still impressive structures known as the Red Pyramid and the Bent Pyramid. The ancient sources disagree as to how many kings there were in this dynasty and the sequence of various reigns.

The Patriarchal Chronology divides this dynasty into two parts, 4A lasting 95 years and 4B lasting 55 years, for a total of 150 years. Although there have been some suggestions in the past that the dynasty may have lasted as long as 160 years, that view is no longer current.[126] Table 5.7, *Various Fourth Dynasty Lengths of Reign*, sets forth the chronologies present in Manetho and the Turin Canon, along with several chronologies by modern Egyptologists. Among the Egyptologists in the Table, Beckareth has the longest duration at 134 years. I omitted Gardiner from the list, but he gives a duration of 140 years. The Patriarchal Chronology's 150-year duration is a little above the higher end of the range, but we will eventually see that the figure is within acceptable bounds when compared with the archaeological record and the ancient king-lists.

The Table also includes a column indicating the High Minimum for each length of reign where we have cattle count information. There is an inscription, which some Egyptologists assign to Radjedef, indicating

Table 5-7. Various Fourth Dynasty Lengths of Reign

King Name	Turin Canon[a]	Manetho	Cattle Count[b]	Kitchen[c]	Beckareth[d]	Shaw[e]	Krauss/ Warburton[f]	CAH[g]
Snofru	24	29	46	24	35	24	33	24
Khufwey/Cheops	23	63	23	23	23	24	23	23
Radjedef	8		21	8	9	8	8	8
Khafre/Chephren	Lost	66	25	25	26	27	25	25
Hardjedef	Lost							
Rabaef								
Menkaure/Mycerinus	18 or 28	63	22	18	28	30	6	28
Shepseskaf	Omitted?		2	4	5	5	5	4
?	4							
?	2							
Ratoises		25						
Bicheris		22			7[h]		2[i]	
Sebercheres		7						
Thampthis		9			2			2
Total/rounded	?	284	139	102	135	119	107	115

[a](Gardiner 1961), 434
[b]Adapted from (Verner 2001), 416. Assumes the biennial value of the highest Occasion of the Count.
[c](Kitchen 1996 [1997])
[d](Beckerath 1997), 159
[e](Shaw 2000), 482.

[f](Hornung, Krauss and Warburton 2006)
[g](Cambridge Ancient History 1971), 995.
[h]Beckerath equates Bicheris with Hardjedef and lists him in Hardjedef's location.
[i]Hornung places Bicheris between Radjedef and Chephren

an 11th cattle count, which, if correctly attributed shows a High Minimum of 21 years.[127] On the other hand, several Egyptologists have rejected the assignment of this cattle count to Radjedef and argue that it should be assigned to Khufu, who also has a 12th Occasion of the Count for his reign.[128] This is due, in part, to the Turin Canon entry indicating that this king had a reign of 8 years. If you look at Table 5.7 you will notice that all the Egyptologists on the list opt for about an 11-year reign. We will work with the lower Turin Canon reign in the below analysis.

Modern Egyptologists agree that the Fourth Dynasty had at least the following six kings serving in the following sequence: Snofru, Khufwey/Cheops, Radjedef, Khafre/Chephren, Menkaure/Mycerinus, and Shepseskaf. However, there is disagreement in the ancient sources and, therefore, among Egyptologists as to whether additional kings also ruled in this dynasty and where in the sequence these additional kings fit in. Beckareth, for example, identifies Manetho's Bicheris with a missing entry in the Turin Canon that was located between Khafre and Menkaure.[129] Krauss/Warburton, on the other hand, places Bicheris between Radjedef and Khafre.[130] Others ignore Bicheris altogether. CAH identifies Manetho's Thampthis with the Turin Canon's missing entry at the end of the list, serving 2 years.[131]

The King-lists

The Turin Canon indicates that there were eight kings in this dynasty and the surviving portions of the list provide lengths of reign for six of those kings, although the length of reign for Menkaure is damaged and could be either 18 or 28 years.[132] The length of reign for Khafre is lost and the list indicates that a king served in between Khafre and Menkaure, but the name and length of reign for Khafre's successor is lost.[133] While we have lengths of reign for the last two kings in the Turin list, the names are missing.[134]

The six preserved lengths of reign add up to either 79 or 89 years, depending on how you resolve the damaged entry for Menkaure. While Khafre's length of reign is missing, we have several inscriptions with an Occasion of the Count during his reign, the highest being 13.[135] If these counts were biennial, and we have no evidence to the contrary, then Khafre reached at least a 25th year of rule. As you can see from Table 5.7, there is a tendency to accept 25 years as his length of reign. In our various reconstructions below, we will assume a 25-year reign for Khafre.

The Turin Canon list is also missing the length of reign for Khafre's successor. It is thought that if any successor intervened between Khafre and Menkaure, that reign would have been brief.[136] Our reconstruction of Manetho will show that his chronology had an intervening gap that lasted 9 years.

The Turin Canon entry for Snofru's reign appears to be significantly shorter than what the archaeological evidence indicates. His highest recorded Occasion of the Count is 24.[137] But there is also one instance of the Occasion of the Count happening in consecutive years.[138] The High Minimum view of how long Snofru ruled would be at least 46 years.[139] The Low Minimum, including three different "Year After the Occasion" inscriptions, would give Snofru at least 27 years of rule.[140] The Turin Canon gives Snofru a 24-year reign. Manetho assigns this king a 29-year reign. Verner suggests that there should be a minimum length of reign of at least 30 years.[141] In my reconstructions below, I will work with a 46-year reign for Snofru.

The Turin Canon indicates that at least two kings ruled after Menkaure and while reigns are given (4 and 2 years) the names are lost. We don't know if either of them was Shepseskaf.

The Table of Sakkara had nine kings listed but no lengths of reign, and differs from the Turin Canon in some areas.[142] It omits the Turin Canon's intervening king between Khafre and Menkaure and places four kings after Menkaure, where the Turin Canon has only two, but the names of these last four kings are lost.

The Table of Abydos has only six kings in the dynasty but no lengths of reign, and agrees with the Sakkara list against the Turin Canon in omitting any intervening king between Khafre and Menkaure.[143] It places only one king after Menkaure, and the list identifies him as Shepseskaf.[144] It is the only one of the king-lists that preserves this king's name, but we have independent archaeological evidence for his existence.[145]

In all three lists, Khafre appears in the fourth position.[146]

We come now to the first of the major problems with the ancient sources, an inscription in the Wady Hammamat that contains a partial sequence of five kings from the Fourth Dynasty, beginning with Khufwey, Radjedef, and Khafre, and continuing with two kings named Hardjedef and Rabaef (also known as Hardjedef and Baufre.)[147] The arrangement places the last two kings after Khafre and, therefore, ahead of Menkaure, the only list to place two kings into this location.

Both Hardjedef and Baufre are well known family members of the dynasty, but other than this inscription there is no other indication that either of these men served as king during the Fourth Dynasty.[148] Radjedef, Chephren, Hardjedef, and Baufre were all brothers, sons of Cheops.[149] Although, neither Hardjedef nor Baufre were otherwise known as kings, Hardjedef was the object of later cult worship.[150] A musician in an Eleventh Dynasty court sang, "I have heard the sayings of Imhotep and Hordjedef with whose words men so often speak."[151] It is often suggested that Hardjedef may be the missing king in the Turin Canon's slot between Khafre and Menkaure.[152]

Citing the Wady Hammamat inscription, Redford says that during the Middle Kingdom great literary interest was shown in Cheops and his sons, and that legends began to grow about them. "Part of this interest," he says, "entailed the assumption, *quite natural for those times*, that each of the sons had been king and reigned in succession to Khufu [= Cheops]. Three of them in fact had done so, and why not the rest [emphasis added.]?"[153]

Redford theorizes that this view of the Fourth Dynasty continued into the New Kingdom's Nineteenth Dynasty, which is when the three major king-lists were created. He writes:

> By the Nineteenth Dynasty this falsification of the 4th Dynasty succession had achieved canonicity. TC [= Turin Canon] and the Sakkara list undoubtedly embody this distortion, the former ending with Shepseskaf, Hordjedef, and Baufre in that order, the latter perhaps

adding a fourth at the end, the enigmatic Vorlage of Thampthis. The tradition to which Manetho fell heir is precisely this one.[154]

Summing up Redford's argument, and that of other Egyptologists, later Egyptians had a mistaken view of who the Fourth Dynasty kings were and added Hardjedef and Baufre to the dynastic list. The ancient sources, they suggest, seem to disagree only as to whether either or both preceded Mycerinus or followed him.

Herodotus

Another problematic king-list comes from the fifth century Greek historian Herodotus. Writing about two centuries before Manetho, he tells of conversations with Egyptian priests that reveal how some later Egyptians viewed the earlier kings of the Fourth Dynasty. He gives the following sequence of kings. Rhampsinitus [presumably Snofru], Cheops, Chephren, Mycerinus, Asychis, and Anysis.[155] This sequence omits Radjedef (belonging between Cheops and Chephren), has no king between Chephren and Mycerinus, and places two unidentifiable kings after Mycerinus.

Of Cheops, second king of the dynasty, he writes, "Cheops (to continue the account which the priests gave me) brought the country into all sorts of misery."[156] Herodotus describes an era of religious persecution and oppressive slavery and adds, "No crime was too great for Cheops; when he needed money, he sent his daughter to a bawdy house with instructions too charge a certain sum—they did not tell me how much."[157] He says Cheops ruled for 50 years.[158]

Herodotus, identifies Chephren as Cheops's immediate successor, omitting Radjedef.[159] (This is the same sequence followed by the Africanus version of Manetho.) Chephren, he says, ruled for 56 years, and continued Cheops's oppressive policies.[160] His length of reign for Chephren is of the same order of size as Manetho's.

After talking about the corruption of Cheops and Chephren, Herodotus turns to the tragic story of Mycerinus, whom, he says, followed after Chephren. This arrangement diverges from the Turin Canon and the Wady Hammamat inscription, both of which indicate at least one ruler serving in between these two kings, but it is consistent with the Tables of Sakkara and Abydos and with Manetho.

Mycerinus, says Herodotus, reversed the cruel policies of his predecessor. Of all the kings of Egypt, he says, "[Mycerinus] had the greatest reputation for justice in the decision of legal causes, and for this the Egyptians give him higher praise than any other monarch."[161] Herodotus preserves a few legends about this king, but one in particular is worth recounting.[162]

An oracle predicted that Mycerinus would live only six more years and die in the seventh. The king was astonished to learn that he would lead such a short life, especially since he had reversed the cruel and oppressive policies of the long-lived Cheops and Chephren. Why then, he asked, should he have such a short life?

In answer to this, Herodotus writes, "there was another message from the oracle, which declared that his life was being shortened precisely because he had not done what he ought to have done: *for it was fated that Egypt should suffer for a hundred and fifty years*—a thing which his two predecessors, unlike himself, understood very well [emphasis added]."[163] In other words, had he continued to follow the evil ways of his predecessors, he would have had a longer life. This anecdote about Mycerinus provides us with two important clues about how ancient Egyptians viewed the Fourth Dynasty.

First, its kings were associated with a period of 150 years, which is the amount of time that Genesis has for this dynasty. However, Herodotus doesn't actually say that the dynasty lasted 150 years, only that a prophecy predicted 150 years of bad times and Mycerinus disrupted the prophecy. I should also note that Herodotus talks about Mycerinus having six years left to live, but he doesn't say if that was the extent of his reign or just a portion of the reign. He also doesn't say whether that prophecy came true.

Second, the transition from Chephren to Mycerinus inaugurated a profound change to the nature of the government, from cruel oppression to great justice. In the minds of later Egyptians, the shift from Chephren to Mycerinus signified a major historical, moral, and political shift. In accounting for the break between Genesis 4A and 4B and in reconstructing the summation lines in Manetho, the division between Chephren and Mycerinus turns out to be the major factor. We will also see that the 56-year reign Herodotus assigned to Chephren is another summation line, like the one in Manetho.

Manetho

The Africanus version of Manetho gives the following list of Fourth Dynasty kings and their lengths of reign.

1. Soris, 29 years
2. Suphis [I], 63 years
3. Suphis [II], 66 years
4. Mencheres, 63
5. Ratoises, 25 years
6. Bicheris, 22 years
7. Sebercheres, 7 years
8: Thampthis, 9 years

He says the dynasty ruled for 277 years but the actual sum is 284 years, a 7-year difference. So, there was probably a transmission error in which either the summation line was mistakenly increased or the lengths of reign were shortened by the 7 years in question or a king was omitted.

Eusebius says there were 17 kings but names only one, Suphis, and provides no lengths of reign. He says the dynasty ruled for 448 years. There is one interesting inconsistency between Africanus and Eusebius. The former has two consecutive kings named Suphis and describes the first Suphis, whom he lists as the second king of the dynasty, as "the builder of the Great Pyramid, which Herodotus says was built by Cheops." Eusebius uses the same description for his Suphis but says that he was the third king of the dynasty, which would correspond to Africanus's second Suphis. This suggests further evidence of a garbled transmission. For the record, Cheops was the second ruler of the dynasty.

In correlating Manetho to the king-lists, it is routinely accepted that his first four kings, Soris, Suphis [I], Suphis [II] and Mencheres, correspond to Snofru, Khufwey/Cheops, Khafre/Chephren and Menkaure/Mycerinus. The other four king names are hard to identify. His sequential order raises some questions. He has no king intervening between Cheops and Chephren, contra to all the Egyptian king-lists but in accord with Herodotus, and no intervening king between Chephren and Mycerinus, contra the Turin Canon. Interestingly, his sequence of four kings after Mycerinus echoes the Table of Sakkara.

Perhaps the most compelling fact in this list is Manetho's three-king sequence beginning with Suphis [I] (corresponding to Cheops), Suphis [II] (corresponding to Chephren), and Mencheres (corresponding to Mycerinus,) ruling respectively for 63, 66, and 63 years. In the Turin Canon, Cheops has a reign of 23 years, Chephren's is lost, and Mycerinus has a reign of 18 or 28 years. Some Egyptologists have suggested that Manetho originally had respective reigns of 23, 26, and 23 years and that during transmission the "20" symbol became a "60" symbol. This would be approximately consistent with the Turin Canon's reigns of 23 for Cheops and 28 for Mycerinus (assuming the damaged figure was 28 and not 18) and with Chephren, as noted above, ruling 25 years. It will be my argument below that the three lengthy Manetho reigns are summation figures that were mistakenly assigned to these kings.

In support of that proposition consider the following. If you add up the lengths of reign for the four kings following after Manetho's Mencheres (= Menkaure/Mycerinus), they add up to 63 years, the same number of years assigned to the reigns of Manetho's Mencheres and Suphis [I]. This seems like quite an extraordinary coincidence and strongly suggests that the three over-60-year reigns are summation lines.

Experimenting with Manetho

On the assumption that the three 60-plus reigns in Manetho are summation totals, let's conduct an experiment. I'm removing the three long-lived reigns form Manetho's list and working with what is left. We would then have the following scheme.

Soris (29 years)
Ratoises (25 years)
Bicheris (22 years)
Sebercheres (7 years)
Thampthis (9 years)

The first four kings in this list have a total of 83 years length of reign. Turn now to the Turin Canon list. If we assign 25 years to the Turin Canon's missing reign for Chephren, the total length of reign for the first four kings would be 80 years. Considering that Manetho's first king has five years more than the Turin Canon's first king, and that Manetho comes closer to that king's reign than does the Turn Canon, we have what is beginning to look like a striking correlation.

Let me now reorder the Manetho list and align it with the Turin Canon list. Table 5.8, *The Fourth Dynasty in Manetho and the Turin Canon Compared*, shows the results.

Except for the slight difference between Manetho and the Turin Canon with respect to Snofru's reign, where Manetho has the more reliable figure, the first four reigns are virtually identical in Manetho and the Turin Canon, the differences in kings 2 and 3 being only a year apart, possible rounding errors. I submit these first four kings and their respective reigns constituted the original Manetho sequence for the start of the Fourth Dynasty and later redactors garbled the text in transmission. Let's take a closer look.

The similarity of the names Ratoises and Radjedef has been noticed by several Egyptologists.[164] But in this re-ordering, he appears in the second position aligned with the length of reign for Cheops. It is my view that Manetho's Ratoises originally corresponded to Radjedef and Manetho's Sebercheres originally corresponded to Khafre/Chephren, but that somehow in transmission the two king

Table 5.8. The Fourth Dynasty in Manetho and the Turin Canon Compared

Manetho King[a]	Reign	Turin Canon King	Reign
(1) Soris	29	Snofru	24
(5) Ratoises	22	Khufwey	23
(7) Sebercheres	7	Radjedef	8
(6) Bicheris	25	Khafre	[25][b]
(8) Thampthis	9	[Hardjedef?]	?

[a]The number in parenthesis indicates what place the king occupied in the Africanus version of Manetho's 4th Dynasty.
[b]This figure is not preserved in the Turin Canon. It is based on the separate existence of a 13th Occasion of the Count for this king.

names were listed in reverse order while their respective lengths of reign remained in the correct sequential order. The 7-year reign should belong to Ratoises and the 22-year to Sebercheres, and the two names should be switched back to their correct sequence.

As to Sebercheres, it is often thought to be a substitute for Shepseskaf. To my eye, though, Sebercheres looks like a closer fit to both Khafre (the Egyptian name) and Chephren (the Greek name) than does Suphis. Both Manetho names substitute the "s" for the "Kh" sound and the "B" in Sebercheres closely aligns with the "PH" in Suphis. But the latter lacks the "R" sound while Sebercheres retains it.

Additionally, Sebercheres actually looks like a garbled concatenation of Chephren in the "Seber" portion and Khafre in the "cheres" portion. In the meantime, the name Suphis is supposed to correspond to two different important king-names, rendering both uses suspicious as a substitute for either.

If my reconstruction is correct, then Sebercheres corresponds to Chephren and we can assign Thampthis to the Turin Canon's missing reign between Chephren and Mycerinus, whom some Egyptologists equate with Hardjedef, from the Wady Hammamat inscription.

Manetho gives him a 9-year reign, which is probably longer that most Egyptologists would accept, and there is the possibility that Thampthis could embody both Hardjedef and Baufre from the Wady list.

This leaves us with a damaged Manetho list in which the original length of reign for Mencheres dropped out, to be replaced by the 63-year summation, and that the original post-Mencheres reigns were pushed out when this group of four preceding reigns was placed after Mencheres. Let's assign Mencheres the 28-year reign belonging to Menkaure/Mycerinus and look at what we have in terms of summations.

We have already seen that the four reigns that Africanus placed after Mencheres (= Menkaure/Mycerinus) had a total number of years equal to 63, the same number of years assigned to Suphis [I] and Mencheres. In the reconstructed and realigned Manetho, these four reigns represent the sequence of kings that runs from Khufwey/Cheops to just before Menkaure/Mycerinus. What we see, therefore, are two different versions of the summation for how many years elapsed from the start of Cheops's reign to the start of Mycerinus's.

This suggests that there may have been different summation totals in the margins, one probably indicating something like "to Mycerinus" and one probably indicating something like "from Cheops." These marginal summations came to be confused with the actual reigns of these kings and inserted into the Manetho list, pushing the other names further down. In both cases, the concern was counting the number of years from the start of Cheops to the start of Mycerinus.

As we saw from Herodotus, Egyptians viewed the transition from Chephren to Mycerinus as an important milestone in their history. It is not surprising, therefore, that later redactors familiar with Herodotus—both Africanus and Eusebius, for example, mention Herodotus in their respective Fourth Dynasty accounts—would have been interested in checking out the numbers and comparing Manetho and Herodotus. Manetho, himself, wrote a now-lost treatise titled *Criticism of Herodotus.*[165]

This leaves us with one more Manetho summation line, the 66 years assigned to Suphis [II]. This is the sum of the lengths of reign for Soris (= Snofru), Thampthis, and Mencheres (= Menkaure/Mycerinus.) The two preserved Manetho reigns for the first two are 29 and 9. If we

assign 28 years to Mencheres, whose true reign is missing from
Manetho, the total for all three reigns comes to 66 years. This is the
sum of all the king-reigns from Snofru through Mycerinus minus the
villainous group of kings in the Cheops-Radjedef-Chephren sequence.
This reconstruction seems to corroborate the suggestion that the damaged entry in the Turin Canon for Mycerinus should be 28 rather
than 18.

I should point out that we placed Thampthis in both summation groups. In the 63-year line of summation he is part of the sequence from the beginning of Cheops to the beginning of
Mycerinus. In the 66-year summation line he is part of the lists of
kings from Snofru to Mycerinus, minus the Cheops-Radjedef-
Chephren period of corruption. Let me emphasize that these two
overlapping summations serve two different functions. One is a
summation line from the beginning of Cheops to the start of
Mycerinus. The other is a summation from Snofru to the end of
Mycerinus, minus the period of corruption. Thampthis, who appears to correspond to the much-admired Hardjedef, falls into
both sequences.

The reign-lengths in Herodotus

Herodotus told us that Cheops ruled for 50 years and Chephren
ruled for 56 years. Here I am going to switch from Manetho's numbers to the Turin Canon numbers. In the latter list, Cheops ruled for
23 years and Radjedef ruled for 8 years, for a total 31 years. If we add
in the 25-years ruled by Chephren, the total is 56 years, the very
same number that Herodotus says he was given by the Egyptian
priests for Chephren's reign.

In Herodotus, this is the sequence from the beginning of Cheops
to the start of Mycerinus. Manetho had the same sequence for his 63-
year summation lines but his list included an additional king, Thampthis, who is missing from the Herodotus list. There is also a very
slight variation between Manetho and Herodotus as to the total duration because Manetho assigns one year less to the reigns of Cheops
and Radjedef than does the Turin Canon.

Since Herodotus got this information from Egyptian priests in the fifth century BCE, about two hundred years earlier than Manetho, we can see there was already a practice of summing up the reigns of Cheops, Radjedef, and Chephren as a single unit down to the start of Mycerinus's reign. What we don't know is whether the information given to Herodotus was intended to be a line of summation that Herodotus misunderstood or whether some Egyptians were already confusing Fourth Dynasty summation lines with lengths of reign for individual kings. It would be interesting to know how Manetho might have addressed this issue in his *Criticisms of Herodotus*.

This brings us to Herodotus's reign of 50 years for Cheops. Since we just saw that this reign was subsumed under the 56 years for Chephren, obviously something is wrong. Here I can only speculate that this 50-year period represented Snofru's reign, which under the maximalist view was at least 46 years long. Snofru preceded Cheops and Herodotus may have confused a description of how many years Snofru ruled before Cheops came to the throne with how many years Cheops ruled. It is also possible that the 50 years was a rounded number rather than a precise number for Snofru's reign, but we have no way to check that.

Reconstructing Fourth Dynasty Chronology

Reconstructing the chronology of the Fourth Dynasty, as viewed by the ancient Egyptians, and modified by archaeological discoveries, leaves us with several inconsistent options regarding the number of kings in the dynasty and how long they reigned.

The Turin Canon, though heavily damaged, appears to have listed eight kings, with one unidentified king serving between Chephren and Mycerinus and two unidentified kings serving after Mycerinus. The lengths of reign are missing for Chephren and the king coming after him. The length of reign for Mycerinus is damaged and is either 18 or 28 years.

The Table of Abydos has only six kings and no lengths of reign. It omits the Turin Canon's reign between Chephren and Mycerinus and has only one king after Mycerinus, Shepseskaf. The other lists are damaged after Mycerinus and we don't know if they included Shep-seskaf among the rulers. But, based on some inscriptions on the Pa-lermo Stone, there is some independent evidence that he ruled for at least one year and perhaps as many as six years.[166] However, the six-year span could encompass more than one king, bringing to mind that the last two rulers in the Turin Canon ruled for 4 and 2 years.[167]

The Table of Sakkara originally listed nine kings but no lengths of reign. The last four names, all serving after Mycerinus, have been lost. Like the Table of Abydos and contra the Turin Canon, it omits any king in the place between Chephren and Mycerinus. Such an ar-rangement opens the possibility that the last four kings in the list include the king that the Turin Canon places before Mycerinus, the two kings the Turin Canon places after Mycerinus, and Shepseskaf.

Manetho introduced some additional problems. As in the Table of Sakkara, he places four kings after Mycerinus, but, as we saw in our reconstruction, two of the four were duplicates for Cheops and Chephren and a third appeared to be Radjedef, the king who ruled between those two kings. These last four kings in Manetho appear to have been a four-king sequence starting with Cheops. This suggested that the fourth king, Thampthis, probably corresponded to the Turin Canon's missing king between Chephren and Mycerinus. Manetho said he ruled for nine years.

Because Manetho's reconstructed lists showed two duplicates, and the last four kings placed after Mycerinus should have preceded Mycerinus, we were left with only six kings in Manetho and no kings after Mycerinus. This recon-struction also left us with no length of reign for Mycerinus, but the suggested reconstruction of the 66-year reign assigned to Suphis [II] appeared to be a summation line incorporating a 28-year reign for Mycerinus.

We also ran into another problem. According to Herodotus, at least as early as the Fifth Century BCE, at least some Egyptian priests had already concatenated the Cheops-Chephren se-quence into the reign of a single king. Herodotus said that the Egyptians assigned a 56-year reign to Chephren. We saw that the 56 years, using the Turin Canon data, incorporated the sequence of Cheops-Radjedef-Chephren.

Manetho had the same sequence summation but extended it through one more reign, adding in Thampthis as the successor to Chephren. Manetho's lengths of reign varied slightly from the Turin Canon's, giving him 54 years for the same three kings. But adding in Thampthis's 9 years brought the total to 63 years.

In the process of concatenating multiple reigns as that of a single king, it appears that Radjedef, between Cheops and Chephren, started getting short shrift. Both Manetho and Herodotus (based on information from Egyptian priests) removed Radjedef from his position. Herodotus omits him from the entire Fourth Dynasty king-list; Manetho appears to have preserved Radjedef's name but placed it among the kings serving after Mycerinus, and somewhere along the line the lengths of reign for Radjedef and Chephren were switched.

For my reconstruction of Fourth Dynasty chronology I am going to use the Table of Sakkara as a template. However, I am going to identify one of the four Sakkara kings with Manetho's Thampthis and, following the Turin Canon, place him between Mycerinus and Chephren. This will leave three kings after Mycerinus, the two listed in the Turin Canon and Shepseskaf.

Using the High Minimum view of the Occasions of the Count, I am going to assign 46 years to Snofru and 25 years to Chephren. I am also going with the higher of the two possible reign-lengths in the Turin Canon for Mycerinus and will assign him 28 years. The reconstructed Manetho and the Turin Canon are only one year apart for each of the reigns of Cheops and Radjedef. Manetho has, respectively, 7 and 22 years; the Turin Canon 8 and 23 years. I will use the Turin Canon data, which appears to be corroborated by the Herodotus summation line he assigned to Chephren as a length of reign.

Several Egyptologists tend to identify Shepseskaf with one of the last two reigns in the Turin Canon, either 4 or 2 years, maybe rounding up one or two years. In my Sakkara template, Shepseskaf is separate from and additional to those last two kings in the Turin Canon. Bear in Mind that Shepseskaf has a length of reign somewhere between one and six years

Here is my initial proposed reconstruction of the Fourth Dynasty chronology. Hardjedef is a stand-in for the Turin Canon king that belongs between Chephren and Mycerinus. Thampthis is the Manetho king corresponding to Hardjedef. Manetho gave him a reign of 9 years. This chronological sequence should be thought of as the High Minimum duration of the Fourth Dynasty consistent with both the archaeological record and the king-lists.

Snofru (46 years)
Cheops (23 years)
Radjedef (8 years)
Chephren (25 years)
Hardjedef/Thampthis (9 years)
Mycerinus (28 years)
Missing Turin Canon king (4 years)
Missing Turin Canon king (2 years)
Shepseskaf (5 years)

The total number of years ruled for this sequence of kings is 150 years, the duration suggested by the Patriarchal chronology. There are admittedly a couple of contentious elements.

The Thampthis reign of 9 years is probably longer than Egyptologists would accept but the reconstructed Manetho makes him the king that served between Chephren and Mycerinus; the 63-year summation line confirms that the 9 years assigned to Thampthis were part of Manetho's history; Manetho's figure is the only hard evidence for the length of the reign for this king; and this establishes the existence of at least one tradition that some Egyptian compilers believed that 9 years was correct. The compiler may have been in error but, nevertheless, it could have been a tradition that the Patriarchal chronographer relied on.

A second issue concerns the alignment of Shepseskaf and the length of reign I have assigned him. I have made him the ninth king in the list and given him a reign of 5 years. The evidence cited above is that Shepseskaf has a length of reign somewhere between 1 and 6 years. It is common among Egyptologists to identify him with one of the last two kings in the Turin Canon. If, for the sake of argument, I did that, then we would have a maximalist total of 145 years, reasonably close to the 150 years in the Patriarchal chronology. I could also under such circumstances consider Herodotus's 50-year reign as an extension of Snofru's reign beyond the 46 years I presently am working with, in which case we could be up to 149 years, virtually identical to the 150 years in Genesis.to year total, off by just one year.

On the other hand, Shepseskaf is the last king of the dynasty. While the Turin Canon has eight kings, the Table of Sakkara has nine. Therefore, I feel justified, from a maximalist point of view, in treating Shepseskaf as the ninth king of the dynasty and adding his length of reign to the 145 year-subtotal.

As to his length of reign, I admit to choosing 5 years to create a nice round 150 years, but whatever specific number we choose between 1 and 6, we would closely approach the 150-year mark, and any slight difference could be explained by nothing more than rounding errors.

The 4A and 4B Break

It is evident from Herodotus's history that later Egyptians had a very negative view of the Cheops-Chephren era. The various reconstructions of Manetho's summation lines clearly frame the Cheops-Chephren problem. In attempting to find a connection between the Patriarchal 4A and 4B, the end of the Chephren era should be the logical breaking point between the two portions of the Fourth Dynasty.

Adding up the years from Snofru through Chephren (46 + 23 + 8 + 25) gives us a total of 102 years. Adding up the five remaining reigns in my proposed chronology (9 + 28 + 4 + 2 + 5) gives a total of 48 years. The two Patriarchal portions, 4A and 4B, separate out with 95 years and 55 years, both of which come quite close to the present division in the proposed Fourth Dynasty chronology. I am going to make one change to the listing.

The Egyptian tradition reflected in Herodotus and repeated in Manetho has clearly marginalized Radjedef. He is missing completely in Herodotus's dynastic listing, subsumed under his 56-year summation line for Chephren. The Manetho listing has also removed him from his position between Cheops and Chephren, although Manetho does preserve a garbled version of Radjedef's reign in a position after Mycerinus.

This evidence suggests that somewhere between the Nineteenth Dynasty, when our known king-lists were created (c. 13th century BCE,) and Herodotus writing in the 5th century BCE, a tradition developed that placed Cheops, Chephren, and Mycerinus into a three-king sequence, causing any intervening kings to be displaced. If correct, then Radjedef may have been moved out of sequence in the later king-lists

Therefore, I am going to reverse the order for Radjedef and Chephren and add his length of reign to the Patriarchal 4B sequence (i.e., post-Chephren) instead of the Patriarchal 4A sequence, where it now stands. Understand, I am not saying this reversal of order is an accurate reflection of the chronological sequence for the Fourth Dynasty. I am merely suggesting that it reflects how Radjedef was marginalized, even eliminated, in various sources and how later compilers might have seen Radjedef as following the Cheops-Chephren sequence rather than being within it.

Radjedef ruled for 8 years in the Turin Canon and 7 years in the reconstructed Manetho. If we switch the order of Radjedef and Chephren, placing Radjedef after Chephren, then we can reduce the period from Snofru to Chephren by 7 or 8 years, resulting in a recalculated duration of 94 or 95 years, and we can increase the post-Chephren period by 7 or 8 years, giving us a new sum of 55 or 56 years. This is virtually a perfect alignment with the Patriarchal Chronology, the differences being nothing more than a rounding error. It is this tradition that I believe the Genesis author worked from.

The Chronology of Dynasty 5

The Patriarchal Chronology dates the Fifth Dynasty to 2471 and indicates a duration of 132 years. Table 5.9, *Various Chronologies for the Fifth Dynasty*, gives several proposed durations for the Fifth Dynasty

Table 5.9: Various Chronologies for the Fifth Dynasty

King	Turin Canon[a]	Manetho	Cattle Count[b]	Verner[c]	Kitchen[d]	Beckerath[e]	Shaw[f]	Krauss/ Warburton[g]	CAH
1. Userkaf	7	28	6	4+x	7	8	7	7	7
2. Sahure	12	13	13/15	8+x	14	14	12	12	14
3. Nefenkare	?	20	10	5+x	10	20	20	10	10
4. Shepseskare	7	7	–		7	7	7	1	7
5. Khanefene	1+X	20	1/3	1+x	7	11	4	1	7
6. Niuserre	11+X	44	13	8+x	31	31	25	29	31
7. Menkauhor	8	9	–		8	9	8	8	8
8. Djedkare	28	44	41/43	28+x	39	39	39	43	39
9. Unis	30	33	15	9+x	30	20	30	15	30
Total		**218**			**153**	**159**	**152**	**126**	**153**

a(Gardiner 1961), 435.
b(Verner, Archaeological Remarks on the 4th and 5th Dynasty Chronology 2001), 385-412. There are some disagreements as to the reading of a highest year date and I have separated the alternatives with a forward slash.
c(Verner, Archaeological Remarks on the 4th and 5th Dynasty Chronology 2001), 416.
d(Kitchen 1996), vol. 67, 11.
e(Beckerath 1997), 155.
f(Shaw 2000), 482.
g(Hornung, Krauss and Warburton 2006), 491.

along with the suggested lengths of reign for each of the kings in that dynasty. The list also includes the data from the Turin Canon, the Africanus version of Manetho, and the Occasions of the Count. The consensus among the listings indicates a duration of about 20 years longer than the Patriarchal Chronology. This difference is mostly due to an opinion about the length of reign for king Niuserre. The analysis below will indicate that the ancient sources had a much shorter reign for Niuserre than that indicated in the various chronologies.

Chronological Markers

There are a few chronological issues that we should deal with, particularly regarding the lengths of reign for Niuserre and Djedkare, the 6th and 8th kings in the Turin Canon and Manetho. (Manetho has different names for the various kings, but, in this analysis, they correspond to the same kings in the Turin Canon order, and I'll use the basic Egyptian names for these kings in the discussion below.)

For Niuserre, the highest known year date comes from a seventh "Occasion of the Count." The High Minimum view indicates that this king ruled for at least 13 years. The Low Minimum perspective indicates only a minimum length of reign of at least 8 years, which includes one reference to a Year After the Count.[168] The Turin Canon entry for Niuserre is damaged and indicates a length of reign higher than 10 years, 11 as a minimum, in between the two boundaries.[169] The Africanus version of Manetho has an entry for the king corresponding to Niuserre of 44 years, much too high to be accepted as the correct length of reign. It will be argued below that Manetho's entry of 44 years for this king is originally a summation figure for several kings that included an 11-year reign for Niuserre.

As Table 5.9 shows, several Egyptologists believe that Niuserre ruled for about 30 years, but, other than the 13 years indicated by the Seventh Occasion of the Count, we have no dated information suggesting more than 11 years.[170] One reason for the high estimate is that this king celebrated a Sed festival, which often, but not always, indicated a king reached his thirtieth year on the throne.[171] Smith says reliance on the Sed festival is insufficient to establish a minimum reign of thirty years as other kings in the Old Kingdom celebrated such festivals earlier than their thirtieth year.[172] Gardiner, who has done extensive work reconstructing the Turin Canon, says the damaged entry would have been 11 years.[173]

If Niuserre only ruled for 11 years, or if ancient sources erroneously indicated that Niuserre ruled for only 11 years, that would reduce the dynastic duration by about 20 years. Except for Krauss/Warburton, such a correction would bring the Patriarchal Chronology into close agreement with the chronologies set forth in Table 5.9.

For Djedkare, the highest known year date comes from an Occasion of the Count that reads either 21 or 22.[174] The High Minimum allows for a reign of at least 41 or 43 years; and the Low Minimum, including seven entries for a "Year after the Occasion," yields at least 28–29 years.[175] Manetho's 44-year entry is consistent with the High Minimum; The Turin Canon's 28 years with the Low Minimum. Table 5.9 shows the listed Egyptologists coalescing near the High Minimum length of reign, closer to Manetho than to the Turin Canon.

We should also look at some other chronological markers.

The second king in the dynasty, Sahure, has a reign of 12 years in the Turin Canon and 13 years in Manetho, showing a very close agreement between the two lists. The cattle count evidence indicates at least a Year after the Sixth Count. although some Egyptologists read this inscription as a Year after the Seventh Count.[176] If the counts remained biennial, Sahure had a reign of at least 12 or 14 years, which is consistent with both Manetho and the Turin Canon.

The Turin Canon is missing the length of reign for the third king, Neferirkare, and Manetho has a 20-year entry for this king. The highest known year for this king is the year after a fifth occasion of the count, indicating a High Minimum of at least 10 years.[177] I will use the 10-year reign for this king in my reconstruction of the dynastic chronology, and argue below that Manetho's 20-year figure is a summation line that originally replaced the 10-year reign.

The Turin Canon also has a damaged entry for the fifth king in the list, Khaneferre, while Manetho has a 20-year reign for this king.

The highest known year for this king is 1 or 3 years, depending on how one reads an Occasion of the Count inscription.[178] Hayes suggests that he may have ruled for at least 7 years because he needed time to build his sun temple.[179] I'll use 3 years in my dynastic reconstruction and suggest that Manetho's 20-year reign here is another summation line erroneously attached to this king.

The Turin Canon

The Turin Canon listed nine kings for the Fifth Dynasty. As shown in Table 5.9, full lengths of reign are preserved for six kings. A damaged length of reign for Niuserre indicates a minimum of at least 11 years. Damage left the third king with no entry. A damaged entry for the fifth king indicates he served at least 1 year.

If we cross-reference the Turin Canon to Manetho we find close agreement between the two with respect to the reigns for four of the six preserved entries, a rather strong correlation suggesting that they were working from similar sets of data for the dynasty. The four close agreements belong to the second, fourth, seventh and ninth reigns, and I have highlighted those reigns in Table 5.9. In the Turin Canon, the respective lengths of reign are 12, 7, 8, and 30 years. In Manetho, the respective figures are 13, 7, 9, and 33 years.

Of the two preserved reigns where they disagree, the first and eighth, the disagreements are large. For the first king, the Turin Canon has 7 years and Manetho 28. There is no evidence for such a long reign as Manetho has. The highest known year, assuming biennial cattle counts, is only 5.[180]

For the eighth king, Djedkare, we have an interesting divergence. The 28 years in the Turin Canon aligns with the Low Minimum view of the cattle counts, at least 28 years; Manetho's 44 years aligns with the High Minimum view of at least 41 or 43 years.

Let's now do some calculations integrating the Turin Canon figures with the High Minimum interpretation of the Occasions of the Count data. Summing the six complete lengths of reign in the Turin Canon (7, 12, 7, 8, 28, 30) gives us a total of 92 years. If we add in the 10 years from the Occasion of the Count for the missing entry for the Turin Canon's third king, the total becomes 102 years. The fifth entry in the Turin Canon is damaged, indicating at least 1 year, but a cattle count (cited above), indicates at least 1 to 3 years. That gives a minimum of 103 to 105 years.

If we add on the 11 years apparently entered for Niuserre in the Turin Canon and include the 15-year difference between the Turin Canon's 28 years for Djedkare and the High Minimum cattle count figure of 43 years, the combined duration would be at least 129 to 131 years, virtually identical to the 132 years indicated by the Patriarchal Chronology.

Manetho

Summing up the individual lengths of reign for Manetho's Fifth Dynasty kings gives us a total of 218 years, far above what the evidence allows. This suggests that, yet again, summation totals have replaced some of the actual lengths of reign. Interestingly, the Africanus summation line says that the dynasty lasted even longer, 248 years, supporting the idea that Manetho's text has been garbled in transmission. The Eusebius version is of no help. It has virtually no information about the Fifth Dynasty, apparently combining it with the Sixth Dynasty and listing no Fifth Dynasty kings and no lengths of reign.

I have already noted above that Manetho and the Turin Canon closely align in sequence and duration for four of the six preserved lengths of reign in the Turin Canon. I have also already pointed out that Manetho's 44 years for Djedkare aligns with the maximalist view of the cattle counts. At the same time, we have seen that the total duration for Manetho's Fifth Dynasty is 218 years, indicating that redactors must have replaced some of the original lengths of reign with summation lines for multiple reigns.

This suggests the possible errors lie with the following group of Manetho kings:

1. Userkaf (28 years)
3. Neferirkare (20 years)
5. Khaneferre (20 years)

6. Niuserre (44 years)

Interestingly, the last three kings in this group are the ones with the damaged entries in the Turin Canon. If we follow the same substitutions for these kings as those we made for the Turin Canon, Manetho and the Turin Canon would, given their alignment on the other four kings, share similar lengths of reign for all of the dynasty's kings except for the first reign.

It is my view that each of these four Manetho reigns are summation lines that came to be confused with individual lengths of reign. Below, I will reconstruct three of the four summation lines, for kings 3, 5, and 6. The one that escapes me is Userkaf's 28 years, which is far too long for that reign. Perhaps the original entry was damaged in transmission. If the original figure was "8" instead of "28" it would be only one year apart for the entry in the Turin Canon.

Let's conduct some experiments by replacing these four unreasonably high lengths of reign with the data from either the High Minimum cattle count evidence or the Turin Canon. As I just mentioned, this should bring the two lists into close agreement, and it could be argued that I am just playing with numbers. However, the purpose of these changes is not to establish a close agreement between Manetho and the Turin Canon, but to see if the corresponding data can give us any meaningful information that will help us figure out what Manetho's proposed summation lines may represent.

Here is a list of the changes I am making.

- Manetho's first king, Userkaf, has an unreasonably long length of reign of 28 years. I'm going to replace it with the 7-year reign from the Turin Canon.
- Manetho's third king, Neferirkare, has a length of reign of 20 years. I'm going to replace it with the 10 years indicated by the cattle counts, just as I did for the Turin Canon's damaged entry for this king.

- Manetho's fifth king, Khaneferre, has a reign of 20 years. I'm going to replace it with the 3 years indicated by the highest known cattle count, just as I did for the Turin Canon's damaged entry.
- Manetho's sixth king, Niuserre, has a length of reign of 44 years. I'm going to replace it with the 11-year minimum duration from the Turin Canon for this reign.

This set of substitutions gives us the following sequence of reigns.

(* = original Manetho figure.)
1. Userkaf (7 years, per Turin Canon)
2. *Sahure (13 years),
3. Neferirkare (3 years, per cattle count)
4. *Shepseskare (7 years)
5. Khaneferre (10 years, per cattle count)
6. Niuserre (11 years, per Turin Canon)
7. *Menkauhor (9 years)
8. *Djedkare (44 years)
9. *Unis (33 years)

The sum for the above reigns equals 137 years, very close to the 132 years proposed by Genesis. If we reduce the last king's reign from 33 to 30, to match the Turin Canon, the total drops to 134 years, virtually identical to the 132 years indicated by the Patriarchal Chronology. Now consider the following lines of summation based on the above data.

- Kings 1 and 2 ruled for 20 years, the number of years assigned to Manetho's third king. This suggests that the current length of reign for Manetho's third king (20 years) is a summation line for the first two kings in the dynasty. The likelihood is that some marginal note said something like "20 years to King 3."
- Kings 3, 4, and 5, after replacing Manetho's 20 years for the fifth king with the 10 years from the cattle count data, ruled for 20 years (=3 + 7 + 10), the number of years assigned to Manetho's fifth king. This suggests that the current length of reign of 20 years

for Manetho's fifth king is a summation line for the lengths of
reign for kings 3–5 in the original Manetho listing. Again, a marginal note may have said something like "20 years to king 5," in-
tending to continue the summation of multiple reigns that
continued from the previous count through king 2.

- Kings 2, 3, 4, 5, and 6, after making the various substitutions,
  ruled for 44 years (13 + 3 +7 + 10 +11), the number of years assigned to Manetho's sixth king. This suggests that the present
  length of reign for Manetho's sixth king, corresponding to Niuserre, is a summation line for the number of years ruled by
  kings 2–6. Note also, this summation line is based on an 11-year
  reign for Niuserre.

This seems like an extraordinary set of coincidences, with the data
controlled by the archaeological information integrated with Manetho
and the Turin Canon. The third summation line, for Niuserre, assumes
a length of reign of 11 years, suggesting that was his original entry for
that king.

Reconstructing the Fifth Dynasty Chronology

Taking the Manetho data, the Turin Canon numbers, and a High Minimum view of the Occasion of the Count, the Fifth Dynasty Chronology
looks something like this.

- Userkaf (7 years, per Turin Canon)
- Sahure (13 years, per the cattle counts)
- Neferirkare (10 years, per the cattle counts)
- Shepseskare (7 years, per Turin Canon and Manetho)
- Khaneferre (3 years, per the cattle counts)
- Niuserre (11 years, per Gardiner's reconstruction of the Turin Can-
  on and Manetho's deconstructed summation line that indicated that
  this king's original Manetho entry was 11 years)
- Menkauhor (8 or 9 years, per either Turin Canon or Manetho)
- Djedkare (41 or 43 years, per the cattle counts)
- Unis (30 years, per Turin Canon)

The sum of these lengths of reigns falls between 130 and 133 years, a virtually perfect agreement with the proposed Patriarchal chronology of 132 years. This arrangement assumes that the 11 years for Niuserre and 41–43 years for Djedkare are valid entries. While Egyptologists may disagree as to whether these two lengths of reign are accurate, the question under consideration is whether an ancient scribe working from Egyptian sources, could reasonably come to such a conclusion. The evidence for our Manetho reconstruction showed that both his original king-list and the Turin Canon (assuming a much shorter reign for Djedkare) both closely paralleled this reconstructed king-list, which implied a length of reign of 11 years for Niuserre.

The Chronology of Dynasties 6-8

In this section we will take the Sixth, Seventh, and Eighth Dynasties together as a single group encompassing all of the Memphite kings following after the Fifth Dynasty. There are two major reasons for this view. First, the Tables of Abydos and Sakkara, the Turin Canon, and Manetho, all radically disagree with each other as to how many Memphite kings ruled after the end of the Fifth Dynasty. Second, only Manetho divides this last group of kings into three dynasties, and his version of the Seventh and Eighth Dynasties, as preserved in heavily redacted accounts, raises a lot of questions as to whether these two dynasties ever existed.

Overview of the King-lists

The Table of Sakkara lists only four kings in the Sixth Dynasty, ending after the long-lived Piopi II.[181] It then jumps to the middle of the Eleventh Dynasty, to the reign of Menthotpe II, who reunified the Egyptian kingdom under Theban rule.[182] The Table of Abydos preserves a list of twenty-two Memphite kings with no indication of a dynastic break.[183] It, too, jumps from the last king in its list to the reign of Menthotpe II.[184] Neither table contains any chronological data.

It seems fair to say that both compilers believed that no legitimate rulers served between the end of their respective lists and the reunification

Table 5.10: The Sixth Dynasty in Manetho and the Turin Canon

King's Name[a]	Manetho Name	TC Duration[b]	Manetho Duration
1. Teti	Othoes	Lost	30
2. Userkare	*omitted*	Lost	
3. Phiops I	Phius	20	53
4. Merenre I	Methusuphis	14/44[c]	7
5. Phiops II	Phiops	90+x	95
6. Merenre II	Menthesuphis	1	1
7. Menkaure	Nitocris	Lost	12
8. Neferka		Lost	
9. Nufe		2 yrs, 1 mo	
10. Ibi		4 yrs, 2 mo	
11. Lost		2 yrs, 1 mo	
12. Lost		1 yr, 1/2d	
Given Total		**181**	**203**
Added years		**6[d]**	
Actual Total		**187**	**198**

[a]Names 1-7 from (Cambridge Ancient History 1971), I:2B,
   995. Names 8-12 from (Gardiner 1961), 436.
[b](Gardiner 1961),436
[c]The Tens figure is damaged. The ones unit is 4.
[d]The Turin Canon has a summation line indicating 181 years and
   6 months. This is followed by an unexplained entry of 6 years.

of Egypt under Menthotpe II. Both lists pass over the Heracleopolitan Ninth and Tenth Dynasties and the earlier portion of the Eleventh Dynasty. That the Abydos author has a longer list of legitimate Memphite kings than the Sakkara compiler suggests that the former was more sympathetic to the later Memphite rulers than was the latter.

The Turin Canon follows the end of the Fifth Dynasty with what was originally a line of summation for the first five dynasties, but the content is lost due to damage.[185] That the Turin Canon author chose to sum up the number of Memphite kings after the Fifth Dynasty instead of the Sixth may reflect the author's concern as to how many legitimate Memphite kings served after the Fifth Dynasty. In line with this view, the Turin Canon listed only twelve Memphite kings, approximately midway between the number of kings in the Tables of Sakkara and Abydos. Table 5.10, *The Sixth Dynasty in Manetho and the Turin Canon*, sets out the Sixth Dynasty chronology in both Manetho and the Turin Canon. The Turin Canon originally had lengths of reign for each of the twelve kings, of which four are completely damaged and two are partially damaged.[186] Of the six fully preserved reigns, four ruled for less than 3 years each. The list concludes with a summation line indicating that the twelve kings ruled for 181 years but the summation is followed by a puzzling unexplained 6-year gap.[187]

Manetho's Sixth Dynasty (Africanus version) has a sequence of six kings of Memphis, each with an individual length of reign. Africanus says it lasted 203 years but when you add up the individual reigns the sum is 198 years. This error is almost certainly due to Manetho's description of the reign of Phiops (= Piopi II,) about whom, he says, "began to reign at the age of six, and continued to his hundredth year." This is the only reign where Manetho doesn't list the specific number of years ruled and you must calculate the length.

A redactor appears to have taken the king's reign as 100 years instead of 95 years, using that higher figure in his summation. Manetho's Seventh Dynasty (Africanus Version) presents only a summary statement indicating that 70 kings of Memphis ruled for 70 days. He names no individual kings and provides no individual lengths of reign. Manetho's Eighth Dynasty (Africanus version) also consists of just a summary line, saying that the dynasty consisted of 27 kings of Memphis who ruled for 146 years.

No serious Egyptologist accepts the credibility of Manetho's descriptions of the Seventh and Eighth Dynasties, but in reconstructing the Old Kingdom chronology and attempting to find some sort of harmony between the various king-lists, many Egyptologists would place some of the Memphite kings mentioned in the Table of Abydos and the Turin Canon into some version of the Seventh and/or Eighth

Dynasties, and limit the total duration of these two dynasties to no more than about 50 years or less.

One interesting feature of the king-lists is that both the Table of Abydos and the Turin Canon say that the second king in the Sixth Dynasty was Userkare, for whom we have some very faint archaeological evidence.[188] On the other hand, The Table of Sakkara and Manetho both omit this ruler from the list of Memphite kings.[189]

It will be my argument below that Manetho's Seventh and Eighth Dynasties are badly garbled summation lines that have been mistakenly treated by the redactors as separate dynasties. When properly reconstructed it will be shown that the original version of Manetho very likely knew of 21 Memphite kings with no indication of a dynastic break. Allowing for the one king in the Turin Canon and Table of Abydos that is missing from Manetho's Sixth Dynasty, and if I am correct about Manetho knowing of a sequence of 21 Memphite kings, we can consider Manetho to corroborate the Table of Abydos as to the total number of Memphite kings that ruled after the Fifth Dynasty ended.

Dynasties 6-8 in Chronological context

In the Patriarchal Chronology, I have proposed that Methuselah's death date (2105) defines the end of the Memphite Kingdom. Above I have dated the end of the Fifth Dynasty to 2339. This give us a period of 234 years for the final group of Memphite kings.

Table 5.11, *Various Proposals for Sixth Dynasty Chronology*, extracts (from Tables 5.2 and 5.3) the estimated dates and durations for the Sixth through Eighth Dynasties as indicated by several Egyptologists and the Patriarchal Chronology. It shows that the indicated starting date for the Sixth Dynasty in the Patriarchal Chronology fits in well with the array of starting dates suggested by Egyptologists.

Gardiner accepts 2340, virtually identical to the Patriarchal 2339. CAH and Shaw both accept 2345, also an excellent fit given how many possible chronological options there may be. Kitchen and Krauss/Warburton are more than 50 years apart

Table 5.11: Various Proposals for Sixth Dynasty Chronology

Dynasties	Gardiner (1961)	CAH (1971-75)	Kitchen (1996)	Beckareth (1997)	Shaw (2000)	Krauss/War-burton (2006)	Genesis 5 Death Dates
6th Dyn. Dates	2340-?	2345-2181	2362-2176	2347-2216	2345-2181	2305-2152	2339-2105[a]
7th Dyn. dates	?	2181-2173	2176- ?	NA	2181- ?		
8th Dyn. dates	?	2173-2160	? -2136	2216-2170	? -2160	2150-2118	
Dyn 6-8 dates	?	2345-2160	2362-2136	2347-2170	2345-2160	2305-2152	2339-2105
6th Dyn. years	?	164	186	131	164	187	234
7th Dyn. years	?	8					
8th Dyn. years	?	14	40[b]	46	21[c]	32	
Dyn. 6-8 years	?	186	126	177	185	219	234

[a] Genesis has no division between the Sixth, Seventh and Eighth Dynasties.
[b] This is Kitchen's total for Dynasties 7-8. He doesn't have a chronological divider.
[c] This is Shaw's total for Dynasties 7-8. He doesn't have a chronological divider.

from each other, with the Patriarchal date falling about midway between the two proposals. We have no smoking gun for the actual starting date, but for all practical purposes, the Patriarchal date is
reasonably consistent with the consensus range among Egyptologists.

When we consider the end date of the Sixth (and Seventh and/or
Eighth) Dynasty, the Patriarchal data encounters a little more turbulence.
Among the various estimates, Krauss/Warburton, including both the Seventh
and Eighth Dynasties, come closest, with a date of 2118. However, if
you look at the Table 5.11 durations proposed for Dynasties 6-8, you
can see how the disparities emerge.

CAH, Shaw and Krauss/Warburton all have a duration of
about 186 years for all three dynasties. This is essentially the
duration taken from the Turin Canon's 181 years plus the extra 6 years immediately following immediately after. Beckareth has a duration of 177 years, which is also built around
the Turin Canon span but with a couple of proposed correc-
tions to the lengths of reign that provide some shortening of
the overall duration.

Kitchen, on the other hand, has a duration of 226 years, which is quite
close to the Patriarchal duration of 234 years. But Kitchen has a substantially earlier starting date (2362). If we move his starting date closer to the
consensus of about 2340 give or take a couple of years, his end date would
be about 2114, not too far off from the Patriarchal date of 2105.

An important feature for you to note in the chronologies concerns the proposed durations of the Seventh and Eighth Dynasties.
The range in Table 5.11 runs from 21 years (CAH, Shaw) to about 46
years (Beckareth.) For the most part, the ranges reflect the number
of years served by the last ten kings in the Table of Abydos and, in
some cases, a couple of kings at the end of the Turin Canon listing.

Two factors explain why the Patriarchal chronology runs slightly
longer than the various chronologies in Tables 5.11. First, Egyptologists
try to avoid as much overlap as possible between the last Memphite
kings and the chaotic First Intermediate Period, which incorporates the
Heracleopolitan Ninth and Tenth Dynasties and part of the Theban
Eleventh Dynasty.

Traditionally, Dynasties 7 and 8 were considered part of the First Intermediate Period, but in more recent times, there has been some effort to exclude them from the period of conflict. If you go back to Table 3.1, you can see that the Egyptologists in our panel have terminated the Eighth Dynasty before the rise of the Ninth Dynasty. This practice is a matter of convention rather than based on significant evidence. Below, in the discussion of the First Intermediate Period, I will argue that the differences between the various king-lists concerning the number of kings in the last Memphite sequence arise from conflicts among the rulers from Memphis, Heracleopolis, and Thebes, and that the Memphite king-line overlapped both sets of rival rulers.

The second factor leading to disparity between the Patriarchal duration and the current consensus arrangement has to do with the conflict between Manetho's chronology and the Turin Canon's. Manetho has a duration of 198 years for the Sixth Dynasty. If you consider only the six kings in the Turin Canon that correspond to the six Manetho kings, it appears that the Turn Canon has about 30 years less for those kings than does Manetho. That thirty-year period is the approximate difference between the Patriarchal chronology and the Egyptological consensus. My analysis of Manetho's evidence will show that the Patriarchal chronology lines up with Manetho's data and the Table of Abydos.

Manetho and the Turin Canon Compared

Michele Baud, in an essay on Sixth Dynasty chronology, says, "Although data are quite abundant for Dynasty 6 and derive from a variety of sources (royal annals and decrees on stone, administrative documents on papyrus, expedition graffiti), the interpretation of the dating system used by the monarchy remains controversial."[190] As to the Turin Canon, he adds, it does not "provide any help for evaluating the dynasty's duration, or the lengths of individual reigns. Most, if not all, of the figures preserved are at odds with contemporaneous OK [= Old Kingdom] data, despite repeated efforts to reconcile the two." [191] A key issue that once again surfaces is whether the cattle count census continued in a regular biennial pattern or on multiple occasions occurred on an annual basis.

Manetho has 6 kings with a total duration of 198 years; the Turin Canon has 12 kings with a duration of either 181 years. Of the latter's 12 kings, five appear after the end of Manetho's list and one (Userkare) falls between Manetho's first and second king. The remaining six kings overlap the Manetho list but substantial damage to the Turin Canon makes a direct one-to-one comparison difficult.

Of the five kings at the end of the Turin Canon list, four individual lengths of reign are preserved, and they add up to 9 years and 4 months. We have no independent evidence as to the validity of these claims. As to the fifth king in this group, with the damaged entry, we lack evidence for this ruler's duration, which suggests that he had an equally short reign. We will assume approximately 2 years for this, consistent with the lengths of reign for the four other members of this group and giving the five kings a total of about 11 years.

Our information regarding Userkare, the one in the Turin Canon's second position, is weak and we have no cattle count data. Gardiner considers his reign virtually ephemeral, with archaeological evidence limited to just two seals and the Table of Abydos.[192] Baud suggests a range of 2–4 years.[193]

Adding the total number of years for the Turin Cannon's six non-Manetho kings gives us about 13–15 years, and if we subtract that from the Turin Canon's dynastic total of 181 years we have a range of about 166–168 years for the remaining six kings that correspond to those in Manetho, indicating that the two lists are about 30–32 years apart. Let's isolate the differences.

Manetho's assigns his first and sixth kings, Othoes and Nitocris, respective reigns of 30 and 12 years. The corresponding reigns in the Turin Canon are damaged and we have no partial data. For Manetho's fourth and fifth kings, Phiops (= Piopi II) and Menthesuphis, the Turin Canon appears to be in reasonable close agreement. Manetho's Phiops ruled for 95 years and the Turin Canon shows a minimum of 90 years for the corresponding king. The Turin

Canon *units* figure for this entry is damaged and unreadable, indicating an even closer correspondence to Manetho's figure. As to Menthesuphis, both Manetho and the Turin Canon's corresponding king have a 1-year reign.

With Manetho's third and fourth kings we encounter a visible and substantial disagreement between the two lists. Manetho gives Phios (= Piopi I) a reign of 53 years and the Turin Canon has a corresponding entry of 20. Manetho's Methusuphis (=Merenre) has a reign of 7 years but the corresponding entry in the Turin Canon is partially damaged. The units figure is 4 but the *tens* unit figure is damaged and various arguments are made for how it should be treated.

Gardiner proposed 44 years.[194] The evidence for such a long reign, however, is missing and few Egyptologists would currently support that. Smith accepts 14 years as the correct reading and at the time he wrote (1960's), he says, it was the common practice.[195] In recent years several scholars, including Beckareth,[196] Krauss,[197] and Shaw,[198] have proposed a reign of less than 10 years.

On the archaeological front, for Piopi I we have a 25th count of the cattle.[199] That indicates a High Minimum reign of 49–50 years and a Low Minimum of at least 27 years (allowing for two additional references to a year after the count.)[200] Baud, says that if the cattle counts were regular then Piopi I probably served a minimum of 50–51 years, quite in line with Manetho's full reign of 53 years and quite contrary to the Turin Canon's 20 years. If the counts were irregular, then the minimum would be closer to the Turin Canon than Manetho. Even if we accept the Low Minimum, the Turin Canon's full reign is still 7 years less than the Low Minimum, and Manetho could still have the more accurate full length of reign. In this study I accept the High Minimum for each king unless there is some contrary evidence.

For Merenre's reign, a "Year After the Fifth Occasion" plus some indicated additional throne time after that cattle count indicates a High Minimum of 11/12 years and a Low Minimum of 7 years.[201] Manetho's 7 years for Merenre is consistent with the Low Minimum and 4 years short of the High Minimum. On the assumption that the Turin Canon figure for this king is more likely to be 14 years rather than 44 years, the Turin Canon figure is consistent with both cattle count minimums. But there is another wrinkle in calculating the length of reign for Merenre.

Smith says that there is evidence of a co-regency between Piopi I and Merenre, citing a pendant bearing the names of both kings along with their titles.[202] Assuming this is the case, Manetho's 7-year figure might represent just the independent portion of Merenre's reign while the Turin Canon entry might signify the full length of reign, including the co-regency.

Of the available data for Manetho and the Turin Canon, the major difference between the two concerns the length of reign for Piopi 1. Manetho has 53 years and the Turin Canon has only 20 years. This 33–year gap between Manetho and the Turin Canon accounts almost completely for the approximately 30-year difference for the total durations of their six corresponding kings. This also has some significance for the Turin Canon's missing data and Manetho's chronology.

If we add up the partial and full lengths of reign that we have for eight Turin Canon kings (assuming a 14-year reign for Piopi I) we have a duration of 134 years for this group. Since the Turin Cannon's 90-year Piopi II reign has a damaged "units figure and Manetho gives him a 95-year reign, we might have perhaps as many as 5 additional years for this group, indicating a possible total of up to 139 years.

The Turin Cannon's dynastic duration is 181 years. That leaves a total of up to 47 years for the four completely damaged entries in the Turin Canon, if we don't count Manetho's additional 5 years for Piopi II, and perhaps as few as 43 years for those four kings if we do. Two of those missing reigns are outside of the Manetho king list and both are considered short, probably totaling no more than 4–6 years. That reduces the available number of years for the remaining two kings corresponding to those on the Manetho's list to 41–43 years, if we don't adjust Piopi II's reign-length, and perhaps as few as 36–38 years if we do count some extra time for Piopi II.

The two corresponding Manetho kings (Othoes and Nitocris) have respective reigns of 30 years and 12 years, adding up to 42 years. This sum is virtually identical to what we get from the Turin

Canon if we don't adjust Piopi II's reign, and just a couple of years short if we do make an adjustment. This suggests that the lost figures for the two kings in the Turin Canon come close to what Manetho has for the same two kings.

The archaeological record shows that Manetho's Othoes, corresponding to king Teti, ruled until at least an Eleventh Occasion of the Count, giving him a High Minimum of at least 21 years and a Low Minimum of at least 13 years.[203] Manetho's 30-year entry for this king, therefore, appears to be a reasonably plausible estimate for the full length of reign, and reinforces the likelihood that the Turin Canon either closely matched Manetho's two reign-lengths of 30 and 12, or came reasonably close (if we allow for slight variations in the other estimated figures for missing entries.)

As to Nitocris, we have virtually no chronological data available and it is generally assumed that this ruler had a very short reign. That may be the case but assuming a regular biennial cattle count, the arithmetic here strongly suggests that the missing Turin Canon entry for the king corresponding to Manetho's Nitocris closely tracked Manetho's 12-year reign or at least within a couple of years, depending upon how many years you want to assign to Othoes. So, whatever the archaeological record may someday show, it appears here that both Manetho and the Turin Canon author had sources suggesting similar lengths of reign for these two kings, with just a slight adjustment down depending on what the Turin Canon entry for Piopi II originally indicated.

So far, then, Manetho has a 198-year reign for six kings in the Sixth Dynasty. On the assumption of regular biennial cattle counts, the Turin Canon appears to have closely, if not precisely, tracked the reigns for five of Manetho's six kings, and appears to have erroneously shortened the length of the other king (Piopi I) by about 33 years. The Turin Canon adds five additional kings after Manetho's last king, and they have an approximate collective duration of about 11 years.

The Table of Abydos lists 22 kings altogether, adding 10 more Memphite kings to the Turin Canon list. There is some question as to whether the second king (Userkare) in the Turin Canon and Table of Abydos belongs in that location or in a later location after the Turin Canon listing. Manetho and the Table of Sakkara both omit Userkare from their respective king-lists. We now need to take up the problems of Manetho's Seventh and Eighth Dynasty before we can start putting all the pieces together.

Manetho's Seventh and Eighth Dynasties

The Turin Canon (12 kings), the Table of Sakkara (4 kings) and the Table of Abydos (22 kings) disagree on how many Memphite kings ruled after the end of the Fifth Dynasty, but none indicate any dynastic divisions within the respective groupings. For all practical purposes, the three sources present three different versions of the Sixth Dynasty.

Only Manetho indicates the existence of a Seventh and Eighth Dynasty, but his descriptions (as transmitted by redactors) raise some problems. Nevertheless, there seems to be a standard practice of identifying most of the Turin Canon list as the Sixth Dynasty and assigning the remaining kings in the Turin Canon and Table of Abydos to one or both of these two additional dynasties. This practice, however, is a convention, and depends solely on the evidence of Manetho, which almost all admit is troubling. Let's look more closely at the Manetho evidence.

According to the Africanus version of Manetho, the Seventh Dynasty consisted of "seventy kings of Memphis, who reigned for 70 days," clearly a bizarre and unacceptable duration, and the Eighth Dynasty consisted of "twenty-seven kings of Memphis, who reigned for 146 years" Eusebius has a slightly different account. He has a Seventh Dynasty that consisted of "five kings of Memphis, who reigned for 75 days" and an Eighth Dynasty that consisted of "five kings of Memphis, who reigned for 100 years."

Table 5.12, *Outline of Manetho's King-list for Dynasties 1–8*, presents an outline of the first eight dynasties, based on the number of kings who served as recorded in both versions of Manetho. For each dynasty it shows how many kings were claimed and how many kings were listed by name. Look first at the Africanus list. There is only one important anomaly.

	Africanus		Eusebius	
Dynasty	Kings Claimed	Kings Listed	Kings Claimed	Kings Listed
1	8	8	8	8
2	9	9	9	9 (3 missing)
3	9	9	8	8 (6 missing)
4	8	8	17	1
5	8	9	31	2 (from D. 6)
6	6	6	?	1
7	70	0	5	0
8	27	0	5	0
Sum 1-5	42	43	73	?
Sum 1-5 + 8	69	70	78	

Table 5:12: Outline of Manetho's King-list for Dynasties 1-8

For the Fifth Dynasty, Africanus has a summation line claiming eight kings, but he lists nine kings. If we count the number of kings Africanus *listed* for the first five dynasties, the total is 43. If we add to that number, the 27 kings in Dynasty 8, we have seventy kings, the exact number of kings claimed for Dynasty 7. This strongly suggests that Dynasty 7 was originally a line of summation, but of what?

The chief clue is in the 27 kings of Dynasty 8. The number 27 is the sum of 21 + 6. The Table of Abydos listed 22 kings beginning with the start of Dynasty 6 but included one king missing from Manetho's Dynasty 6. If that king were omitted by Manetho and he knew of the remaining kings in the Memphite line, he would have had a total of 21 kings beginning with Dynasty 6.

This suggests that Manetho's Eighth Dynasty was originally a garbled transmission of a Sixth Dynasty line of summation. What seems to have happened is that after the list of Manetho's first 6 Memphite kings, there must have been a line of summation that referred to the sequence of all 21 Memphite kings known to Manetho. One of Manetho's earlier redactors must have misread the text and thought the 21 kings were in addition to the 6 listed kings, getting a total of

27 kings in all. He may have then written that the last Memphite dynasty had 27 kings. This line of summation was later misread as a separate dynasty apart from the six listed Memphite kings. Because of its description as the last Memphite dynasty, it was placed at the end of the Memphite list and became identified as the Eighth Dynasty.

If Africanus's Eighth Dynasty was originally a garbled line of summation for the Sixth Dynasty, where, then, did he get the figure of 146 years for that dynasty's duration? It is my suggestion that this figure is a line of summation for the latter part of the Memphite line, beginning with the 95-year reign of Piopi II. Let's conduct an experiment.

The three kings who preceded Manetho's Piopi II had a collective reign of 90 years (30 + 53 + 7.) If the 146-year period began with the start of Piopi II and continued to the end of the Memphite line, the total duration of the Memphite line of kings would be 236 years (90 +146), virtually identical to the 234 years suggested by the Patriarchal chronology. The two-year difference could be no more than rounding off errors for partial years. If my explanation for Manetho's 146-year period is correct, then the Patriarchal Chronology and Manetho are in virtual agreement as to how long the post-Fifth Dynasty Memphite kings ruled.

The Patriarchal Chronology places the start of the Sixth Dynasty in 2339 and ends the Memphite line at 2105, a period of 234 years. Now plug the Manetho figures into this timeframe. If 146 years indicates the period running from the beginning of Piopi II and continuing to the end of what I contend was Manetho's list of 21 Memphite kings (correlating to the 22 kings in the Table of Abydos that included one king missing from Manetho), then adding 146 years to the 2105 end year gives us a proposed starting date of 2251 for Piopi II. The three Manetho kings preceding Piopi II, had a collective reign of 90 years (30 + 53 + 7). That would mark the start of Manetho's Sixth Dynasty at 2341, versus the 2339 in the Patriarchal chronology, virtually equivalent given the likelihood of rounding errors for partial years at the beginning and end of a king's reign. Nevertheless, the Manetho duration is only two years longer than that suggested by the Patriarchal chronology.

That Manetho's 146-year summation line falls precisely where the Patriarchal Chronology would place the start of Piopi II's reign (minus 2 years, i.e., 2249) and that the beginning of Manetho's Sixth Dynasty would therefore begin precisely where the Patriarchal Chronology places it, seems like an extraordinary coincidence. To validate the idea that the Patriarchal chronology for the Sixth Dynasty corresponds to Manetho's Chronology it would be helpful if some evidence could explain why Manetho would have chosen the start of Piopi II's reign for a summation line. The Table of Sakkara seems to supply that evidence.

As you will recall, the Table of Sakkara has only four Memphite kings, the last of which is Piopi II. The Table also agrees with Manetho in omitting Userkare from the list of kings. Since the Sakkara compiler has implicitly declared all kings between Piopi II and Menthotpe II in the Eleventh Dynasty to be illegitimate, we can reasonably assume that some major conflict broke out between Memphis and some other political entity either during or immediately after the reign of this monarch who appears to have ruled for over 90 years.

The most likely explanation for this conflict would be the rising of the Heracleopolitan rival sometime during or after the reign of Piopi II. We'll look at these issues more closely in our review of the First Intermediate Period below. What this suggests to me is that Manetho, like the author of the Table of Sakkara, saw the period running from Piopi II to the end of the Memphite Kingdom as a significant political era, and Manetho thought it should be identified by a line of summation indicating how long the challenge to Memphis lasted before the kingdom completely collapsed.

Let's now take a second look at the Manetho chronology without reference to the Patriarchal Chronology. From Piopi II to the end of Manetho's Sixth Dynasty we have a total of 108 years (95 + 12 + 1.) The Turin Canon's last five kings add about 11 more years to the total, bringing us to about 119 years. Subtracting that from the 146 years in Manetho's Eighth Dynasty leaves us with about 27 to 28 years for the last 10 kings in the Abydos list.

This is reasonably consistent with the broad consensus view of Egyptologists. Using the estimate of about 30 years for the final group of 10 Memphite kings, the average length of reign is about 3 years, approximately consistent with the lengths of reigns of the last five kings in the Turin Canon list, which range from 2–4 years.

While this doesn't give us a precise count of the years from Piopi II to the end of the Sixth Dynasty, the circumstantial evidence strongly shows that Manetho's 146 years is reasonably consistent with the timeframe encompassing the start of Piopi II's reign to the end of the Memphite kingdom. Taking this into consideration, strongly corroborates the apparent correlation between Manetho and the Patriarchal chronology.

If I am correct in this analysis, it suggests that the original version of Manetho had no Seventh or Eighth Dynasty. What became the Eighth Dynasty was a garbled transmission of a summation line that indicated the Sixth Dynasty had 21 kings and that there was a period of 146 years, beginning with the reign of Piopi II, in which the Memphite Kingdom fought with political rivals before it was finally extinguished.

Having analyzed the Africanus version of the Seventh and Eighth Dynasty, let's briefly look at the much more corrupted Eusebius account. (See Table 5.12.) Eusebius's claimed that 73 kings ruled through Dynasties 1–5. But his Third Dynasty has only 8 kings where Africanus has 9 kings. If we make that upward adjustment, the new total is 74 kings. Additionally, Eusebius's Sixth Dynasty contains only one king. Adding on the single Sixth Dynasty king to the previous total for the first five dynasties indicates that 75 kings ruled in the first six dynasties.

This shows that Eusebius' version of the Seventh Dynasty is a summation line for the number of king's in the Memphite kingdom. Despite having different numbers from Africanus, we can see that both versions of the Seventh Dynasty are nothing more than badly garbled accounts of a summation line for the number of kings who ruled from Memphis, from the start of the First Dynasty to the end of the Memphite line of kings. It also suggests that the use of the term "days," in both Africanus and Eusebius, to define the length of time they ruled was some sort of metaphor for individual reigns.

Lastly, we look at Eusebius's Eighth Dynasty, to which he assigns a duration of 100 years where Africanus had 146 years. I suggested earlier that the Africanus figure represented the sum of Memphite years beginning with Piopi II. We note, however, that in the Africanus list, Africanus's source mistakenly confused Piopi II's 100th birthday with his 100th year on the throne.[204] The Eusebius figure, therefore, may represent the erroneous total for Piopi II's reign. This would reinforce the idea that the Manetho Eighth Dynasty was intended as a line of summation for the period running from Piopi II to the end of the Memphite line. The redacted version reaching Eusebius must have confused the reference to the years from Piopi II to the end of the dynasty with a reference to just the number of years for Piopi II reign.

The First Intermediate Period

At some point after the start the Memphite Sixth Dynasty, a political entity, identified with Dynasties 9 and/or 10, arose in the city of Heracleopolis, and another dynastic entity, the Eleventh Dynasty, arose in the city of Thebes. The First Intermediate Period can be loosely defined as that period when the Heracleopolitan dynasties ruled part of Egypt. However, as Seidlmayer observes, "Determining the length of the Heracleopolitan period is fraught with all but unsurmountable difficulties. Data for the length of individual reigns or of the entire dynasty are not preserved."[205]

The Turin Canon had allowed for a sequence of 18 kings but most of the data is lost.[206] But some names are preserved and there is archaeological evidence for the existence of some of the earlier members of the roster.[207] We also know that the Heracleopolitan kingdom was defeated sometime during the reign of Menthotpe II in the Eleventh Dynasty, but it is not clear as to when during the reign that occurred.[208]

It is widely accepted that the Heracleopolitan period of rule overlapped the Theban period of rule for about a century. Seidlmayer estimates the period of overlap at 87 to 114 years, depending upon the exact date of reunification.[209] In our panel of Egyptologists in Table 3.1, the estimated periods of overlap run between 93 and 100 years.

The more difficult problem is how long before the rise of Thebes did the Heracleopolitans come to the fore. Seidlmayer says that the only chronological data that we have for this comes from Manetho's account of the Tenth Dynasty.[210] Manetho (Africanus version) says the Tenth Dynasty had 19 kings ruling 185 years. This total includes both the period of overlap and the period that preceded the overlap. Many Egyptologists reject Manetho's Tenth Dynasty duration and opt for a much shorter period for the pre-Theban period.

Commenting on the duration of the Heracleopolitans, Gardiner says, "here we may fairly well choose between Ed. Meyer's estimate of 200 years and a lower one of, say 100 years."[211] Seidlmayer, writing more recently, says, "The customary 'short model' and the Manethonian 'long model' result in two profoundly different views about the FIP."[212] There is a split among Egyptologists over this issue, with several citing archaeological data pointing to a long period of Heracleopolitan rule prior to the beginning of the Eleventh Dynasty.[213]

A separate problem is the date of unification under Menthotpe II. There is some disagreement over this issue and no precise data. There is also a division among Egyptologists as to whether we should use the High or Low Chronology for Dynasties 11–12. In this study we continue to follow the High Chronology. Within that range, several Egyptologists have settled on the year 2040 for the unification date.[214] That is the date we will use below.

Another question we need to answer is whether there was any overlap between the last group of Memphite kings and the Heracleopolitans and whether there was any Memphite and Theban overlap. There is a tendency among Egyptologists to cut off the Memphite line of kings at the start of the Heracleopolitan era. In the present study, we follow the "long" Manethonian model and show some corroboration in the Patriarchal Chronology for the Manetho tradition. I will show below that the Memphite kingdom overlapped the Heracleopolitan Tenth Dynasty and the Theban Eleventh Dynasty.

Dynasties 9 and 10

The archaeological record shows a string of rulers from Heracleopolis associated with a "House of Akhtoy but shows no clear dynastic break among these rulers.[215] We have no chronological evidence for the individual lengths of reign of these kings nor for how long the dynasty lasted.[216] As noted above the basic choice is between the "long" Manetho model of about 200 years and a "short" model of about 100 years.

The Heracleopolitan section of the Turin Canon is badly damaged, with just a few names preserved and no lengths of reign.[217] It did however once contain a list of 18 kings, including a couple of kings named Akhtoy.[218] The dynastic summation line is also damaged, and the number of years is missing.[219]

Manetho, on the other hand, lists a Ninth and Tenth Dynasty from Heracleopolis. The Africanus version states that there were 19 kings in each dynasty but provides no names except for the first one, Achthoes (i.e., Akhtoy.). He says the Ninth Dynasty ruled for 409 years and the Tenth for 185 years. The Eusebius version says that the Ninth Dynasty had 5 kings ruling for 100 years, also naming Achthoes as the first king, and he follows the Africanus version for the Tenth Dynasty.

That Africanus has two separate Heracleopolitan dynasties each having 19 kings, where the Turin Canon has one dynasty with 18 kings, strongly suggests that Manetho (or his redactors) confused two separate lists of the same dynasty for an indication that there were two separate dynasties with the same number of kings. Both agree that the Tenth Dynasty lasted 185 years, but they disagree on how long the Ninth Dynasty lasted. Africanus's 409 years for the Ninth Dynasty is clearly out of order, possibly an erroneous transmission or a summation line of some sort that has yet to be untangled. Eusebius's 100 years for the Ninth Dynasty is less problematic, but if we accept that there was only one dynasty, the Tenth, as most Egyptologists do, that makes the matter moot.

If we accept Manetho's 185-year period as the duration of the Heracleopolitan Tenth Dynasty and count back from the High

Chronology date of 2040 for the reunification of Egypt under Theban rule, the Heracleopolitans began their reign in 2225.

Based on the Patriarchal chronology we have dated the beginning of Piopi II's 95-year reign to about 2249/51. This means he was on the throne until 2154/56. If the Tenth Dynasty started at 2225, per the Manetho/Patriarchal chronology for this dynasty, then the Heracleopolitans came to power approximately 25 years after Piopi II started his reign. This would help explain why the Table of Sakkara omitted all kings after Piopi II and before Menthotpe II. Piopi II was the last ruler of a unified Egypt before the Heracleopolitans established a base of rule and Menthotpe II was the first king to rule a unified Egypt after the Heracleopolitans were gone from the scene.

The Sons of God and the Daughters of Man Problem

The Manetho date of 2225, assuming a 185-year duration of the Heracleopolitans that ended in 2040, raises an interesting solution for a problematic incident in Genesis related to the Flood story. As you may remember, Methuselah's death date of 2105 coincides with the onset of the Great Flood. But there is puzzling piece of chronological data associated with why God chose to unleash the Great Flood.

> When people began to multiply on the face of the ground, and daughters were born to them, the sons of God saw that they were fair; and they took wives for themselves of all that they chose. Then the LORD said, "My spirit shall not abide in mortals forever, for they are flesh; their days shall be one hundred twenty years."[220]

Who are the sons of God in this monotheistic religion? Why did their marriage to the daughters of man cause God to wipe out the human race with a great flood? And most interestingly, why did God decide to wait 120 years before acting?

If the great flood occurred on the death of Methuselah, in 2105, the year in which the millennium-long kingdom of Memphis ended, and we count back 120 years, we arrive at a date of 2225, the year in which, according to the Manetho data, the Heracleopolitan kingdom began. This suggests a context for the conflict between Memphis and Heracleopolis.

In Egypt, the legitimate ruler was equated with the god Horus. His sons/princes are the children of the god. A rival king in a different region couldn't be Horus while the existing Horus remained on the throne. The Horus status continued for whomever the Egyptians recognized as the legitimate god.

What we may be seeing behind this Genesis story is a bit of Egyptian history. The sons of God would be the children of the legitimate Horus-king and the daughters of man would be the children of a family that intermarried with Horus' sons, setting up a potential rivalry for the throne and constant conflict over who the legitimate ruler was.

This suggests that the god in question may be either Piopi II's father, Merenre, or Piopi II himself. If Merenre was the Horus king, then it is possible that one or more of his sons married into a rival family, establishing a legal claim for one of the children of those marriages to claim a right over the five-year-old Piopi II to succeed Merenre. Alternatively, if Piopi II were the god-king, a similar set of marriages may have led to a variety of intrigues for political power in the royal court.

The Heracleopolitan claim to power occurred in approximately the 25th year of Piopi II's reign, when he was only 30 years old. It is conceivable that a failed attempt at supplanting Piopi II led to a military challenge to his reign, giving the Heracleopolitans a strong rival claim to the throne.

Whatever the background to this conflict, we have an astonishing set of chronological coincidences. The Heracleopolitans arise 120 years before the complete collapse of the legitimate Memphite kingdom; In Genesis, God says the marriage between the sons of God and daughters of man will lead to the destruction of society in 120 years. Both events are dated to 2225–2105.

The Dynasty 11 Foundation Date

To resolve various chronological disputes, it would be helpful if we could establish some sort of anchor date to which we could connect other events. The most helpful evidence available comes from the Turin Canon, which says the Eleventh Dynasty ruled for 143 years.[221] Manetho assigns 43 years to this dynasty but it is often assumed that the "hundreds" figure was lost in transition. If correct, the two lists corroborate each other.

In the high chronology, the Twelfth Dynasty began in 1991.[222] Counting back 143 years establishes a starting date of 2134. The precision of the date should be taken with caution, but it is a reasonably reliable estimate.

In our reconstruction above of Manetho's Memphite chronology for Dynasties 6-8, we saw that he originally had a list of 21 kings with a combined reign of 236 years. We also saw that the Patriarchal chronology for the Sixth Dynasty ran from 2339 to 2105, a period of 234 years, virtually identical with the Manetho timeframe. The Patriarchal Chronology, therefore, indicates that the Theban Eleventh Dynasty began 29 years before the end of the Memphite Sixth (through Eighth) Dynasty.

If we subtract Manetho's 198 years for the Sixth Dynasty from 2339, we arrive at the year 2141, about 7 years before the start of the Eleventh Dynasty. If we subtract from that the Turin Canon's 13–15 years for its six kings missing from the Manetho list, we arrive at about 2128–2126, about 7 years after the start of the Eleventh Dynasty. This suggests to me that both Manetho and the author of the Turin Canon sought to end their list of Sixth Dynasty kings at about the point where they thought the Eleventh Dynasty began but that they were each off by about 7 years, but in opposite directions.

If we can rely on the Patriarchal chronology, the Theban overlap lasted 29 years (2134–2105). That indicates that the Sixth Dynasty Memphite kings ruled for 205 years prior to the start of the Eleventh Dynasty (2339–2134). This is 7 years longer than Manetho's Sixth Dynasty, suggesting that the Theban Dynasty arose at about the time of either the ninth or tenth king listed in the Turin Canon.

This 29-year timeframe for the last 10–13 Memphite kings is consistent with conventional Egyptological estimates. Baud says that the 10 kings following the Turin Canon list lasted about a generation, perhaps as much as 50 years.[223] Krauss, however, says he follows Baud's estimate of about one generation but assigns about 30 years to the period.[224] Gardiner estimates that the period shouldn't be much more than about 25 years.[225]

Conclusions

Despite several damaged entries, Egyptologists generally rely on the Turin Canon as a template for Sixth Dynasty chronology. However, on the assumption of regularity for the biennial cattle counts for the Sixth Dynasty, we saw that Manetho's 53-year reign for Piopi I, whose reign included a 24th or 25th cattle count was much more likely to reflect Piopi I's length of reign than the Turin Canon's 20-year total.

Once we corrected for this 30+-year error, an arithmetic analysis of the minimum number of years in the Turin Canon showed that two missing entries in the Turin Canon ruled collectively for approximately the same number of years as the corresponding two kings in the Manetho list. This indicated that the Turin Canon corresponded chronologically with five out of six Manetho king reigns. Correcting for the one Turin Canon error showed that Manetho's 198-year reign for six kings provided a better chronological template than the Turin Canon.

The analysis also showed that Manetho's Seventh and Eighth Dynasties were originally summation lines. The Seventh Dynasty summed up the total number of kings ruling from Memphis, beginning with the first king of the First Dynasty and ending with the last king of the Sixth Dynasty. Analysis of Manetho's Eighth Dynasty suggested that he knew of 21 Memphite kings (in parallel to the Table of Abydos which had 22 kings that included 1 king missing from the Manetho sequence.) Manetho also included an Eighth Dynasty summation line of 146 years.

On the assumption that the 146-year figure signified the number of years from the beginning of the reign of Piopi II to the end of the Memphite line of kings, we saw that Manetho originally had a duration of 21 Memphite kings ruling for 236 years. The evidence also showed that the conflict between Memphis and Heracleopolis broke out during Piopi II's reign.

The Patriarchal chronology indicated a beginning date of 2339 and an end date of 2105 for what I suggested was the Memphite line of kings following the Fifth Dynasty. This indicated a duration of 234 years, coinciding almost exactly with the reconstructed 236 years for the corresponding line of kings in the original version of Manetho. The proposed starting date was consistent with other Egyptological estimates, but the dynasty was somewhat longer than most Egyptologists preferred.

This difference in length, however, was due to the prior reliance on the damaged Turin Canon than on what appears to be the more accurate Manetho account of the Sixth Dynasty. Using the Manetho chronology of 198 years for the first six kings left 36 years for the remaining 15 kings, a figure consistent with both the Turin Canon and the archaeological evidence that suggested a series of short reigns for the last fifteen kings.

Accepting the Patriarchal-Manetho correlation for the Memphite line of kings showed that there was some overlap between the Memphis line of kings and both the Heracleopolitan Ninth and/or Tenth dynasty and the Theban Eleventh Dynasty. For all practical purposes, this meant that the First Intermediate Period could best be described by the Table of Sakkara, which showed Piopi II to be the last Memphite king to rule over a united Egypt and Menthotpe II to be the first Theban king to rule over a united Egypt.

The Heracleopolitan regime overlapped both part of Piopi II's reign and part of Menthotpe II's reign. Establishing the true length of the Heracleopolitan reigns is difficult due to the lack of archaeological evidence. This leads Egyptologists to choose between a "long" Manetho period of about 185 years and a "short" period of about 100 years. Opinion is divided on this issue. This raises an interesting chronological coincidence between Genesis 6:1–3, a Flood warning date, and Manetho's 185-year Heracleopolitan Tenth Dynasty

According to that passage, God determined that the marriage of the sons of God with the daughters of man would result in the destruction of mankind in 120 years. Since the Flood occurred in 2105, the year that the Memphite line of kings ended, the Flood warning occurred in the year 2225. At the same time, if we counted back 185 years for the Heracleopolitan Tenth Dynasty, beginning with the High Chronology date of 2040 for the Theban victory over Heracleopolis, we arrive at 2225 as the starting date for the Heracleopolitans, the year in which the sons of Man married the daughters of man. This suggests that the Genesis warning and the Flood date may have originally been a literary device to describe the rise of the Heracleopolitan dynasty and the collapse of the Memphite line of kings, leading into a period of post-Flood chaos.

Some Loose Ends

We come now to four dates that fall within Methuselah's life span but which we have not yet touched upon. These are the birth and death dates for Lamech (2887–2110), and the birth dates for Noah (2705) and Shem (2205). Lamech is the son of Methuselah, Noah is the son of Lamech, and Shem is the son of Noah. All three, therefore, were all born *after* Methuselah. The above study of the Memphite Kingdom and the rise of its rivals depended upon an analysis of the death dates of all those born *before* Methuselah. So, they don't fit into the above literary scheme.

Additionally, the death dates for the last two fall outside of Genesis 5 and outside of Methuselah's life span. The dates in question must relate to something other than the specific dynastic dating scheme described in the preceding analysis. As we shall see, we lack sufficient chronological data to determine what events they mark off.

Lamech (2887-2110)

Lamech's life span presents something of a textual problem. In the standard Hebrew text, Lamech lived for 777 years. In the Greek Septuagint text, he lived for 753 years, a difference of 24 years. For all eight of Lamech's ancestors, the Hebrew and Greek texts agree on the life spans.[226]

Complicating the problem further, the first century Jewish historian Josephus, who very likely used a Septuagint version of the Jewish scriptures, gives Lamech a life span of 707 years.[227] This looks more like a variation of the Hebrew figure than it does of the Septuagint version. Since the Hebrew text is based on source documents that were produced after the time Josephus wrote,[228] it is possible that Josephus may have the more accurate figure. It is also likely that in transmission of the Josephus text the Greek letter for "70" (= O, omicron) dropped out and the Hebrew source text is more accurate.

The Septuagint source text also dates to an earlier time than the Hebrew source text and could also reflect a more accurate figure. The Josephus variation, however, could also indicate an alternative version of the Septuagint translation.

As it presently stands in the Hebrew text, Lamech died in 2110, five years before the end of the Memphite line. We have no chronological guidelines to relate this to. It could correspond to dates within the Memphite, Heracleopolitan or Theban line of kings. We have no way to resolve this issue.

If Josephus preserves the correct figure, then Lamech died in 2180, towards the latter part of the reign of Piopi II. Again, we have no chronological clue as to what this date represents. Again, it could correspond to dates within the Memphite, Heracleopolitan or Theban line of kings. We have no way to resolve this issue.

A more intriguing solution would use the life span in the Septuagint version, 753 years. If we use that figure, then Lamech died in the year 2134, the foundation date of the Eleventh Dynasty. I find the coincidence highly interesting and would like to accept this, but we have no way of knowing if the Septuagint had the correct original figure, and I think there is a different issue in play here. I think Lamech's life span may have been shortened so that he would appear to have died before the Flood.

As I pointed out above, there is some evidence that the Flood story may have some literary parallels to events during Egypt's First Intermediate Period, marking off both the start of an era of chaos following the death of Methuselah, and an interesting hint that the events triggering God's wrath may have been associated with the rise of the Heracleopolitan Tenth Dynasty. This would suggest that the Flood story may have been moved out of its original location and inserted into its present location for literary effect.

Some scholars have argued that the Flood story was originally an alternative Creation story that had been redacted into its present form to avoid conflict with the current Creation story in Genesis 1. I currently plan to make such an argument in Volume III of this study. If the Flood story had been moved into its present place that could have led to a shortening of Lamech's reign such that he didn't survive the Flood.

In support of a shortening of Lamech's life I would note that other than Enoch (who serves a symbolic purpose as a chronological pointer to the start of a Sothic Cycle,) Lamech is the only Genesis 5 Patriarch to die before his father. The birth of Lamech also departs slightly from the basic template language for the Genesis 5 chronology in that it inserts a commentary as to why Lamech named Noah as he did and connects Lamech to the Flood narrative.[229] Genesis also contains a passage about a person named Lamech who appears to be a separate (but genealogical parallel) to Lamech who is associated with a lot of "7" numbers. "If Cain is avenged sevenfold, truly Lamech seventy-sevenfold."[230] This may account for why Lamech is given a life span of 777 years.

For now, I simply take the position that we don't have sufficient data to identify what event Lamech's present death date of 2110 signifies nor can we be sure that Lamech's death date hasn't been altered to accommodate the Flood story.

As to Lamech's birth date in 2887, we again have very flimsy data as to what it may mean. The date falls into the First Dynasty. During my analysis of the First Dynasty above, I pointed out that a redactor may have misread a "47" as a "57" by confusing a Greek letter "mu" for the letter "nu." If we make that adjustment and assign 47 years to the second king, then the sixth king in Manetho's First Dynasty, Miebidos, would have come to the throne in the year 2991, just before the birth of Lamech. Manetho gives him a reign of 26 years, placing Lamech's birth date early in that king's lengthy reign.

As you may recall, the Table of Sakkara omitted the first five kings of the First Dynasty, suggesting some sort of illegitimacy issue. Lamech's birth date could be pointing to the reign of Miebidos as the first ruler of the First Dynasty to be considered legitimate, with the birth date signifying some form of political consolidation during this king's reign. This is a highly speculative conclusion and I just note the possibility. I am not endorsing this conclusion.

Noah (2705-1755)

The Patriarchal chronology indicates a starting date for the Third Dynasty of 2719. Noah was born in 2705. The Turin Canon assigned 19 years to the first king of the dynasty, Nebka. The cattle count data gave him a High Minimum reign of at least 15 years. Manetho indicated that this king reigned for 28 years but this appeared to be a concatenated reign including a portion of his successors' time on the throne. There are some questions as to how long this king actually reigned, and how much of that reign was independent of the last king of the Second Dynasty, Khasekhemwy. I also suggested that the 19-year reign may have belonged to Khasekhemwy rather than Nebka.

Nevertheless, let's work with what we have, a High Minimum reign for Nebka of at least 15 years and a potential duration of 19 years. Nebka was succeeded by Djoser, whom the Turin Canon author singled out for special attention by the unique use of red ink. It was my suggestion that Djoser may have reunified Egypt after a period of conflict between Nebka and Khasekhemwy.

If we subtract Nebka's High Minimum reign of 15 years from the 2719 starting date in the Patriarchal Chronology, and allow for rounding off partial years, we arrive at a starting date for Djoser of 2705, the year of Noah's birth. Even if we accept a 19-year reign for Nebka, Noah's birth date is very close to the start of Djoser's reign and could signal that Djoser's unification occurred shortly after taking the throne. That Noah's birth date falls on or just after Djoser's ascension to the throne (based on the Patriarchal Chronology) is highly suggestive and, at a minimum, together with the Turin Canon's use of red ink, signifies that Djoser, for whatever reason, was highly revered by later Egyptians.

Noah's death date doesn't appear in the Genesis 5 or Genesis 11 birth-death chronology. We will look at it later in this study.

Shem (2205-1605)

Shem's birth date, 2205, is also a problem. He was born 20 years after the proposed date for the start of the Heracleopolitan Dynasty. We have no data that will enable us to identify any event that corresponds to his birth date. His death date falls outside of the Methuselah timeframe and will be reviewed later in this study.

Summary

In this chapter I examined the thesis that the death dates of each Patriarch born before Methuselah (except for Enoch) defined dynastic break points in the chronology of the Memphite Kingdom. Our three main chronological tools were the Turin Canon of Kings; the writings of Manetho (primarily the more complete Africanus version); and several inscriptions relating to Occasions of the Count, a cattle census that Egyptians used to mark when events occurred within a king's reign. This material was supplemented by archaeological evidence and interpretations of the data by several Egyptologists. To validate the thesis, I started with two data screens.

First, we checked to see how the proposed starting and ending dates in the Patriarchal Chronology corresponded with what Egyptologists believed to be the proper chronology. However, because of the large number of gaps and disagreements among Egyptologists regarding several issues we have no agreed upon dated chronological sequence. Nevertheless, we listed some alternative chronologies from leading Egyptologists in order to establish some chronological parameters for each dynasty's dates. The Patriarchal data for each dynasty showed significant evidence of correlation within these guidelines.

Second, since we had no absolute anchor dates for any of the Memphite dynasties, and because there were numerous disagreements among Egyptologists as to how long various kings ruled and how long each dynasty lasted, I set up the second screen. Instead of working with dates, I worked with durations for each dynasty, using the above dates given by each Egyptologist to see how long that Egyptologist assigned to each dynasty.

Again, given the variations among Egyptologists with estimated durations, there appeared to be significant correlation between the duration of Patriarchal dynasty breaks and the acceptable range of dynastic durations. In this regard, I also found that longer dynasties in the Egyptological lists are longer in the Patriarchal Chronology, and shorter dynasties are shorter. But given the wide range of disagreements among Egyptologists, further refinements were needed, leading to a dynasty by dynasty analysis.

As we moved through the chronological evidence available for each dynasty we made three major discoveries that provided strong evidence that the Patriarchal Chronology for the Old Kingdom (Dynasties 1–8) coincided precisely with what the evidence of ancient sources and archaeological evidence indicated.

- **Identifying numerical pattern errors in Manetho's unreasonably long dynastic durations and king-lists**: From the analysis above, I established that redactors of Manetho's text frequently confused lines of summation, either from embedded summation lines or marginal notations, with either additional lengths of reign for additional kings or with corrected lengths of reign to be substituted for that originally assigned to listed kings. This enabled me to show clearly and logically what Manetho's original king-list chronology looked like.
- **Correlation between Manetho and the Turin Canon**: As we proceeded to reconstruct Manetho's original king-list, on a dynasty by dynasty basis, we also established a very high degree of chronological correlation between Manetho and the Turin Canon for most (but not all) of the lengths of reign for each of the kings. This indicated that, for the most part, Manetho and the Turin Canon

worked from similar archived data sources regarding the chronological history of Old Kingdom monarchs. Nevertheless, both lists
exhibited an occasional departure from each other and/or what
we know from archaeological evidence.

- **Correlation between the Patriarchal Chronology, Manetho, and
  the Turin Canon:** Using the reconstructed Manetho chronology
  we were able to demonstrate an almost perfect correlation between the Patriarchal Chronology and Manetho, with substantial
  implicit corroboration from the Turin Canon.

For the first three dynasties, after reconstructing Manetho's chronology, I established the following correlations between Manetho and
the Patriarchal Chronology for the duration of each dynasty. Both had
243 years duration for Dynasty 1, 112 years for Dynasty 2, and 98 years
for Dynasty 3. Such a perfect correlation is astounding and clear evidence that the Genesis chronographer worked from ancient archived
records similar to what Manetho used.

For the First Dynasty, the non-Genesis chronological evidence
consisted solely of Manetho's history. For the Second Dynasty, we
were able to add a small amount of data from the Turin Canon that
seemed to partially corroborate the reconstructed Manetho record.
For the Third Dynasty, the Turin Canon had more substantial data
but there was some conflicting data.

The Turin Canon indicated that the Third Dynasty lasted 74 years,
but several Egyptologists believed that the archaeological evidence
supported a duration of about 100 years. The Patriarchal Chronology
and the reconstructed Manetho both indicated a duration of 98 years.

The chief critique of the Turin Canon had to do with the length of
reign of King Djoser. The Turin Canon assigned him 19 years, but
several Egyptologists thought that was much too short to encompass
this king's accomplishments. Gardiner had about 44 years for this
king and both Manetho and the Genesis author both appear to have
come close to a similar conclusion.

For the Sixth Dynasty, the Patriarchal Chronology indicated 232
years, but, based on the chronological analysis, the Patriarchal

Chronology implicitly included an additional group of kings missing from the Manetho and the Turin Canon accounts of the Sixth Dynasty but present in the Table of Abydos. Manetho had six kings ruling 198 years, the Turin Canon had 12 kings ruling 181 years, the Table of Abydos indicated 22 kings but lacked chronological data.

The primary chronological conflict between Manetho and the Turin Canon concerned the length of reign for Piopi I. Manetho had 53 years and the Turin Canon had 20 years. This difference accounts for the primary disagreement over Sixth Dynasty chronology between Manetho and the Turin Canon. The archaeological evidence showed a 25th Occasion of the Count, indicating a High Minimum of 49 years and a low minimum of 27 years.

Manetho's 53 years is consistent with the High Minimum of 49 years; the Turin Canon is seven years too short for the Low Minimum. In this study, I follow the High Minimum indicated for each king unless there is evidence to the contrary. If we upped the Turin Canon length of reign for Piopi I to match Manetho's, the two lists would be in relative chronological harmony for each of the six kings present in both lists.

As part of the Sixth Dynasty study, I looked at Manetho's Seventh and Eighth Dynasties. I showed that the Seventh Dynasty was nothing more than a garbled summary of how many Memphite kings ruled from the start of the First Dynasty to the end of the Sixth Dynasty. Manetho's Eighth Dynasty was also a garbled summary, but of just the Sixth Dynasty. The analysis showed that Manetho's Sixth Dynasty originally consisted of 21 kings, of which only the first six appear to have been listed by name.

Manetho's Eighth Dynasty also included a summation line of 146 years, which could in no way be considered even remotely reliable for a post Sixth Dynasty Memphis king-list. On the assumption that this summation line signified the number of years from the beginning of Piopi II's reign to the end of the Memphite line, the same time-period that troubled the compilers of the Table of Abydos and the Table of Sakkara, I integrated the 146-year duration with the 198-year Sixth Dynasty, eliminating the overlaid duplicate lengths of reign. This indicated that the total number of years for the Sixth Dynasty, encompassing 21 or 22 kings, would be 234 years, virtually identical to the Patriarchal Chronology figure of 232 years for the Sixth Dynasty.

This precise correspondence between the Patriarchal Chronology and the reconstructed Manetho for the durations of Dynasties 1, 2, 3, and 6, should leave little doubt that the Patriarchal Chronology for the Memphite kingdom is based on the sort of ancient archival evidence known to the compilers of the various ancient Egyptian king-lists.

For Dynasties 4 and 5, we had slightly more difficult problems to overcome. In reconstructing the Manetho data for these two dynasties, we saw that the redactors replaced some of Manetho's lengths of reign with summation lines, and in doing so eliminated some of the original data for those reigns and some of the kings that Manetho originally included. We also had some damaged data in the Turin Canon, making a complete Manetho-Turin Canon comparison problematic.

Although attempting a reconstruction of Manetho's dynastic durations, I was more concerned with establishing a reliable chronology for both the Fourth and Fifth Dynasties. To do this, I relied on the combination of data from Manetho, the Turin Canon, and the High Minimum cattle count, as well as other king-lists to determine how many kings belonged to each of the dynasties and how long they ruled.

For the Fourth Dynasty, the Patriarchal Chronology indicated 150 years, a little longer than most Egyptologists would allow. I also indicated that the Patriarchal Chronology divided the dynasty into two portions, which I labeled 4A and 4B, the former lasting 95 years and the latter lasting 55 years. Egyptologists do not recognize this division. I noted, however, that this division wasn't intended to be a dynastic division but a political division that separated King Chephren from King Mycerinus.

A chief source of conflict for this dynasty concerned the length of reign for King Snofru. The cattle count data indicates a High Minimum of 46 years and a Low Minimum of 27 years. Both Manetho and the Turin Canon have significantly shorter durations,

29 years and 24 years, respectively. Egyptologists, as shown in Table 5.7 tend to assign a range from the mid-30s to the mid-20s. This is probably because there was one incident in which the cattle counts came in consecutive years during Snofru's reign, giving them an excuse to accept the Low Minimum instead of the High Minimum. Sticking with the High Minimum, as I have done, accounts for just about the entire difference between the accepted chronology and my slightly higher duration.

Reconstructing Manetho's chronology for this dynasty showed that lines of summation replaced much shorter lengths of reigns for each of three major kings in this dynasty. While I was able to reconstruct most of Manetho's Fourth Dynasty, the redactors had damaged the original list such that some of the kings that originally populated his list had been removed, along with their lengths of reign. Therefore, we could not compare the Patriarchal data to a completed Manetho king-list. Nevertheless, Herodotus also provided some indication that the dynasty was associated with a period of 150 years, and that, prior to Manetho, some king reigns were already being concatenated as if they constituted a single king ruling for the combined lengths of reign.

A separate issue with respect to the Fourth Dynasty concerned the Patriarchal Chronology division into two parts, 4A and 4B. Evidence from the writings of Herodotus showed a major cultural and political shift in the transition from King Chephren to King Mycerinus. The Patriarchal Chronology split signified the break between these two kings but there was one intervening king that had to be accounted for. When we moved that king out of sequence, the reconstructed chronology divided precisely as the Patriarchal Chronology had it, 95 years down though Chephren and 55 years from Mycerinus to the end of the dynasty.

For the Fifth Dynasty, the Patriarchal Chronology indicated a duration of 132 years. I had to do reconstructions of both Manetho and the Turin Canon. We also had significant conflicts between Manetho, the Turin Canon, and the High Minimum cattle count data for two kings, Djedkare and Niuserre. To establish an accurate dynastic chronology required that we integrate all three data sources.

The reconstructed Turin Canon had a duration of 129–131 years. The reconstructed Manetho had a duration of 134–137 years. The integrated data from all the sources suggested that the Fifth Dynasty, with the High Minimums available, gave a duration of 130–133 years. Overall, the reconstructed Fifth Dynasty duration coincided almost precisely with what was indicated by the Patriarchal Chronology.

Having established this chronological base, I went on to examine the chronological interaction of the Memphite Kingdom with the Heracleopolitan and Theban dynasties. The High Egyptian chronology showed that the Theban Eleventh Dynasty began in 2134, twenty-nine years *before* the collapse of the Memphite Kingdom. As to the start of the Heracleopolitan dynasties, we had some additional clues.

When we looked at Manetho's Tenth Dynasty, based in Heracleopolis, it had a duration of 185 years. According to the Egyptian High Chronology, the Tenth Dynasty ended in 2040. Counting back 185 years from 2040 gave us a Tenth Dynasty date of 2225. This meshed with another piece of Genesis chronology. Genesis 6:1–3 indicates that 120 years before the Flood a moral crisis triggered the disaster, when the Sons of God married the daughters of man. Methuselah died in 2105, the year of the Flood.

Counting back 120 years before the Flood gave us a date of 2225, the very same year we established for the start of the Heracleopolitan Tenth Dynasty. The Flood warning date and the Flood date both chronologically coincide with the Egyptian crisis that saw the threatening rise of Heracleopolis and the later fall of Memphis, a coincidence that is not easily explained by random chance. This is not to say that there was a flood in Egypt, but rather that the flood story may have been deliberately placed into its present position in Genesis to serve as a literary parallel to the collapse of the Memphite kingdom and the chaos that followed.

The evidence above clearly demonstrates that the dated life span of Methuselah and the death dates of his patriarchal predecessors constitute a chronological record of Memphite dynasties that closely tracks the type of archived resources available to the ancient Egyptian scribes who produced our various king-lists. While some light tweaking may be necessary to conform small portions of the Patriarchal Chronology to what we now know from modern archaeological evidence, much as we now do for the Turin Canon and Manetho, Genesis 5 preserves a chronological history of the Old Kingdom just as valuable, if not more so, then any other ancient king-list and chronological record. With dates tied to a Sothic Year, indicated durations for each dynasty, and strong correlations with a reconstructed Manetho, the Patriarchal Chronology must be considered in any debates over Old Kingdom chronology, particularly regarding the issues of High Chronology versus Low Chronology and the debates over the regularity of the cattle counts.

6 Eber and Thebes: Part I
The Middle Kingdom

EGYPTOLOGISTS IDENTIFY THE THEBAN-BASED ELEVENTH AND TWELFTH Dynasties as the Middle Kingdom. It was succeeded by the Theban-based Thirteenth Dynasty, which enjoyed a few years of peace before the onset of the massive political disruption known as the Second Intermediate Period. Some Egyptologists would include the early part of Dyn. 13 within the Middle Kingdom.

Most Egyptologists divided this chaotic era into five dynasties, three consecutive dynasties in Thebes (Dyns. 13, 16, and 17) and two non-Theban dynasties (Dyns.14 and 15). At least one of the non-Theban dynasties (Dyn. 15), if not both, was ruled by a group of foreign kings known as the Hyksos. There is some issue as to whether the Hyksos dynasty established control over all of Egypt for at least some period or only captured the northern portion of the country in the Delta region. This era ended during the reign of the Theban king Ahmose, who expelled the Hyksos from Egypt and is considered the founder of the Eighteenth Dynasty.

The Second Intermediate Period has long been thought of as a graveyard for chronological theories about the era's history.[231] We'll take up that challenge in the next chapter. In this chapter we will concentrate on the Middle Kingdom. But first, a few chronological notes.

For the Twelfth Dynasty we have enough data to paint an almost complete chronological portrait of its kings, including lengths of reign and co-regencies. This is the dynasty for which we have a Sothic date in the seventh-year of King Senwosre III. What year that date should be assigned to is one of the flash points in the argument over Egypt's High versus Low Chronology. In this study, we will, as usual, work with the High Chronology.

Richard A. Parker, one of the leading experts on Twelfth Dynasty chronology, established the foundation for the High Chronology dating of the Twelfth Dynasty. Before the growing movement in support of the Low Chronology, His dating of the Twelfth Dynasty kings had been used in almost every general study of Egyptian history. It is the one used by Gardiner and the CAH.[232] Subsequent to his study, as he himself acknowledges, a discovery of a Year 13 inscription for King Amenemhe IV, extended the dynastic range by four years, but the discovery had no impact on the issue of Sothic dating or the start and end dates for any of the kings except for the one king who followed after Amenemhe IV.[233]

In the High Chronology, the Twelfth Dynasty lasted from 1991 to 1782.[234] As noted in the previous chapter, based on the Turin Canon, the Eleventh Dynasty lasted for 143 years. Counting back from 1991 gives a starting date of 2134. A second key date for the Eleventh Dynasty is the date of unification under King Menthotpe II.

Based on the High Chronology, and using the Turin Canon lengths of reign for Menthotpe II and his successor, (51 years + 12 years), gives us a starting date of 2154.[235] The archaeological evidence indicates that the last stage of his campaign to defeat the Heracleopolitans began in the fourteenth year of his reign.[236] This yields a date of 2040, which several Egyptologists accept as the date of unification.[237]

As to calculating the starting date for the Eighteenth Dynasty, three issues are important. In what year did the Sothic sighting for the ninth Year of Amenhotep I occur? How long did Ahmose, the founding king of the Eighteenth Dynasty, rule? Did Ahmose share a coregency with his successor, Amenhotep I?

As to the year of the Sothic sighting, we not have only a conflict between the High Chronology and the Low Chronology, but within the High Chronology there is a lot of room for chronological disagreements. Again, we follow the High Chronology in this study. Within that framework, the Sothic sighting occurred sometime between 1544 and 1537.[238] That places the start of Ahmoses' reign somewhere between 1553 and 1546.

For Ahmose, the highest known year date in the archaeological record is 21.[239] The Manetho sources, however, award him 25 years[240] and many Egyptologists accept that as his full length of reign.[241] Some scholars have argued for a 6-year co-regency between Ahmose and Amenhotep I, but that is not well received.[242]

If there is no co-regency, then the earliest High Chronology date allowable for the start of the Eighteenth Dynasty would fall between 1578 and 1574, depending upon whether you accept the 21-year marker as the highest year for Ahmose or the 25-year Manetho figure. Gardiner dates the Ahmose ascension to 1575.[243] Wente and Van Siclen proposed a starting date of 1570 but they included a six-year co-regency. Removing the coregency gives a starting date of 1576.[244] Moving to a later date along the Sothic date range in both the High and Low Chronology allows significantly later starting dates for the Eighteenth Dynasty, and within the Low Chronology dynastic starting dates of 1550 to 1540 are common.

The Patriarchal Data

In the previous chapter, we saw that all the birth dates before Methuselah fell into the predynastic period and the death dates of those same individuals corresponded to the starting dates of the Memphite Dynasties. We will now move from the Genesis 5 chronology to the Genesis 11 chronology. I placed that data in Table 6.1, *Genesis 11 Chronology*. Let me draw your attention to some details.

If you look at the birth dates, you will note that they all fall within the Middle Kingdom timeframe. In like manner, all the death dates fall within the Second Intermediate Period. Given the pattern in the Genesis 5 chronology, this suggests that we should expect the birth dates to give us information about Middle Kingdom events and the death dates to give us important correlations to the Second Intermediate Period. For the Middle Kingdom, however, we have only two dynasties, and we have nine dates. The birth dates, then, will include dates other than dynastic starting dates.

Table 6.1: Genesis 11 Chronology		
Generation	Birth Year	Death Year
Arphaxad	2105	1667
Shelah	2070	1637
Eber	2040	1576
Peleg	2006	1767
Reu	1976	1737
Serug	1944	1714
Nahor	1914	1766
Terah	1885	1680
Abram	1815	

Now look at Eber's birth and death dates, 2040 and 1576. In the High Chronology, 2040 is the unification date of Egypt during the reign of Eleventh Dynasty Theban king Menthotpe II, and, politically, the effective starting date of the Eleventh Dynasty; 1576 is one of the plausible dates accepted by several Egyptologists for the year that King Ahmose ascended the throne before he unified Egypt, and while the conflict continued within Egyptian borders for a short while, Ahmose was effectively the Egyptian ruler from the time he took the throne. Eber, then, appears to embody two of the most important dates in the history of Theban rule, the effective starting dates and reunifications of Egypt under Menthotpe II and Ahmose. In this regard, Eber's life span plays a literary role like Methuselah's, defining the beginning (2040) and end (1576) of a major political era in Egyptian history.

Let's now look at how the Patriarchal Chronology intersects with the High Chronology of the Middle Kingdom. I'll begin with the Twelfth Dynasty and follow with the Eleventh Dynasty.

Patriarchal Chronology and the Twelfth Dynasty

Table 6.2, *The Twelfth Dynasty and Genesis 11*, sets up a comparison between the standard High Chronology for the Twelfth Dynasty and the last six Patriarchal birth dates in Genesis 11. It requires some explanations.

King Name	Start	End	Coregency with Successor	Start of sole reign	Patriarch	Birth year	Minus 15 years
Table 6.2: The Twelfth Dynasty and Genesis 11[a]							
1. Amenemhe I	1991	1962	9-10 years	1991	Peleg	2006	1991
2. Senwosre I	1971	1928	1-2 years	1961	Reu	1976	1961
3. Amenemhe II	1929	1895	2-3 years	1927	Serug	1944	1929
4. Senwosre II	1897	1877	1-2 years	1894	Nahor	1914	1899
5. Senwosre III	1878	1843	0 years	1876	Terah	1885	1870
6. Amenemhe III	1842	1797	1-2 years	1842			
7. Amenemhe IV	1798	1786	0 years	1796	Abram	1815	1800
8. Sebeknofru	1785	1782	0 years	1785			

[a]Twelfth Dynasty chronology from (Gardiner 1961), 439, except for the extension of the reign for Amenemhe IV per (Parker 1977), 188-189.

The Twelfth Dynasty has several coregencies, mostly short but one lengthy 10-year co-rule between the first two kings. Because years are rounded off, it is hard to precisely establish how long the much shorter coregencies lasted and I have given approximations that reflect the possibility of different short durations depending upon how partial years may have been rounded off. In setting the starting dates for each king's reign, I include the coregency period for each king's successor, but I also provide a column indicating in what year each king began his solo reign.

Following that column, I have listed all the Genesis 11 Patriarchs born after Eber and aligned them with six specific kings. The first five Patriarchs are aligned with the first five kings in the dynasty. The sixth Patriarch, for reasons that will become apparent in a moment, is aligned with the seventh king in the dynasty. Next to each Patriarch is the date of birth and next to the date of births I have a column that subtracts 15 years from all six Patriarchal birth dates.

This 15-year adjustment functions like the alignment of tumblers in a lock, opening a portal into an astounding collection of chronological correlations for five of the six Patriarchs. Let's take a closer look.

From the revised birth dates, we find the following alignments.

- Peleg's revised birth date of 1991 coincides with Amenemhe's ascension date of 1991.

- Reu's revised birth date of 1961 coincides with the start of Senwosre I's independent rule in 1961.
- Serug's revised birth date of 1929 coincides with Senwosre II's ascension date of 1929.
- Nahor's revised birth date of 1899 falls just two years earlier than Senwosre III's ascension date of 1897.
- Abram's revised birth date of 1800 falls just two years earlier than Amenemhe IV's ascension date of 1798.

For the first three kings and Patriarchs we have precise dated matchups. For the fourth and sixth Patriarch, the dates were each just 2 years higher than the corresponding king's starting date, close enough to be the result of rounding errors, or disagreements as to whether to count a king's reign from the date of his ascension to the throne, the first full calendar year after he ascended to the throne, or the first full calendar year for the year he ascended the throne.

We do have one outlier in the correlations. The fifth patriarch, Terah, is badly misaligned with the fifth king, Senwosre III. It doesn't matter whether we use the original birth date or the adjusted birth date. It is possible that the "units" figure dropped out during transmission, or it may simply be a mistake. The impact, though, just blurs the dividing line between Senwosre II and Senwosre III.

Both kings have the same name and there is some evidence that the ancient compilers also had problems identifying where the boundaries between the two rulers belong. In the High Chronology, Senwosre II had a reign of 20 years and Senwosre III had a reign of 35 years. They shared a coregency of 1-2 years. The combined duration for both kings would be 53-55 years depending on the duration of the coregency. Manetho, it is widely thought, combined both reigns together under a single ruler named Sesostris.[245] He gives this monarch a reign of 43 years, about 10 years short of the true number.

Despite Terah's misalignment, if we sum up the number of years ruled by the first six kings (1991-1797/98) and the number of years between the birth date for Peleg and the birth date for Abram (2006-1815), we get respective totals of 193/194 and 191, virtually identical durations. If we calculate the durations for just kings 4-6 (1897-1797/98), the ones surrounding Terah's misalignment, and the corresponding duration between Nahor's birth date and Abram's birth date (1914-1815), we get respective durations of 99/100 years and 99 years. So, while Terah's misalignment gives an erroneous dividing point between Senwosre II and Senwosre III, it does not affect the overall correlations between the Twelfth Dynasty Chronology and the Patriarchal Chronology.

The set of chronological alignments between five Patriarchal birth dates and the starting dates for five Twelfth Dynasty kings cannot reasonably be explained away by coincidence. This is highly unlikely to be a random event. Beyond the impact for biblical studies, it should have a profound effect on the debate over High Chronology and Low Chronology. Clearly, the Patriarchal data proves that the High Chronology for the Twelfth Dynasty is correct.

Let me finish the Twelfth Dynasty analysis with just a brief remark on the 15-year adjustment. While it obviously proves that the birth dates were intended to correspond to the ascension dates of various Twelfth Dynasty kings, there is no clear explanation why this initial error is present in the Patriarchal Chronology. My best explanation is that if you look at the co-regencies column, there may be about 15 years of coregencies. It is not unlikely, therefore, that the Genesis compiler (or his source) did not clearly recognize the existence of coregencies and found a 15-year gap between the dates he came up with and the full lengths of reign for each king without regard to the coregencies. The compiler, therefore, may have pushed the dates back 15 years to account for what he may have (erroneously) thought to be 15 missing years.

Patriarchal Chronology and the Eleventh Dynasty

I turn now to the Eleventh Dynasty. We have only three remaining birth dates, Arphaxad's 2105, Shelah's 2070, and Eber's 2040. I'll start with Shelah and subtract the same 15-year correction to his birth date that I did for the other Patriarchal birth dates. That gives us a revised birth date of 2055. As noted above, this is the date for the ascension of

Menthotpe II to the throne, the king who unified Egypt under Theban rule. This adds one more astonishing correlation to the earlier collection of five direct alignments with Dyn. 12 kings.

Menthotpe II's feat of reuniting Egypt made him one of the more celebrated Egyptian kings. Almost a thousand years later, during the Nineteenth Dynasty, a temple inscription brought together the names of Menes, Nebhepetre (a portion of Menthotpe II's full name) and Ahmose, obviously, Hayes notes, as a recognition of the three great unifiers who inaugurated the three greatest Egyptian epochs.[246] Menthotpe II was so revered that as late as the Twentieth Dynasty numerous tomb inscriptions celebrated his role as founder of the Middle Kingdom.[247]

This brings us to the date of Menthotpe II's victory. As indicated above, in the High Chronology, that is 2040, the date of Eber's birth. A question that could be raised here is why I don't subtract 15 years from this birth date also. It is my view that this date doesn't come from king-lists. This was an important celebrated event for over a thousand years and I am sure it was well-documented in Egyptian records. I can't imagine that for such an achievement there wouldn't have been a Sothic dating for this event, although, obviously, we haven't found one yet. So, I don't think this date came from the king-lists. It must have been well preserved in independent archival records. I will leave it untouched and consider this as a further remarkable correlation between the Patriarchal Chronology and the Middle Kingdom chronology.

This leaves only one more date, Arphaxad's birth at 2105. Let me begin with a reminder that there was a slight chronological discrepancy surrounding his birth date. His father, Shem, was born in 2205. According to Genesis 11:10, "These are the descendants of Shem. When Shem was *one hundred years* old, he became the father of Arpachshad *two years after the flood* [emphasis added.]" The problem here is that Shem's one hundredth year is the year *of* the flood, not *two years after* the Flood. Clearly some sort of error occurred in calculating this birth date.

I have no qualms about subtracting 15 years from the birth date, but neither 2105 nor 2090 coincides with any Eleventh Dynasty starting dates for kings. On the other hand, the date of 2105 is specifically linked to the Flood chronology and may not actually be part of the king-list. As it presently stands, 2105, is the year of the Flood and the end of the Memphite kingdom.

In Genesis, Arphaxad is the first child specifically identified (and chronologically identified) as being born after the Flood. His birth, therefore, may symbolize the rise of a new generation to lead Egypt. In that context, a birth date of 2105, or a revised birth date of 2090, may symbolize a public declaration by Thebes to be the legitimate rulers of Egypt and the beginning of Theban efforts to defeat Heracleopolis.

I'm content to leave that as the explanation but I suspect that something else is in play. I believe that Arphaxad originally had a birth date before the Flood and the date was cut off to just after the Flood to accommodate the need to wipe out humanity. I suspect that, originally, Arphaxad was born in 2134 and signified the start of the Eleventh Dynasty but the date was shortened so that the end of the Memphite Kingdom led into the start of the Theban Kingdom. But here I am speculating.

Arphaxad's birth date only has meaning as a mark of continuity between the end of the Memphis Kingdom and the start of the Theban Kingdom. Therefore, I don't think the date was generated from a king-list but rather that it was deliberately chosen to be the dividing line between the two kingdoms. If we do subtract 15 years from this date, it would have to be because it was generated from a king-list, in which case it would be an outlier.

Summary

In this chapter we looked at the nine Genesis 11 birth dates and discovered an extraordinarily high degree of correlation between six of those dates and the starting dates for six middle kingdom rulers. A key to the analysis was the recognition that the birth dates were 15 years out of synchronization with the Twelfth Dynasty High Chronology. Once we adjusted the birth rates by 15 years, everything fell into place.

Four of the revised birth dates coincided with the very same year in which a king began his reign. (In one of these instances, the correlation was to the start of the independent reign after a co-regency.) Two of the revised birth dates were just two years off a king's starting date on the throne. A seventh date, Eber's, coincided with the same year in which Menthotpe II reunited Egypt.

One date, Arphaxad's, identified that portion of the Theban Eleventh Dynasty that followed immediately after the collapse the Memphite Kingdom. The only outlier in the sequence of birth dates belonged to Terah, misplacing the dividing line between Senwosre II and Senwosre III. These two kings had similar names and evidence indicated that Manetho also had difficulty separating out these same two kings, combining them together as a single ruler.

Lastly, we saw that the duration of the Twelfth Dynasty, from the start of the first reign to the beginning of the seventh reign lasted 193 years and the corresponding duration for the Patriarchal birth dates lasted 191 years, a virtually perfect match.

This agreement between so many Genesis 11 birth dates and the Middle Kingdom chronology of kings is astounding and can leave little doubt that there must be some connection between the Patriarchal Chronology and Egyptian king-lists. The correlations also suggest that the High Chronology probably represents a more accurate chronology of Egypt than does the Low Chronology.

7 Eber and Thebes: Part II The Second Intermediate Period

WE WILL NOW LOOK AT HOW THE PATRIARCHAL CHRONOLOGY INTERACTS with what Egyptologists identify as the Second Intermediate Period, that amorphous historical stretch bridging the gap between the end of the Twelfth Dynasty and the beginning of the Eighteenth Dynasty. Kitchen has observed, "the Second Intermediate Period (Thirteenth–Seventeenth Dynasties) is the graveyard of many chronological essays."[248] So, I proceed forward with a bit of trepidation.

The Second Intermediate Period was a time of great chaos from which we have few contemporaneous records to flesh out more than a skeletal overview of this problematic era's dynastic divisions, political rivalries, and precise chronological boundaries. The meager archaeological and epigraphic record for this period has resulted in many debates and disagreements among Egyptologists as to how to reconstruct the era's dynastic and chronological record. Before looking at the Patriarchal Chronology, let's review the evidence and arguments.

A Political Outline of the Second Intermediate Period

The Second Intermediate Period encompasses Dynasties 13–17, but this arrangement is primarily a product of the Manetho tradition.[249] We have little independent verification that the ancient Egyptians endorsed this specific structure. Still, Egyptologists have attempted to describe the dynastic history of this era in accord with the Manetho Model, although there is still a substantial amount of disagreement over what that historical model should look like. The Manetho record for this era, as we will see below, is a massive chronological mess that has so far defied taming. Nevertheless, as we have previously seen, once we understand how the Manetho redactors abused and misunderstood summation lines and marginal notes, most of Manetho's original data can be restored, and we will do so here.

The chief political feature of this puzzling era is the rise of a group of non-native Egyptian kings (of indefinite origin and identity) who at times ruled over various and different parts of Egypt in conflict with the Theban rulers in Upper Egypt, and, perhaps, at other times ruled over all of Egypt, subjecting the Theban rulers to vassal status.

Historians usually identify these foreign rulers as the Hyksos or Shepherd Kings, both terms introduced by Josephus who erroneously identifies the latter as a translation of the former.[250] Gardiner derives the name *Hyksos* from an Egyptian phrase that he gives as *hikkhase*, which he translates as "chieftain of a foreign hill country."[251] Problems in the transliteration of Egyptian words have resulted in alternative spellings and variations in translations. David O'Connor, for instance, renders the Egyptian term as *hekaw khaset* and translates it as "rulers of a foreign land."[252]

The conventional view holds that the Hyksos disruption began sometime after a peaceful start to the Theban Thirteenth Dynasty and that during the Thirteenth Dynasty a preliminary Hyksos group came to power in parts of northern Egypt. At some point after this first group of Hyksos kings came to power, it established its capitol in the city of Avaris. Subsequently, a second group of Hyksos kings extended its reach beyond that of the earlier Hyksos group, capturing the city of Memphis and possibly all of Egypt. Egyptologists usually identify the earlier Hyksos group as the Fourteenth Dynasty and the later Hyksos group as the Fifteenth Dynasty, which they also refer to as the Great Hyksos Dynasty. It is not clear from the evidence if the Fourteenth Dynasty ended with the rise of the Fifteenth or continued in a vassal status.

Egyptologists also agree that that the Thirteenth and Seventeenth Dynasties should be identified as Theban, but where the Thirteenth Dynasty ends and the Seventeenth Dynasty begins remains unresolved. The difficulty is caused in part by the problematic nature of identifying and classifying the Sixteenth Dynasty. Fueled by inconsistencies in the Manetho sources, some scholars believe that the Sixteenth Dynasty was Theban, fitting in between the Thirteenth and Seventeenth Dynasties, and some that it was a Hyksos Dynasty concurrent with the Hyksos Fourteenth and/or the Hyksos Fifteenth Dynasties. Others consider it a catchall term for a mixture of concurrent dynasties, both Theban and Hyksos, while still others propose that it was purely spurious, non-existent, a figment of the Manetho tradition.

The Second Intermediate period ended when the last few pharaohs of the Seventeenth Dynasty waged war against the Hyksos and drove them out of Egypt. This last group of Seventeenth Dynasty kings appears to have been 5 in number and the Turin Canon appears to have separated them out from the group of Theban kings immediately preceding them.[253] The final victor was Ahmose, considered the founder of the Theban Eighteenth Dynasty. His brother, Kamose, was the last of the Seventeenth Dynasty kings. The conclusion of the Theban-Hyksos war came sometime during Ahmose's reign but when during that reign the war concluded is not clear from the existing evidence.

Non-Manetho King-lists

The difficulties inherent in reconstructing the dynastic divisions and lists of kings in the various dynasties can be seen from the fact that two of the major king-lists, the Tables of Abydos and Sakkara, completely ignore Dynasties 13–17.[254] The Abydos list even omits the last king of the Twelfth Dynasty.[255]

Despite the claims that the transition from the Twelfth to Thirteenth Dynasties was peaceful, the absence of any Thirteenth Dynasty kings in these two lists suggests that some ancient Egyptians may have seen this as a more politically divisive time than do the modern Egyptologists. The omission of king names can be interpreted as a sign that some Egyptian factions did not see anyone in this period as having clear (and legitimate) dominion over all of Egypt.

The absence of Sebeknofru, the last king of the Twelfth Dynasty, from the Abydos list further suggests that possible conflict began during that reign. Ryholt has argued that Sebeknofru may have usurped the throne from the heirs of Amenemhe IV, and this may have triggered some internecine struggles for power into the Thirteenth Dynasty.[256] It may also indicate, as Ryholt has proposed, that foreign disruption in the Delta may have begun as early as the end of the Twelfth Dynasty.[257]

The Karnak list mentions some of the kings from this period but they do not appear in chronological order.[258] In its original state, says Gardiner, it may have mentioned as many as thirty kings from the Second Intermediate Period, mostly Theban, only about half of whom have been authenticated from monuments or other artifacts.[259]

The most important ancient source for our purposes is the Turin Canon of Kings, which, unfortunately, is badly damaged with pieces missing. There is even debate over which pieces go where, having some slight effect on the historical debate about events in this period.

The Turin Canon appears to have recorded the kings for the Second Intermediate Period in six columns, (numbers VI–XI), each of which may have consisted of up to thirty lines of text, most of which contained an individual king's name and length of reign and some of which consisted of summation lines for a group of kings.[260] Whether any of the entries for a particular king spilled over onto more than one line we can't say and Gardiner warns against assuming that the original document had as many as 180 names or that all of the names listed were authentic.[261] In any event, he says, the present state of the manuscript allows us to read no more than about sixty names, of which perhaps only a third or so have been authenticated from monuments.[262] While most names are missing due to the damaged state of the list, it contains many other entries for the lengths of reigns, although a number of the corresponding king names are missing.

Nevertheless, there is one key and very important section of the document that opens a window into the political difficulties of the period. Line X:21 (i.e., located on column X at line 21) says, according to Gardiner, "[Total, Chieftains of] a foreign country, 6, they made 108 years."[263] This entry signifies that a group of six foreign kings ruled for 108 years. The preceding line, X:20, appears to identify the last of these six rulers as Khamudy, but, so far, no independent authentication of that name has surfaced.[264] None of the five other remaining kings are identified in this document.

Because the Manetho sources only mention six Hyksos kings by name (although none have the name Khamudy or a recognizable variation of that name) and identify them as the conquerors of Egypt, these six Manetho Hyksos kings have been equated with the six foreign kings in the Turin Canon, and both sets of six are identified as the Great Hyksos Dynasty. Based on Africanus's identification of these kings as the Fifteenth Dynasty, Egyptologists have followed the convention of identifying this Great Hyksos Dynasty as Dynasty 15. Eusebius, however, identified the same group of kings as the Seventeenth Dynasty.

By implication, the Turin Canon kings appearing after the six Hyksos kings must be Thebans, including at least all the members of the Seventeenth Dynasty, and perhaps some Theban predecessors. As there were 30 lines per column and the Hyksos summation line occurred at X:21, there remain a total of 39 possible lines for this list of Theban kings, at least one of which, and perhaps others, must have been a summation line saying how many Theban kings were in that sequence. This would indicate a sequence of Theban kings containing no more than 38 names and perhaps as few as 36 or 37.

Preceding these six foreign kings, we have a section that seems to have a number of Semitic or foreign sounding names in the king-list and many Egyptologists identify this portion of the Canon with the Hyksos Fourteenth Dynasty, although Redford has argued that the individuals named were only an ancestor list for the Fifteenth Dynasty Hyksos kings and they never ruled in Egypt.[265] It is important to note for our subsequent discussion that this portion of the Turin Canon, which immediately precedes the sequence of six foreign kings, contains 32 names.[266]

Students of the Turin Canon note that beginning with the start of the Thirteenth Dynasty there appears to be a sequence of about 50 to 60 Theban kings, after which there appears to be a break in the Theban sequence.[267] Hayes adds that the list has omitted some names known from the archaeological record.[268] A number of Egyptologists believe that this Theban sequence lasted about 150 years.[269] Kitchen argues that his Thirteenth Dynasty contains 50 kings ruling for about 150 to 155 years and cites von Beckerath for the proposition that the period encompassed 50 kings ruling for about 146 to 152 years.[270]

Beginning sometime around the 24th through 27th king in this Theban sequence the archaeological and epigraphic materials show a distinct lack of evidence for Theban king-names in the northern and central portions of Egypt.[271] For this reason, many Egyptologists believe the Hyksos kings came to power in the northern delta somewhere around the time of the 24th through 27th king in the Theban sequence, and are inclined to believe that the Thebans started losing ground to the Hyksos Fourteenth Dynasty at about this time (although the Hyksos dynasty may have started earlier.)

Kitchen estimates that these first 24 to 27 kings ruled for about 75 to 100 years,[272] but he relies on several estimates and guesses, and the duration might be shorter. If Kitchen is correct, this leaves about 50 to 75 years for the balance of this Theban sequence. In the high chronology the break falls between about 1707–1682 and in the low chronology between about 1720–1695, although in either case it might be moved back a decade or more.[273]

Sources Other Than the King-lists

Outside of the king-lists, several kings are mentioned on monuments and other artifacts, some of whose names correspond to those in the Turin Canon and others who are known from no other king-lists. (Some might correspond to missing names from the Turin Canon, but we can't say.) Only a handful of Hyksos names (not all of them necessarily kings) are known to us from outside Manetho and the Turin Canon, and most of these are the subject of speculation as to when or if they ever ruled or if they correspond to any of the names in the king-lists.

The most important for purposes of our chronological reconstruction are the references to the Hyksos king Awaserre Apopi, who was on the throne during Year 3 of the Theban King Kamose, who was the predecessor and brother of the Ahmose who expelled the Hyksos.[274] Year 3 is the highest recorded year for Kamose.[275] In addition, we know from an entry on the *Rhind Mathematical Papyrus* that this Apopi served at least 33 years.[276] Apopi's name was also found written on a temple wall together with that of a Hyksos king named Khayan, who was, presumably, Apopi's predecessor on the throne. [277] Hayes says that the fourth of the six Hyksos kings listed in the Turin Canon ruled for over 40 years, and the length of reign suggests that he is probably Apopi.[278]

In the Manetho sources, one of the six named Hyksos kings is Aphophis (or Apophis according to the Josephus version), clearly identifiable as Apopi, but the sources are inconsistent as to his placement within the order of the six kings and the length of his reign. (See below.) Some have also suggested a connection between Khayan and the Iannas appearing in the Josephus listing of Manetho's six Hyksos kings. However, in the Josephus list, Iannas appears after his Apophis.

The Conquest of Avaris

Sometime before the rise of the Great Hyksos Fifteenth Dynasty, the Hyksos kings of the Fourteenth Dynasty established their capitol at Avaris, in the Delta region, where they also adopted the Egyptian god Set as their national deity. Later, during the Nineteenth Dynasty, Ramesses II changed the name of Avaris to Pi-Ramesse, which may be the biblical city of Raamses where, allegedly, Hebrew slaves were kept captive.[279]

The connection between Ramesses II and Avaris is interesting, not only because his father was named Sethos, after the same Egyptian deity worshipped by the Hyksos, but because an inscription from the time of Ramesses II, and discovered near Avaris, relates how Sethos, while a commander in the army of Pharaoh Horemheb, came in the four hundredth year of the god Set to do him honor.[280]

This text has been widely interpreted as referring to the four hundredth anniversary of the founding of Avaris as the Hyksos capitol.[281] If true, and we can only speculate that it is so, then we can establish a chronological boundary for the foundation of Avaris. Horemheb ruled from about 1342–1316 in the high chronology and from about 1317–1291 in the low chronology, although there is still some debate in both camps as to where to place the starting date for Horemheb's reign and whether this king reigned for 27 years or 14 years.

Within large margins for error, then, Avaris would have been founded somewhere between either 1742–1716 or 1717–1691, depending upon the chronological scheme adopted. As the Hyksos would not have been able to establish Avaris as their capitol unless they had earlier established a stronghold in the north, we can probably place the origins of the Fourteenth Dynasty at least a decade or two earlier.

The Great Hyksos Dynasty

Egyptologists credit Dynasty 15, the Great Hyksos Dynasty, with the capture of Memphis and the extension of the Hyksos reach far into the south.[282] The dynasty ended sometime after the start of the Eighteenth Dynasty, during the reign of King Ahmose, who expelled the Hyksos from Egypt.

Ahmose, the first king of the Eighteenth Dynasty, ruled according to Manetho for 25 years, and for at least 22 years according to the archaeological evidence. This gives us a parameter for the termination of Hyksos rule but not a precise date. We have, though, some entries on the *Rhind Mathematical Papyrus* that provide some further guidance but that are the subject of some interpretive disputes.

That document indicates that in Year 11 of the reign of Ahmose, the king defeated the Hyksos at the city of Sharuhen,[283] a military fortress located outside of Egypt, where the Hyksos had established a military presence.[284] The struggle lasted for at least three years.

Another document tells us that Ahmose defeated the Hyksos at Avaris.[285] Unfortunately, we do not have any definitive evidence regarding the sequence of these two events. Did Avaris fall first or Sharuhen? Some have argued that after defeating the Hyksos at Sharuhen, the Egyptians returned south and attacked Avaris.[286] If correct, then Dynasty Fifteen ended sometime after the eleventh year of Ahmose, possibly as late as the fifteenth or twentieth year.

Others have argued that Avaris must have fallen first.[287] One rational for that view is that it is not likely that the Thebans could have staged a three-year siege at Sharuhen while the Hyksos still maintained a strong presence at Avaris, which lay between Sharuhen and the Thebans. If this latter proposition is the case, then Avaris must have fallen no later than the eighth or ninth year of Ahmose, when the siege on Sharuhen began, and probably a couple of years before the siege started.

Several Egyptologists would date the defeat at Avaris to about the third or fourth year of Ahmose's reign.[288] My chronological reconstruction, partially confirmed by Eusebius's version of Manetho, assumes that Ahmose defeated the Hyksos in Avaris in about his fourth year, 1572 in my present chronological scheme. In this latter scenario, the Great Hyksos Dynasty ended with the fall of Avaris. The later defeat at Sharuhen, outside of Egypt, simply delivered the decisive blow that eliminated them as a political force.

As this dynasty is believed to have arisen with the conquest of Memphis and lasted 108 years, we can date the fall of Memphis into Hyksos hands to no earlier than about 1680 according to the high chronology or about 1655 according to the low chronology. In either case, this suggests that the Great Hyksos Dynasty originated between about 35 and 65 years after the establishment of Avaris as the Hyksos capitol. However, there is also an issue as to whether the 108 years terminates at the fall of Avaris or the fall of Sharuhen, which could have the effect of moving the capture of Memphis forward by a few years.

A Summary of the Non-Manetho Chronological Evidence

The above overview gives us several chronological clues about events in the Second Intermediate Period and I think it would be helpful to summarize them before proceeding further.

- According to the Turin Canon, Dynasty 15, the Great Hyksos Dynasty, lasted 108 years and had six kings.

- The Turin Canon has 32 kings with foreign sounding names immediately preceding the Great Hyksos Dynasty.

- The Turin Canon allows for up to 38 Theban kings and a summation line following immediately after the Great Hyksos Dynasty. The last 5 kings in this sequence, who waged the war against the Hyksos kings, appear to be separated out from the preceding kings.

- The Turin Canon has a sequence of about 50 to 60 Theban kings beginning with the start of the Thirteenth Dynasty. This sequence of Theban kings may have lasted about 150 years but there are some questions as to the validity of this estimate and the duration may have been as much as a couple of decades shorter.

- Ahmose, first king of the Eighteenth Dynasty defeated the Fifteenth Dynasty sometime after he came to the throne. He defeated them at Avaris, probably around Year 4 in his reign and at Sharuhen in Year 11 of his reign after a 3-year siege.

- Apopi, one of the Great Hyksos kings, was on the throne during Year 3 of Kamose, last Theban king of the Seventeenth Dynasty. He appears to have ruled at least 33 years. This Year 3 of Kamose is the highest year recorded for this king.

- An inscription suggests that the Hyksos established Avaris as their capitol 400 years before some year in the reign of Horemheb. This event would have occurred prior to the Hyksos capture of Memphis by the Fifteenth Dynasty.

- The Hyksos must have had time to establish a political base in Egypt prior to the establishment of Avaris as their capitol.

- Many Egyptologists believe that somewhere around the reign of the 24th through 27th Theban king, the Thebans lost control of the northern territories and perhaps the middle territories as well. the territories probably fell to the pre-Fifteenth Dynasty Hyksos kings. The division between the earlier and later group of Theban kings may have fallen somewhere near the midpoint of this 150-year range.

The Manetho Sources

With the start of the Second Intermediate Period we can add a third source for our Manetho text, the writings of Josephus, the first century Jewish historian. As noted above, Josephus appears to have known at least two copies of Manetho and there were some differences between them. Josephus wrote more than a century earlier than Africanus and Eusebius.

Josephus's works were widely circulated in early Christian circles and we know that Eusebius was familiar with his writings, having quoted him on occasion. We can be reasonably certain that Africanus, who wrote on ancient chronology, also knew of Josephus's history, either directly or indirectly through other sources.

Africanus's account of the Hyksos dynasties, as we shall see, closely parallels that of Josephus but Eusebius departs significantly from both. Either Eusebius represents a radically different line of transmission or Africanus modified a source similar to Eusebius's so that it reflected what Josephus wrote about the Hyksos.

An interesting feature of Josephus's account is that he includes a lot of narrative history in addition to king-lists. Also, he doesn't present numbered dynastic breaks. His account focuses primarily on the Hyksos portion of the Second Intermediate Period and transitions along the way to the Eighteenth and Nineteenth Dynasties, but he doesn't number them as such.

Table 7.1, *Summary of Manetho Sources for the Second Intermediate Period*, displays summaries of the Second Intermediate Period as they appear in Josephus, Africanus and Eusebius. There are several salient factors that we should take notice of. For starters, all three display extraordinarily long durations for the Second Intermediate Period. Even if we allow for concurrent dynasties between the Thebans and the Hyksos, the numbers are still too high.

Josephus, whose chronology focuses solely on the Hyksos, says that the collective reign for all the Hyksos kings was 511 years long and consisted of two consecutive groups. Africanus says that the Theban

Thirteenth Dynasty lasted 453 years and that a mixed Hyksos-Theban Seventeenth Dynasty lasted another 151 years, a 600-year duration for the Thebans. For the Hyksos as sole rulers, Africanus has three dynasties, Fourteenth through Sixteenth, with respective durations of 184 years, 284 years, and 518 years, for a total of 986 years. Eusebius has three Theban dynasties, Thirteen, Fifteen, and Sixteen, with respective durations of 453 years, 250 years, and 190 years, for a total of 893 years, and two Hyksos dynasties, Fourteen and Seventeen, lasting respectively 184 years and 103 years. It should be pointed out, that Eusebius disagrees with Africanus as to whether Dynasties 15 through 17 were Theban or Hyksos. Where one says Theban, the other says Hyksos. Evidently, the source material must have been quite confusing.

As we have learned repeatedly above, when the Manetho figures are radically too high, we are very likely looking at summation lines or marginal notes that have been added on to the totals or which have replaced individual lengths of reign. This will be seen to be the case here. When we get done with the reconstruction, we will see that there is a very tight fit between the original Manetho and the Patriarchal Chronology.

Josephus only gives us a chronology for the Hyksos kings, which he divides into two groups. The first, based on the names given, corresponds to the six kings of the Great Hyksos dynasty, whose individual lengths of reign add up to 259 years and 10 months, but he does not give us the total number of years they ruled in the form of a summation line.[289] He then says these six kings were followed by a second group of Hyksos kings, none of whose names are given and no specific duration is given, But, he says, the two groups had a collective reign of 511 years.

Subtracting the duration of the first group of kings from the total group of all the Hyksos kings, leaves 251 years and 2 months for the second group of kings. That the two groups had almost equal durations over a very long period of just over 250 years each, suggests that Josephus may have confused a line of summation for the first group of kings as if it were a reference to a second line of kings. I'll suggest later that the "511" figure is an erroneous transmission of "518," which number would be exactly twice as large as the duration of the first group of kings.

Table 7.1 Summary of Manetho Sources for the Second Intermediate Period

Dynasty	Josephus	Africanus	Eusebius
13		Diospolis (=Thebes) 453 years 60 kings	Diospolis (=Thebes) 453 years 60 kings
14		Hyksos rule in Xois 184 years 76 Kings	Hyksos rule in Xois 184 years[a] 76 kings
15	Hyksos[b] 259 years/10mo 6 kings Salites 19 yrs Bnon 44 yrs Apachnan 36 yrs/7mo Aphophis 61 yrs Iannas 50 yrs/1mo Assis 49 yrs/2mo	Hyksos 284 years 6 kings Saites 19 yrs Bnon 44 yrs Pachnan 61 yrs Staan 50 yrs Archles 49 yrs Aphophis 61 yrs	Diospolis (=Thebes) 250 years Number not given. See Dyn. 17 below.
	Hyksos[c] 251 years/2 mo. Number of kings not given		
16	Hyksos Total 511 years[d]	Hyksos 518 years 32 kings	Thebes 190 years 5 kings
17		Hyksos and Thebes or Diospolis[e] 151 years 43 Hyksos kings 43 Theban kings	Hyksos 103 years 4 kings Saites 19 yrs Bnon 40 Aphophis 14 yrs Archles 30 yrs

[a]The Armenian version of Eusebius gives the reign as 484 years.

[b]Josephus does not divide the kings into numbered dynasties. Although I have aligned Josephus with Africanus's Fifteenth Dynasty instead of Eusebius's Seventeenth, this is only for convenience in comparing all the sources.

[c]Josephus says this Hyksos group followed the previous Hyksos group but doesn't indicate any dynastic break

[d]This is only a summation line for the two Hyksos groups of kings. It is argued in the main text that the original duration should be 518 years.

[e]Africanus has a very confused account of this dynasty and doesn't appear able to distinguish Theban kings from Hyksos kings.

Since Josephus doesn't give dynastic numbers for the two group of kings or indicate they were separate dynasties, I have, for convenience of comparison, placed both groups of kings into the Fifteenth Dynasty but separated the two groups within the listing. I also placed the total duration for both Hyksos dynasties, 511 years, in alignment with Africanus' Sixteenth Dynasty, lasting 518 years. However, In Josephus, the "511" figure is a summation line for the two Hyksos Dynasties whereas in Africanus, the "518" year figure is a separate dynasty listing. We will see later that Africanus's 518 years, like Josephus's 511 years, is due to confusing a line of summation with a separate listing for a dynasty of kings.

Africanus and Eusebius both agree as to the nature of Dynasties 13 and 14. To the former, they assign 453 years to 60 kings from the city of Diospolis, which is a Greek variant of the Greek name Thebes. Both also agree that the Fourteenth Dynasty consisted of 76 Hyksos kings ruling for 184 years from the city of Xois. For the last three dynasties we find thoroughly inconsistent data.

Africanus assigns the Fifteenth Dynasty to six Hyksos kings and names them and gives their lengths of reign. The Africanus listing very closely tracks the Josephus listing but radically departs from Eusebius. Africanus's listing has rounded off Josephus's partial years, and, with one exception, lists the same lengths of reign for five of the six Josephus kings. Africanus gives the sixth king, Apachnan/Pachman an extra 25 years. Josephus and Africanus give this dynasty, respectively, 259 years and 284 years of rule.

Eusebius, on the other hand, says the Fifteenth Dynasty was from Diospolis (= Thebes) and ruled 250 years but doesn't say how many kings there were. In addition, Eusebius has a parallel to Africanus's Fifteenth Dynasty but identifies it as the Seventeenth Dynasty. He lists only four kings, three of whose names match those of Africanus and Josephus but gives the dynasty a duration of only 103 years. As we shall soon see, this conforms almost precisely with the Turin Canon account of this dynasty and will provide an important clue to reconstructing the chronology of the Second Intermediate Period.

Let me return for a moment to Africanus's 25-year increase in the reign of Apachnan/Pachnan. Curiously, Ahmose, the first king of the Eighteenth Dynasty, who defeated the Hyksos, has a reign of 25 years in Josephus and Eusebius. Africanus mentions this king by name but omits the 25-year reign. This suggests the possibility that 1) the 25 years may have been erroneously attached to Apachnan's reign, 2) Apachnan may have originally been the last king in the list, the one defeated by Ahmose, and, therefore, 3) Manetho may have originally placed the Great Hyksos Dynasty immediately before the Eighteenth Dynasty, as Eusebius has it. In support of this, I would note that after the second king in the Great Hyksos Dynasty, all three sources are in disagreement over the order of the kings and the names of some of the kings. Admittedly, this is very speculative and the validity of this proposal in no way impacts the underlying analysis of the Patriarchal Chronology, but I bring it up for consideration.

With the Sixteenth Dynasty, Africanus says there are 32 Hyksos kings ruling 518 years and Eusebius says the dynasty consisted of 5 Theban kings ruling 190 years.

I've already discussed Eusebius's version of the Seventeenth Dynasty as a Hyksos dynasty. Africanus, on the other hand seems terribly confused about its makeup. He says the kings were either Hyksos, Theban, or Diospolitan, they ruled for 151 years, and consisted of 43 Hyksos kings and/or 43 Theban kings. (Thebes and Diospolis are different Greek names for the same city, but it is not clear that the Manetho redactors knew this. The Egyptian name for the city was Waset.)

I will deal with most of these difficulties in due course and reconstruct the original Manetho chronology. First, however, we should look at the Patriarchal Chronology to see what it has to say about the era.

The Patriarchal Chronology

In the previous chapter we have already established some boundaries for the Second Intermediate Period. In the High Chronology, the Twelfth Dynasty ended in 1782 and the Eighteenth Dynasty began in

1576 (also Eber's death date). Our reconstruction of the chronology for the in-between era must reasonably fit into this context.

Here's a list of Patriarchal death dates for those individuals in Genesis 11 who were born after Eber. (I'm omitting Abram from this list because his death date doesn't appear in Genesis 11.)

Peleg died in 1767
Reu died in 1737
Serug died in 1714
Nahor died in 1766
Terah died in 1680

The first thing I want to point out is that Peleg and Nahor died at virtually the same time, 1777/1776. Second, Nahor's death date is out of sequential order, suggesting that Nahor-Terah may represent one grouping and Peleg-Reu-Serug may represent a different grouping. In this regard, there is a peculiar statement in Genesis about Peleg that has troubled biblical scholars.

Just prior to the Genesis 11 chronology, Genesis 10 contains a non-chronological genealogical account of the descendants of Noah, in the course of which we are told, "To Eber were born two sons: the name of the one was *Peleg, for in his days the earth was divided,* and his brother's name was Joktan [emphasis added]."[290] Peleg was so-named because in his time the land was divided.

E. A. Speiser, in his commentary on Genesis, says that Peleg's name derives from the Hebrew word *niplega,* which he says has the literal meaning of "divided, broke up."[291] Since this passage is part of the Genesis account of the distribution of Noah's descendants and the nations they founded, it is often thought the passage is just a general reference to the division of the world into nations. But, chronologically, Peleg is born about 100 years after the flood, and that distribution of peoples was well underway before his birth, not in his time. What was it that was divided in Peleg's time? The answer is Egypt in the Second Intermediate Period.

Peleg died in 1767, 15–16 years after the end of the Twelfth Dynasty, in the early stages of the Thirteenth Dynasty. Gardiner says that the first two kings of the Thirteenth Dynasty ruled for about 10 years, although data for the second king is weak.[292] Following these two kings, the Turin Canon has a period of six years without a ruler.[293] A period of kinglessness in Thebes is the sort of situation that would tempt political rivals to challenge the Theban administration. If we take 10 years for the first two kings and add the six years without a king, we arrive at the very interesting year of 1766/67, the years in which Peleg and Nahor were born.

Let's now approach these birth dates from the other direction. Eusebius says the Sixteenth Dynasty consisted of five kings who ruled for 190 years. In Eusebius, this is end of the Theban line in the Second Intermediate Period. If we count back 190 years from 1576, we arrive at 1766/1767, the year in which Peleg and Nahor died. This is a strong clue that Eusebius's Sixteenth Dynasty is nothing more than a summation line for the period running from the split between Thebes and the Hyksos to the beginning of the reign of Ahmose, the king who reunited Egypt by driving out the Hyksos.

The reference to five kings in a summation line defining the start of Ahmose's reign reminds us that the Turn Canon singled out the last five kings from Thebes, the family that started the war to drive out the Hyksos. The Eusebius Sixteenth Dynasty appears to be a simple mashup that references the five Theban kings at the end of the Seventeenth Dynasty (the same five referenced by the Turin Canon) and the duration of the split between Thebes and the Hyksos. This suggests that some original source said something like "5 Theban kings fought the Hyksos, 190 years for Theban kings."

Our next important clue comes from Eusebius's Seventeenth Dynasty. In Eusebius, this is the Great Hyksos Dynasty, but he lists only four of the six kings indicated in Josephus, Africanus, and the Turin Canon. This appears to me to be the result of ending the Great Hyksos Dynasty in the year that Ahmose became the Theban King. Since the final defeat of the Hyksos at Avaris came in about the fourth year, and the Turin Canon gives these six kings a duration of

108 years, Eusebius's truncation aligns at just about the point where Ahmose became the king.

That Eusebius's Seventeenth Dynasty coincides so precisely with the Turin Canon and that his Sixteenth Dynasty seems to closely align with the duration of the Hyksos-Thebes split suggests that underlying the original Manetho there appears to be a reliable guide to the chronology of the Second Intermediate Period. Yet, this data doesn't appear in Africanus or Josephus. How did this happen? We will explain shortly when we look at the matter of summation lines.

Before going to the next step in the Manetho reconstruction, lets return for a moment to the Patriarchal Chronology. In the Patriarchal sequence, Terah died in 1680. If the Eighteenth Dynasty started in 1576 and the Hyksos were defeated in the fourth or fifth year, and the Great Hyksos Dynasty lasted 108 years, then the starting date for the Hyksos Dynasty would 1680/1679, the year in which Terah died.

This leaves us with the following suggested framework for the Patriarchal Chronology and the Second Intermediate Period. The death dates of Peleg and Nahor, 1767 and 1766, appear consistent with the split between Thebes and the Hyksos, and the death date of Terah, 1680, coincides with the start of the Great Hyksos Dynasty. The dates for Reu and Serug, 1737 and 1714, are still open to investigation. Before proceeding further on the Patriarchal Chronology, I want to reconstruct the Manetho chronology and establish its parameters.

Reconstructing Manetho's Second Intermediate Period Chronology

As noted above, The Eusebius Sixteenth Dynasty consisted of 5 Theban kings ruling for 190 years. This is a summation line for whatever group of Theban kings preceded the start of the Eighteenth Dynasty. His Seventeenth Dynasty consisted of four named kings ruling for 103 years, and these four kings coincide with the Great Hyksos Dynasty that lasted 108 years, Josephus assigns 259 years to this same dynasty but doesn't number it. Africanus identifies it as the Fifteenth Dynasty and assigns 284 years, although that sum appears to include 25 years wrongfully taken from Ahmose, reducing Africanus's Fifteenth Dynasty total to the Josephus total of 259 years. In almost all other respects, Africanus agrees with Josephus's lengths of reign for the other five kings.

I showed above that if we count back 190 years from 1576, we arrive at 1766. In the Patriarchal Chronology, Peleg, whose name is associated with "division," died in 1767 and Nahor died in 1766. I also pointed out that the first two kings of the Thirteenth Dynasty may have served up to 10 years and they were followed by a period of six years with no king, ending in 1766/67, a period of instability that would encourage political rivals. It was my suggestion, therefore, that 1767/1766 is the year of the split between Thebes and the first group of Hyksos kings.

In addition, I pointed out that Terah died in 1680, the year in which the Great Hyksos Dynasty came into being. The dynasty ended in 1572. This would give the Hyksos era a period of 194 years. Since the Eusebius data fits so well with the chronological parameters, I'll use it as a framework for reconstructing Manetho's Second Intermediate Period. Turn now to Africanus's versions of the Sixteenth and Seventeenth Dynasties.

Where Eusebius describes the Seventeenth Dynasty as Hyksos, Africanus has a very confused account. He doesn't seem to know if it was Hyksos, Theban, or a mixture of both. This suggests he (or his source) had been looking at either some sort of listing that included both Hyksos and Thebans and/or saw a summation line for such a list that said something like "Hyksos and Theban kings, X years." In either case, he understood this source material as one dynasty including Hyksos and Thebans.

If a list was involved, and we can rely on Eusebius, the Theban group came first and the Hyksos group came last. In either event, this referenced Hyksos group, appearing as the final group of Hyksos kings would have to be a duplicate account of the Great Hyksos Dynasty, which Africanus earlier identified as the Fifteenth Dynasty lasting 259 years. Africanus, therefore, has two separate dynasties referencing the same group of Hyksos kings.

Africanus says the total number of Hyksos and/or Theban kings equaled 43. If the Hyksos group, as we know, consisted of six kings, then the remaining 37 kings must be Theban. As you may recall, after the Turin Canon listing of six foreign kings, there remained 39 spaces available, at least one of which must have been a summation line. If there were two summation lines, one for the Thebans and one for both the Thebans and Hyksos, we would have 37 kings in the remaining spaces. The Africanus listing, therefore, appears to reflect what's in the Turin Canon, a group of six Hyksos kings in sequence with a group of 37/38 Theban kings.

This indicates that the original Manetho agreed with the Turin Canon (give or take one Theban king) as to the number of kings that made up the final listing of Hyksos and Theban rulers. Couple this with Eusebius's apparent alignment, contra Africanus and Josephus, with the Turin Canon as to the duration of the Great Hyksos Dynasty, and we have solid ground for the proposition that the original Manetho was largely consistent with the Turin Canon, at least for this portion of the Second Intermediate Period.

Africanus gives the Seventeenth Dynasty a duration of 151 years. In our chronology, the Second Intermediate Period runs from 1782 to 1576, about 206 years. If the first group of Theban kings in the Turin Canon ruled for about 150 years, that leaves only about 56 years for the second group of Theban kings in the Turin Canon. Africanus's 151 years for his final group of Theban kings, then, can't be referencing the same sequential group as the Turin Canon. Is it a combined total for both the Hyksos kings and the Theban kings, or is it a separate total for a specific group of Theban kings tied to a specific event?

If the 151 years includes both Hyksos and Thebans, and we subtract 108 years for the Hyksos, we have about 43 years left for the Theban kings. Our calculations showed there should be about 56 years for this group, so the assignment of 43 years seems too short. I'm going to treat the 151 years as a total for some group of Theban kings but not necessarily to the second group of Theban kings in the Turin Canon.

If we take Africanus's 151-year period for his last group of Theban kings and the Turin Canon's 108 years for the last group of Hyksos kings (corroborated by Eusebius 103 years for the Great Hyksos

Dynasty up to the start of Ahmose's reign) and add them together we would have 259 years for the combined list of Hyksos-Theban kings. Africanus's Seventeenth Dynasty appears to be the Theban half of this list and Eusebius's Seventeenth Dynasty appears to be the Hyksos half of this list.

Interestingly, "259" is the number of years Josephus assigned to the Great Hyksos Dynasty. Africanus, as noted above, has what appears to be a 25-year error in this dynasty and when corrected, it also gives 259 years. But the Josephus and Africanus lengths of reign for the six kings are much too long. What appears to have happened is that the Josephus and Africanus line of transmission had what was originally a list of individual kings with individual lengths of reign that included Theban kings ruling for 151 years and Hyksos kings ruling for 108 years, but the list became garbled through transmission and marginal summations came to be confused with the lengths of reign for the first six kings.

In other words, The Africanus-Josephus Fifteenth Dynasty derives from miscalculated lengths of reign for the list of Theban kings and Hyksos kings, with individual reigns totaling 151 years for the Thebans and 108 years for the Hyksos. The Africanus-Eusebius Seventeenth Dynasties consists of the summation lines appended to this list of Theban and Hyksos kings, with Africanus preserving the Theban half and Eusebius preserving the Hyksos half (along with some of the king-names.) This brings us to Africanus's Sixteenth Dynasty with 518 years and Josephus's Hyksos total of 511 years.

Africanus's Sixteenth Dynasty consists of 32 Hyksos kings serving 518 years. We are clearly dealing with another confused summation line. More specifically, the sums of 108 + 151 + 259, which adds up to 518 years. So, we are floating around the same confused mashup of Theban and Hyksos kings. This summation derives from the total length of reigns for the individual kings in the Theban-Hyksos list plus the summation lines for each set of kings.

Africanus presents this as a Hyksos dynasty with 32 kings. But 32 is the number of kings in the first Hyksos Dynasty so somehow in transmission a redactor saw the summation line for 108 + 151 + 259 as defining a separate group of Hyksos kings that preceded the first group of Hyksos kings. Consistent with this, Joseph says the total duration of all Hyksos kings was 511 years, listing the Great Hyksos Dynasty first and the earlier Hyksos dynasty as following after. I suspect that the 511 years was originally 518 years and accidentally altered in transmission. If it was 518 years, then Josephus had two groups of Hyksos kings each ruling 259 years, obviously the same error that found its way into Africanus, although each misidentified it in different ways.

Africanus's Sixteenth Dynasty and Josephus's total Hyksos duration both suggest that confusion developed over what was originally a chronology of the second group of Theban and Hyksos kings (as arranged in the Turin Canon) that somehow came to be confused with the first group of Hyksos kings. With that though in mind, let's look at Eusebius's Fifteenth Dynasty.

Eusebius describes the Fifteenth Dynasty as a Theban dynasty ruling for 250 years but omits the number of kings. If 190 years is the total duration for the Theban kings beginning with the split between Thebes and the Hyksos, and Manetho's second group of Theban kings ruled for 151 years, that leaves 39 years for the Theban kings running from the split between the Hyksos and Thebans to the start of the 151-year period. If 194 years is the total duration for the Hyksos kings, and the Great Hyksos Dynasty lasted 108 years, that leaves a total of 86 years for the first Hyksos Dynasty.

If we add up the 39 Theban years and the 86 Hyksos years, the sum is 125 years. If we add up the sequence 39 + 89 + 125, the total is 250 years. Once again, a line of summation adding up the number of years ruled by a group of kings has been confused with an additional group of kings. What is interesting is that the Fifteenth Dynasty in Africanus involves the second group of Theban and Hyksos kings and Eusebius's Fifteenth Dynasty involves the first group of Hyksos kings and Theban kings. So Africanus's Sixteenth Dynasty has confused a list of the second group of Hyksos and Theban kings with a first group of Hyksos kings and Eusebius has replaced Africanus's Fifteenth Dynasty account of the second group of Hyksos and Theban kings with an account of the first group of Hyksos and Theban kings.

Africanus and Eusebius both have a Theban Thirteenth Dynasty lasting 453 years that included 60 kings. That is the approximate number of kings in the Turin Canon for the Theban kings beginning with the Thirteenth Dynasty and continuing to the listing of the first group of Hyksos kings. The consensus estimates for the duration of this Theban grouping is about 150 years, give or take a few years in either direction. This suggests we are now looking at a confusion of events involving the earlier portion of the king-lists.

The standard approach to Manetho's Thirteenth Dynasty is to assume that there is an error in transmission in which 153 years came to be written as 453 years. In support of this, the argument goes, Eusebius has 184 years for the Fourteenth Dynasty whereas the Armenian version of Eusebius has 484 years. I, however, believe "453" years is a summation line

First, recall that Eusebius had a 190-year period for the Theban kings preceding the Eighteenth Dynasty, which we dated to 1766/67. I argued that this was the year of the split between Thebes and the Hyksos. Since the Great Hyksos Dynasty extended 4 years past the start of the Eighteenth Dynasty, the Hyksos duration from 1766/67, would be 194 years. If we add up the 108 (Hyksos)+ 151 (Theban) + 194 (Total Hyksos), we have a garbled summation line that double-counts the Great Hyksos and adds up to 453 years.

This garbled account mistakenly assumed that the total duration for all the Hyksos kings was just the duration of the first group of Hyksos kings. In effect, the Thirteenth Dynasty is a garbled summation line for the total number of years ruled by all the Theban kings since the break with the Hyksos combined with the total number of years ruled by all of the Hyksos kings.

For this reason, I strongly suspect that the 184 years Africanus and Eusebius assign to the Hyksos Fourteenth Dynasty is an erroneous transmission of 194 years, which should be the summation line for the total duration of the Hyksos kings. In support of this notion, consider the following.

Manetho's Fourteenth Dynasty has 76 Hyksos kings. According to the Turion Canon, the first Hyksos dynasty had 32 kings and the

Great Hyksos Dynasty had 6 kings, for a total of 38 kings. This suggests that the original Manetho had a reference to 32 Hyksos kings followed by 6 Hyksos kings, followed by a summation indicating 38 Hyksos kings in total. Again, the summation line was thought of as an additional group of kings, yielding 76 kings in total. If we are dealing with what appears to be the full group of Hyksos kings, then we are dealing with a period of 194 years, not 184 years. I would change the 184 to 194 in order to recover the original Manetho.

The one issue left open with the Manetho Chronology is where to place dividing lines for the Theban dynasties. Manetho appears to have divided the Theban experience into two groups, an earlier group lasting 39 years and a second group lasting 151 years. This diverges from the Turin Canon arrangement. There should also be a period of time that runs from the end of the Twelfth Dynasty until the split between Thebes and the Hyksos. This has not been accounted for in the Manetho reconstruction.

This runs counter to the Turin Canon, in which the first group lasted approximately 150 years and a second group about 50 years, almost the reverse of the Manetho numbers. It is my suggestion, admittedly speculative at this point, that the dividing date of 1727 is the year in which the Hyksos kings established Avaris as their capitol. The lack of an anchor date makes this difficult to resolve but 1727 is consistent with the high chronology range of dates (1742–1716) for the capture of Avaris. If I am correct, then one of the redactors confused the dividing point between the two groups of Theban kings, as presently indicated in the Turin Canon, with the dividing point for the capture of Avaris, and mistakenly assigned the latter's number of years to the 37 Theban kings that preceded the Eighteenth Dynasty.

Summary

This brings us to the end of the reconstruction of Manetho's Second Intermediate Period. I won't reiterate the unraveling of the many summation-line errors in the transmission of the original Manetho text but let me summarize the chronological results. Dates given assume a starting date of 1576 for the Eighteenth Dynasty.

In summarizing Manetho's chronology, we should note that he appears to have omitted the fifteen-year period between the end of the Twelfth Dynasty and the start of the Thebes-Hyksos split. This may be a product of the same error made by the Genesis chronographer, who raised the Twelfth Dynasty dates by 15 years. The error, in both cases, may have been the result of failing to properly account for Twelfth Dynasty co-regencies.

- The duration of Theban kings from the start of the Hyksos-Theban split (1766/67) to the beginning of the Eighteenth Dynasty (1576) was 190 years.
- Manetho's original text appeared to allow for 60 kings in the first group of Theban rulers and 37 kings in the second group of rulers, consistent with the Turin Canon's division of the groups of Theban rulers.
- Manetho has divided the Theban kings into two groups, separating them at the year 1727. The first group ruled for 39 years (1766/7–1727/28), the second for 151 years (1727–1576). This is not consistent with any dynastic arrangements presently suggested by our current knowledge of Second Intermediate Chronology and may represent some other event, such as the capture of Avaris.
- The duration of the Hyksos kings from the split with Thebes (1766/67) to the expulsion from Avaris in Ahmose's fourth year (1572) was 194 years. There appears to be a ten-year error in the Manetho transmission of the Fourteenth Dynasty, which only indicates a duration of 184 years. Evidence of the error was presented above in the summation line analysis.
- Manetho divided the Hyksos kings into two groups, a first group ruling 86 years (1766–1680) and a second group ruling 108 years (1680–1572). The original Manetho chronology agreed with the Turin Canon in allotting 32 kings to the first group and 6 kings to the second group.

Aligning the Patriarchal Chronology

In considering the alignment of the Patriarchal Chronology with the chronological evidence I have to admit that I am partially stymied by the lack of meaningful anchor dates to align with. The only meaningful hard data comes from the Turin Canon account of the Great Hyksos Dynasty. Other than that, the Turin Canon is heavily damaged with few reliable king names and lengths of reign. It gives us a list of Theban kings followed by a list of Hyksos kings followed by a list of more Theban kings. The experts simply cannot agree on where Theban dynasties begin or end, or how the Hyksos dynasties, however many there may be, align with each other.

The other constraint on the evidence is Manetho's badly garbled account of the Second Intermediate Period, which forms something of a template for dynastic divisions. As we saw, this template is relatively useless as a reasonable guide to dynastic divisions in the Second Intermediate Period. Within these parameters, we have some very good alignments, some highly speculative alignments, and some alignments that can't be made.

On the assumption that I have accurately worked out the original Manetho model for the Second Intermediate Period, we have three excellent alignment that clearly show that the Genesis chronographer had some good source knowledge of events in this era,

Peleg, whose name means "division," died in 1767 and Nahor died in 1766. Our Manetho reconstruction showed a Theban period of 190 years before the Eighteenth Dynasty and a Hyksos Period of 194 years down to the fourth year of King Ahmose, first king of the Eighteenth Dynasty. These two Manetho dates converge at 1767/1766, a strong indication that Peleg and Nahor constitute the "division" dates between the Thebans and the Hyksos.

Additionally, Nahor's son, Terah, died in 1680. The Turin Canon and the Manetho reconstruction both give the Great Hyksos Dynasty a duration of 108 years, which probably ended in the fourth year of king Ahmose (corroborated by Eusebius's indication that the Eighteenth Dynasty cut off during about the fourth/fifth year in Ahmose's reign.) This indicates a dynastic starting date of 1680. So, Nahor aligns precisely with the start of the first Hyksos dynasty, and his son aligns precisely with the start of the Great Hyksos Dynasty. It's hard to do much better than this.

Speculative Alignments

These three above alignments with Manetho and the Turin Canon provide an excellent chronological template that corresponds to the chronological evidence. This actually places us slightly ahead of the agreed upon consensus for the Second Intermediate Period. Unfortunately, that's as far as we can take the precision alignments. Because we lack sufficient dynastic data, I have to move into a more speculative mode.

Here is a list of the remaining Genesis 11 death dates still in issue.

- Reu, 1737
- Serug, 1714
- Arphaxad, 1667
- Shelah, 1637
- Shem, 1605

Of these names, only the first two fall within the Eber framework, that is people who were born after Eber and died before him. For these two, we have no clear and convincing evidence as to what the dates signify. As to Reu, I remain stymied. As to Serug, I have a speculative suggestion,

As noted above, there appears to have been a strong Hyksos expansion during the reigns of the 24th through 27th king in the Turin Canon. If we estimate a timeframe for the start of this Theban grouping it would probably begin somewhere between 65–75 years after the start of the Thirteenth Dynasty, or about 1717–1707. In the Patriarchal Chronology, Serug died in 1714 and this would be consistent with the timeframe in which Thebes may have been subdued by the Hyksos. Whether the ancient Egyptians considered this a dynastic division we can't say. Because this is a highly speculative theory, I am not including it in my final alignments, but offer it as a thesis still to be pursued.

As to the other three names on the above list, we are also in highly speculative territory. Arphaxad's death date, like his birth date, cannot be clearly associated with any specific event Egyptian event. As to Shelah and Shem, I have some very speculative thoughts that I offer only for consideration and I do not adopt these proposals at this time.

The Turin Canon, beginning with the end of the Twelfth Dynasty, has a sequence of 50 to 60 Theban kings and these are thought to encompass the Thirteenth Dynasty. As noted above, this group had a duration of 150 years, give or take a few years. Beckareth estimates a duration of about 145 years.[294] Kitchen suggests a period of 150–155 years.[295] If we take these as parameters, the Thirteenth Dynasty would have ended at about 1627 to 1637. Coincidentally, Shelah has a death date of 1637, consistent with Beckareth's estimated length. This suggests that Shelah may define the start of whatever Theban dynasty comes after the Thirteenth.

Shelah's death date, if we take it as the end point of the first group of Theban kings, defines the start of the Turn Canon's second group of Theban kings, ending with the last kings of the Seventeenth Dynasty. This date falls about 60 years before the start of the Eighteenth Dynasty. By convention, many Egyptologists refer to this second group of Theban kings as the Seventeenth Dynasty, but this is more a matter of convention and speculation than based on any actual dynastic declarations in the record. The one source we do have, the Turin Canon, singles out the last five kings in the list, these being members of the family that eventually ousted the Hyksos kings. Whether these last five kings should be considered a separate dynasty, or a continuation of the existing dynasty is a matter of speculation.

Unfortunately, we don't know how long these five kings ruled. The only data we have is that the last of the five, Kamose, reached at least a Year 3. It is my suggestion that Shem's death date, 1605, might demark the start of this family group. This is a tight squeeze. It allots about 29 years to this group of five kings. That leaves us with only about 32 years (1637–1605) for about 32 more kings, about one year each. If we did not allot the 30 years to the last five kings, the average length of reign would be about 2 years. So, very short reigns are clearly the trend. Given the rapid turnover, it's possible that there may have been some coregencies to ensure family continuity on the throne.

With the speculative date alignments for, Serug, Shelah, and Shem, we have gone as far as we can go for the relationship between the Patriarchal Chronology and the Second Intermediate Period. Let me now review what other Genesis dates fall within the Second Intermediate Period but which can't be aligned.

Patriarchal Dates That Can't Be Aligned

Outside of Genesis 5 and 11, we have several dates that fall within Eber's time span, but which cannot be reasonably aligned with Egyptian events. Their presence outside of Genesis 5 and 11 may indicate that they are only filler events for the purpose of continuity. They include the following Patriarchal Chronology dates.

- Noah's death date in 1755, shortly after the break between Thebes and the Hyksos
- Abram's death date in 1640, during the Great Hyksos Dynasty
- Isaac's birth date in 1715
- Jacob's birth date in 1655

Summary

The analysis above showed that the original version of Manetho's chronology had an almost uncanny correspondence to the Turin Canon. Once we removed the various layers of concatenated summation lines created by Manetho's redactors, we could establish the following similarities between the original Manetho and the Turin Canon.

- Both lists were subdivided into two groups of Theban kings (Thebes 1 and Thebes 2) and two groups of Hyksos kings (Hyksos 1 and Hyksos 2, the latter being the Great Hyksos Dynasty.)
- Both lists indicated that Thebes 1 had between 50–60 kings. Manetho specifically said there were 60 kings. The Turin Canon has room for 50–60 kings.
- Both lists indicated that Thebes 2 had 37–38 kings. Manetho had 37 kings. The Turin Canon had space for 37 to 38 kings depending upon

how many summation lines there were at the end of the list. (This count assumes at least one summation line in the 39th space.)

- Both lists indicated that Hyksos 1 had 32 kings.
- Both lists indicated that Hyksos 2 had 6 kings.
- Both lists indicated that Hyksos 2 ruled for 108 years.
- Both lists appear to have separated out the last five kings of Thebes 2, who were the members of the family that ousted Hyksos 2.

This degree of coincidence between the number of kings in the two lists is so close that there can be little doubt that both Manetho and the author of the Turin Canon had nearly identical archival data for the construction of the king-lists for the Second Intermediate Period.

Nevertheless, aside from the many redactional flaws in the transmission of Manetho regarding the duration of the various dynasties, two important differences between the Manetho redactions and the Turin Canon need to be mentioned.

First, the redacted Manetho disagrees with the Turin Canon as to how many years should be assigned to Thebes 1 and Thebes 2. The Turin Canon indicates that Thebes 1 lasted about 150 years, and Thebes 2 lasted about 56 years or so (assuming chronological boundaries of 1782 and 1576.) The Manetho redaction indicated that Thebes 1 lasted about 39 years and Thebes 2 lasted 151 years.

Since both lists are in close agreement as to the number of kings who populated Thebes 1 and Thebes 2, the Manetho dividing line is based on some other division than the separation between Thebes 1 and Thebes 2. What specific event it may reflect cannot be presently determined.

Second, the Turin Canon starts with the first king after the Twelfth Dynasty (or, at least, we assume this is the case,) and Manetho appears to have omitted the brief period of about 15–16 years between the end of the Twelfth Dynasty and the break between Thebes and the Hyksos. We should acknowledge, however, that both the Table of Abydos and the Table of Sakkara also omit this brief period, along with everything else between the end of the Twelfth Dynasty and the start of the Eighteenth Dynasty. This suggest a good deal more turmoil and confusion in this brief period following the Thirteenth Dynasty than is usually acknowledged. We should also acknowledge that for at least 6 of these years, the Turin Canon shows no king ruling in Thebes.

It is also possible that Manetho's error may be a mirror-image of the Genesis chronographer's 15-year error in the Twelfth Dynasty, which, I suggested, were the result of confusion over how to account for the coregencies in that dynasty. The Genesis author pushed the dates back from their original position. Manetho may have pushed the dates 15 years forward in the succeeding dynasty.

Whatever the explanation, our analysis of the Manetho redactions showed that the original Manetho indicated that the total duration of the Theban period, from the break with the Hyksos to the start of the Eighteenth Dynasty lasted 190 years (1767–1576) and the corresponding Hyksos period lasted 194 years (1766–1572.) It also showed that Hyksos 2 lasted 108 years, from 1680–1572.

We also saw from the Turin Canon, that following the start of Dynasty 13 there was a six-year period without a king in Thebes, that also appears to have ended at about 1766/67, although the duration is not precisely fixed. And, of course, the Turn Canon also showed that Hyksos 2 lasted 108 years.

The Patriarchal Chronology, when considered with other chronological data, established boundaries of 1782 for the end of the Twelfth Dynasty and 1576 for the start of the Eighteenth Dynasty. In that context, we saw that Peleg and Nahor had death dates of 1767 and 1766 respectively, coinciding precisely with the Manetho data for the split between Thebes and the Hyksos. Intriguingly, Peleg's name translates into English as "division, break-up."

Additionally, we saw that Nahor's son, Terah, had a death date of 1680. This indicated that Nahor's death signified the start of Hyksos 1 and his son's death date signified the start of Hyksos 2. The Patriarchal Chronology seemed to acknowledge this by placing Nahor's death date out of order in the chronological sequence of births.

Of the five Patriarchal Chronology death dates that belonged to the Eber framework, three provided us with starting dates for Thebes 1, Hyksos 1, and Hyksos 2, with durations identical to Manetho's original figures for the Second Intermediate Period, Eber's own death date provided us with the High Chronology the date for the start of the Eighteenth Dynasty, This provides strong proof that the Genesis chronographer had access to accurate accounts of the Second Intermediate Period, as understood by Manetho and the author of the Turin Canon, and that his chronological scheme was consistent with the dynastic history of this era, a period that is still notably difficult to untangle from the available evidence.

8 Joseph and the Rise of Egyptian Empire

AHMOSE'S DEFEAT OF THE HYKSOS MARKED HIM AS THE FOUNDER OF THE Eighteenth Dynasty, the beginning of the New Kingdom. The Eighteenth Dynasty, based on choices over High and Low chronologies and various theories to fill in some gaps, lasted about 250 years, give or take a decade or two. In the present study, I am only concerned with approximately the first half of the Eighteenth Dynasty.

Table 8.1, *Alternative chronologies for the first seven rulers of the Eighteenth Dynasty*, shows several alternative chronologies for that group of kings within the Eighteenth Dynasty. As you can see, even within the High and Low Chronologies there are some disagreements as to how long various pharaohs ruled and in what years they served.

Chronological Overview

For the Eighteenth Dynasty we have three key astronomically determined dates that define the debate over the correct chronology for this dynasty, but there is some argument over what these three dates should be. One is the Sothic date for the ninth year of Amenhotep I. The other two involve lunar dates for the first years of Thutmose III and the Nineteenth Dynasty pharaoh Ramesses II. Despite the differences of opinion, the high and low chronologies differ by no more than about twenty-five years.

We have already reviewed the Sothic date data for the ninth year of Amenhotep I and based on that data we have associated 1576, the year of Eber's death, with the year that Ahmose became the king of

Table 8.1: Alternative chronologies for the first seven rulers of the Eighteenth Dynasty

King/Queen	High Chronologies				Low Chronologies			
	Gardiner[a] (1961)	CAH[b] (1973)	Wente/ van Siclen[c] (1977)	Redford[d] (1984)	Kitchen[e] (1996)	Beckerath[f] (1997)	Shaw[g] (2000)	Krauss/ Warburton[h] (2006)
Ahmose	1575-1550	1570-1546	1570-1546	1569-1545	1540-1515	1550-1525	1550-1525	1539-1515
Amenhotep I	1550-1528	1546-1526	1551-1524	1545-1525	1515-1494	1525-1504	1525-1504	1514-1494
Thutmose I	1528-1510	1525-1512	1524-1518	1525-1514	1494-1482	1504-1492	1504-1492	1493-1483
Thutmose II	1510-1490	1512-1504	1518-1504	1514-1504	1482-1479	1492-1479	1492-1479	1482-1480
Hatshepsut	1490-1468	1503-1482	1503-1483	1502-1483	1478-1457	1473-1458	1473-1458	1479-1458
Thutmose III	1490-1436	1504-1450	1504-1450	1504-1451	1478-1424	1479-1425	1479-1425	1479-1425
Amenhotep II	1436-1413	1450-1425	1453-1419	1453-1426	1424-1398	1428-1397	1427-1400	1425-1400

[a] (Gardiner 1961), 443.
[b] (Cambridge Ancient History 1971), Vol II: Part 1.
[c] (Wente and Van Siclen III 1977), 218.
[d] (Redford 1984), 13.

[e] (Kitchen 1996), 12.
[f] (Beckerath 1997), 119-123.
[g] (Shaw 2000), 484-485.
[h] (Krauss and Warburton 2006), 492.

Thebes. For Thutmose III, based on the lunar data, the advocates of the High Chronology see 1504 or 1490 as the starting date for this pharaoh, with most favoring 1504;[296] and, as seen in Table 8.1, advocates of the Low Chronology accept 1479 as the likely date. For Ramesses II, based on the lunar dates, likely starting dates are either 1304, 1290, or 1279.[297]

For the Ramesses starting date, there is no perfect solution to this problem because all three choices assume that there was an observational error made by the person recording the lunar date.[298] According to Wente and Van Siclen III, one type of error "could easily be caused by unfavorable atmospheric conditions, when cloudiness, haze, or smoke from village fires might obscure the visibility of a final lunar crescent with the result that New Moon day would be declared one day in advance of actual conjunction."[299] The 1304 and 1279 dates assume just such an error.[300] Advocates of the 1290 date propose an error where the observer thought they saw a final crescent when none was actually present.[301]

On the assumption that it is more likely that a trained observer might fail to see a crescent due to blockage than to mistakenly see one when it wasn't there, the 1304 and 1279 dates are generally preferred among Egyptologists. Because these dates are twenty-five years apart, which one is chosen can have a substantial impact on the dates for the Eighteenth Dynasty. Because this study follows the High Chronology, I accept 1304 as the starting date for Ramesses II.

In addition to the lunar and Sothic dates, we have several inscriptions that give us high year marks for many of the pharaohs and in several cases final year markers for the last year of reign. We also have a few gaps in the record that have to be filled in by guesswork, the decisions being controlled primarily by what choices one makes regarding the astronomically determined dates.

For our purposes in this chapter, the most problematic issue concerns the lengths of reign for Thutmose I and his successor Thutmose II. For Thutmose I, the highest certain year marker is Year 4, with a less certain possibility of a Year 9.[302] However, many Egyptologists are concerned that 4 years is too short a period for this pharaoh's military accomplishments, and 9 years or more might be appropriate. Gardiner has proposed a reign of 18 years but that has little support.[303] Wente and Van Siclen, on the other hand, propose a reign of 6 or 7 years.[304]

For Thutmose II, we have a Year 1 marker and a controversial possibility of a Year 14 or 18. At the center of the dispute is a lost copy of an inscription prepared by George Daressy, a prominent Egyptologist. Daressy's copy of the inscription indicated a high-year marker of 18 for Thutmose II, but, unfortunately, his papers have been lost.

Wente and Van Siclen III discuss this lost inscription.[305] Though admitting that it cannot easily be dismissed they add that Daressy was not noted for epigraphic accuracy and may have miscopied "14" as "18", a mistake which may have arisen from damage to the broken stele from which the inscription was copied.[306] On the other hand, some argue that this "18-year" marker belongs to a different king.[307] As a practical matter, the dividing point between Thutmose I and Thutmose II is uncertain and the decision is made on the basis of how one resolves issues related to the reigns of other pharaohs and whether you work with the High or Low Chronologies.

Ahmose's successor, Amenhotep I, has a high-year marker of 21.[308] Assuming no coregencies between Amenhotep I and either his predecessor and his successor, we would have the following chronological sequence, give or take a year or so depending on rounding errors.

- Ahmose (1576–1551)
- Amenhotep I (1550–1529)
- Thutmose I (1528 starting date)

For now, we skip over the end date for Thutmose I and the starting date for Thutmose II and build back to establish an end date for the latter. In the High Chronology, Thutmose III came to the throne in 1504. Because this pharaoh came to the throne as a child, Hatshepsut, his Queen-mother, served as a coregent for the first part of his reign. This establishes an end date of 1505/4 for Thutmose II. Therefore, assuming a dynastic starting date of about 1576,

Thutmose I and II ruled in sequence from 1528 to 1505, and any solution to the dividing point between the two requires that we take these parameters into question.

Thutmose III ruled in total just short of fifty-four years, giving him an end date of 1450.[309] His successor was Amenhotep II and there is a question of whether Thutmose III and Amenhotep II shared a period of coregency. Several Egyptologists, including Redford, Wente, Van Siclen and Parker, believe there was a coregency that lasted 2 years and 4 months.[310] Others dispute this, and the issue remains unresolved.[311] Assuming the coregency, Amenhotep II came to the throne at about 1453.

Our specific chronological concerns in this chapter end with the ascension of Amenhotep II to the throne. Before returning to the Patriarchal Chronology, I want to touch on a few historical issues involving this group of Pharaohs.

The Rise of Egyptian Empire

Egypt's Eighteenth Dynasty arose in the context of an 11-year war to expel the foreign Hyksos rulers. Something like this had never happened in Egypt before and the impact may have inadvertently led to major changes in the nature of Egyptian kingship. Hayes writes, "Out of the struggles to regain her independence and her ascendancy over the warlike nations of Western Asia, Egypt during the Eighteenth Dynasty emerged, for the first time in her history, as a predominantly military state under the rule of a king dedicated from early youth to the leadership of the army and navy and to the expansion and consolidation of his empire by force of arms."[312] The young heirs-apparent to the throne received extensive training in the arts of war, becoming quite skilled in archery, charioteering, and ship-handling.[313]

Redford attributes the empire of the New Kingdom to three kings, Thutmose I, Thutmose III, and Amenhotep II.[314] "The first" he said, "established an ideal, the second lived up to the ideal and won an empire, the third nearly lost it."[315] Thutmose I engaged in several foreign battles, including a campaign in which the Egyptian army crossed over the Euphrates.[316] For several centuries thereafter, only Thutmose III was able to venture that far to the north-east.[317] Thutmose II put down rebellions in Nubia and waged campaigns in Canaan.[318] Under Thutmose III, Egypt reached the highest stage of its military influence, with military conquests in Nubia, northern Sudan and south-western Asia.[319] Hayes says, "during the thirty-two years of his independent reign (1482–1450 B.C) Thutmose III proved himself to be, incontestably, the greatest pharaoh ever to occupy the throne of Egypt."[320] (Hayes dates the independent reign to 1450 because he rejects the coregency between Thutmose III and Amenhotep II.)

Militarism and military conquest, however, was not the only major change introduced under the Thutmoses. Thutmose III launched a major exploitation of the nation's resources, augmented by his many conquests.[321] He ruled the kingdom with absolute power, and paid great personal attention to the details of administration.[322] While a king's power usually rested on the idea that he was a god, Thutmose III took further steps. According to Hayes, he took direct control over the machinery of government, including the army and navy, the legislative and judicial branches of government, and probably the priesthood.[323] Hayes adds, that while this description of government power rests primarily on what we know about Thutmose III, "it is clear that this pattern of kingship followed by Thutmose III had already been established by his grandfather, Thutmose I, and was maintained, in so far as their abilities permitted, by his son and grandson, Amenhotep II and Thutmose IV, and, in the early years of his reign, by his great-grandson Amenhotep III."[324]

In the biblical stories about Joseph, who became prime minister of Egypt, his policies on behalf of the pharaoh also transformed the Egyptian monarch into an almost absolute ruler with unpresented power over the people and resources of the nation. It would be interesting, therefore, to see how the Joseph chronology coincides with Thutmose III and the rise of Egyptian empire.

The Joseph Chronology

Joseph is arguably the most important character in the Book of Genesis. Because of him the Israelites moved to Egypt and through him the covenant with God passed to the nation of Israel. His death marks the final event in the Book of Genesis.

Although he was the eleventh of Jacob's twelve sons, he was the first-born of Rachel, Jacob's beloved wife, and Joseph rapidly became Jacob's favorite son. At an early age he demonstrated a facility for dream interpretation, an indication that he had a close connection with God. A somewhat precocious and rather obnoxious child, at an early age he interpreted several dreams to mean that he would become the family leader and that all would bow down before him, even (to their disappointment and shock) Jacob and Rachel.

His brothers grew to hate him and his grandiose prophecies and plotted to kill him, but at the last minute the idea repelled even them. Instead, they sold him into slavery. To explain his disappearance to his father, they soaked Joseph's famous multi-colored robe in blood and told their father that an evil beast had devoured his favorite son.

The slave traders carried Joseph to Egypt and sold him to Potipher, a high official in the Egyptian court. Joseph served Potipher well, running the household and managing his affairs, and Potipher prospered. Unfortunately, Potipher's wife took a liking to Joseph and tried to seduce him. Joseph, loyal to his master, rejected her enticements and angered her. To get even, she told her husband that Joseph had tried to force himself on her. Potipher couldn't quite believe this about his trusted servant but couldn't allow his wife to be thought of as a liar. So, he had Joseph imprisoned.

While in prison, Joseph continued to demonstrate his ability to interpret dreams and his reputation spread to the pharaoh, who was deeply disturbed by some of the visions in his sleep, the meanings of which defied his own counselors. As a last desperate measure Pharaoh sent for Joseph and put the dreams to him. In his first dream,

> [Pharaoh] stood by the river. And, behold, there came up out of the river seven well favoured kine and fatfleshed; and they fed in a meadow. And, behold, seven other kine came up after them out of the river, ill favoured and leanfleshed; and stood by the other kine upon the brink of the river. And the ill favoured and

leanfleshed kine did eat up the seven well favoured and fat kine.[325]

And, in his second dream

[S]even ears of corn came up upon one stalk, rank and good. And, behold, seven thin ears and blasted with the east wind sprung up after them. And the seven thin ears devoured the seven rank and full ears.[326]

Joseph listened carefully to what the pharaoh had to say and then explained to him the meaning of the dreams. Egypt was about to enter a seven-year period of great prosperity. However, these seven "fat" years will be followed by seven "lean" years in which famine spreads throughout the land. That the two dreams followed so closely upon each other, he said, indicated that the period in question was close in hand. Joseph gave Pharaoh the following advice:

Now therefore let Pharaoh look out a man discreet and wise, and set him over the land of Egypt. Let Pharaoh do this, and let him appoint officers over the land, and take up the fifth part of the land of Egypt in the seven plenteous years. And let them gather all the food of those good years that come, and lay up corn under the hand of Pharaoh, and let them keep food in the cities. And that food shall be for store to the land against the seven years of famine, which shall be in the land of Egypt; that the land perish not through the famine.[327]

The pharaoh, thoroughly impressed with Joseph's performance and advice, appointed Joseph to the post of Prime Minister. Joseph was 30 years old when appointed pharaoh and served with distinction.[328] In accord with his prophesy, Egypt experienced seven wonderful years of prosperity and, on cue, the famine arrived in the eighth year. The famine devastated Egypt but the pharaoh, pursuant to Joseph's advice, had vast grain storages. This had some consequences for the land of Egypt.

Now there was no food in all the land, for the famine was very severe. The land of Egypt and the land of Canaan languished because of the famine. Joseph collected all the money to be found in the land of Egypt and in the land of Canaan, in exchange for the grain that they bought; and

Joseph brought the money into Pharaoh's house. When the money from the land of Egypt and from the land of Canaan was spent, all the Egyptians came to Joseph, and said, "Give us food! Why should we die before your eyes? For our money is gone." And Joseph answered, "Give me your livestock, and I will give you food in exchange for your livestock, if your money is gone." So they brought their livestock to Joseph; and Joseph gave them food in exchange for the horses, the flocks, the herds, and the donkeys. That year he supplied them with food in exchange for all their livestock. When that year was ended, they came to him the following year, and said to him, "We can not hide from my lord that our money is all spent; and the herds of cattle are my lord's. There is nothing left in the sight of my lord but our bodies and our lands. Shall we die before your eyes, both we and our land? Buy us and our land in exchange for food. We with our land will become slaves to Pharaoh; just give us seed, so that we may live and not die, and that the land may not become desolate." So Joseph bought all the land of Egypt for Pharaoh. All the Egyptians sold their fields, because the famine was severe upon them; and the land became Pharaoh's. As for the people, he made slaves of them from one end of Egypt to the other. Only the land of the priests he did not buy; for the priests had a fixed allowance from Pharaoh, and lived on the allowance that Pharaoh gave them; therefore they did not sell their land. Then Joseph said to the people, "Now that I have this day bought you and your land for Pharaoh, here is seed for you; sow the land. And at the harvests you shall give one-fifth to Pharaoh, and four-fifths shall be your own, as seed for the field and as food for yourselves and your households, and as food for your little ones." They said, "You have saved our lives; may it please my lord, we will be slaves to Pharaoh." So Joseph made it a statute concerning the land of Egypt, and it stands to this day, that Pharaoh should have the fifth. The land of the priests alone did not become Pharaoh's.329

If this description of the Pharaoh's accumulation of power and authority over all of Egypt's land and resources sounds suspiciously parallel to the rise of the all-powerful state under the Thutmoses, we will see in a moment that this is no coincidence.

The famine had a second consequence. It reached into Canaan, in the land where Jacob and his children dwelled. Needing grain, Jacob sent his children to Egypt to buy some provisions. When they arrived in the Pharaoh's court, Joseph immediately recognized them, but they did not recognize him. Seeing an opportunity to explore their ethical and moral status, Joseph subjected them to several dramatic tests, generating fear and tension both among his brothers and his father. Finally, Joseph revealed his identity, made peace with his brothers, and invited his family to live in Egypt where Pharaoh gave them a land of their own.

Joseph's Birth and Death Chronology

We have already established the birth and death dates for Joseph as 1564 and 1454. The dates are significant. Ahmose's battle to crush the Hyksos lasted about 11 years. We have dated the start of his reign to 1576. Allowing for rounding off partial years, Joseph's birth date corresponds to the year in Ahmose's reign when the Hyksos threat to Egypt ended.

As indicated above, there is some disagreement over whether Thutmose III and his successor, Amenhotep II, shared a short coregency. Hornung, in his summary of some of the arguments, says that many authors side with Redford and Parker in advocating a coregency of 2 years and 4 months but the issue remains unresolved.[330] Thutmose III died sometime during 1450. If we accept the existence of this coregency, then Amenhotep II came to the throne at about1453, marking Joseph's death date as the last independent year of reign of Thutmose III before the start of the co-regency with his successor.

Genesis ends with the death of Joseph and, therefore, at the height of Egypt's greatest power. The next book of the bible, Exodus, tells of Egypt's crushing fall in its failed challenge to the god of Moses. I suspect, therefore, that choosing this end date for Joseph was an intentional act to serve as a contrast for what follows next in Egypt's confrontation with the people of Israel.

Having established the chronological boundaries of Joseph's birth and death, the defeat of the Hyksos and Egypt's rise to its political height, we should now turn our attention to the internal chronology within the life of Joseph.

The Famine Chronology

We have three dates in the Joseph story related to the famine. Joseph became Prime Minster of Egypt at the age of thirty, which would be 1534. The seven 'fat" years would begin at this time, with the pharaoh accumulating grain as a reserve for the seven lean years. The good years ended in 1527/28; the bad years in 1520/21.

If we look at Table 8.1 at the various Thutmose I High Chronologies, we see some proposed starting dates of 1528, 1525, and 1524. I suggest that the 1527/28 date for the beginning of the famine, during which the pharaoh started to increase his power over the Egyptian government, makes an excellent fit as the High Chronology starting date for Thutmose I, when a similar rise of power began to occur.

How long Thutmose I ruled is one of the problematic gaps in our record. The only certain high-year mark we have is 4 years.[331] There is a possible high-year mark of 9 years, but it is not considered reliable. The chief objection to a four-year reign is that this pharaoh's military campaigns seem to extensive for such a short period.

It is my suggestion that the end of the seven famine years, 1520/21, marks the end of Thutmose I's reign. Wente and Van Siclen give this pharaoh a reign of 6–7 years in their chronology,[332] Unfortunately, due to the lack of more definite archaeological evidence, we can only say that the 7-year period is plausible, and consistent with the archaeological evidence, but not certain.

As to what event coincides with the start of the 7 good years and Joseph's elevation to Prime Minister of Egypt at the age of 30, in the year 1534, we have no good answer. The date falls at the start of the last seven years of Amenhotep I, and we have no reasonable known event to relate the date to. It may reflect some political transformation taking place in Amenhotep's reign that led to the increased drive for political power or some event in Thutmose I's career prior to taking the throne, but we can only guess that this is the case.

A date that we should have expected to find, would have been the start of the reign for Thutmose III in 1504. The closest we can come is the death date for Jacob, who died in 1508. The 4-year gap is too large to accept. I'd like to think that perhaps there was an error in transmission, but it seems unlikely that a required life-span of 151 years would accidentally become the 147 years assigned to Jacob.

The only other Patriarchal date in the Eighteenth Dynasty is the year of Isaac's death, 1535. That it is virtually identical to the 1534 date for Joseph's rise to Prime Minister and the start of the seven good years, further suggesting that something important in Egyptian history happened at about 1534/35. For now, what that was remains an open issue.

Summary

For Joseph, we have the following chronology. His birth date, 1564, coincides with the final defeat of the Hyksos by the founder of the Eighteenth Dynasty, a battle that lasted about 11 years. His death date, 1454, coincides with the last year of independent reign by Thutmose III, if the dynasty began in 1576 and there was a coregency of 2 years and 4 months with Amenhotep II.

The start of the 7 lean years begin in 1527/28, which date closely aligns with the start of the reign of Thutmose I. The end of the 7 lean years, 1521/20, is a plausible date for the beginning of the reign of Thutmose II, but we lack sufficient information to determine the true dividing point between Thutmose I and Thutmose II.

Joseph's birth and death dates coincide, respectively, with Ahmose's final victory over the Great Hyksos dynasty and the end of the independent reign of Thutmose III, considered by many Egyptologists as the greatest emperor in Egyptian history. This period, in both Egyptian history and in the Genesis Joseph stories marks a massive transformation in the nature and power of the Egyptian pharaoh over the Egyptian people and the nation's resources. Joseph's death mark's off Egypt's rise to its greatest power and influence in that country's history. Exodus, the succeeding book of the bible, depicts the fall of this great empire at the hands of the Hebrew God and the rise of Israel as an independent political entity.

Based on the Patriarchal chronology, we have the following key dates for the Eighteenth Dynasty chronology. (Bolded dates indicate a match with Genesis events.)

1576, Ahmose, founder of the Eighteenth Dynasty becomes king of Thebes.

1564, Ahmose administers final defeat the Great Hyksos Fifteenth Dynasty.

1550, start of Amenhotep I, second king.

1528, start of Thutmose I, third king of the dynasty.

1521, possible start of Thutmose II, fourth king of the dynasty.

1504, start of Thutmose III, fifth king of the dynasty, (and coregency with Hatshepsut).

1454, start of coregency between Thutmose III and his successor, Amenhotep II.

We had dates in the Patriarchal chronology in the Eighteenth Dynasty, that we couldn't identify with specific political events. Isaac died in 1535 and Jacob died in 1508. Neither date appears in the Genesis 5 or Genesis 11 sequence and are, therefore, less secure as specific political dates, and may be just connective filler to Joseph. However, Isaac's death date coincides with Joseph's rise to prime minister in 1534, reinforcing the idea that 1534/5 may have signified the date of some important event seven years before the end of Amenhotep I's reign. Jacob's death date of 1508 is close to, but not close enough to, the 1504 starting date for Thutmose III, and we would expect that that king's starting date should have been memorialized. It is possible, therefore, that there was an error in calculating the number of years Jacob lived in order to match Thutmose III's starting date. Given the lack of certainty, we will leave the 1534/35 and 1508 dates open for future discussion.

9 Conclusions

IN CHAPTER ONE, I SAID, "WHEN THE EVIDENCE IS FULLY PRESENTED, there should be no reasonable doubt that the Patriarchal Chronology is a document based on Egyptian chronology and that the author must have been working from Egyptian archival records." I am satisfied that I have met that burden. Let me set out the evidence and show what it proved.

Methodology Issues

Apart from Manetho's chronology, about which more below, I have stayed strictly within the confines of traditional mainstream Egyptian studies. Where relevant, I have noted those issues where the experts agree or disagree, explained the nature of such disagreements, and showed how those issues affected my analysis. Two major disagreements dominate Egyptian chronological studies.

From the Twelfth Dynasty on, the primary conflict is over what anchor dates to use for the Twelfth and Eighteenth Dynasties. There are two kings, one in the Twelfth Dynasty and one in the Eighteenth Dynasty, for which we have a Sothic sighting in a specific year of that king's reign. For a third king, also in the Eighteenth Dynasty, we have a Sothic sighting not tied down to a year, but we have a lunar sighting that provides some parameters.

The problem is that Egyptologists disagree as to where the Sothic sightings occurred and in which of three possible years (over a 25-year range) the lunar sighting occurred. If the Sothic sighting occurred in Memphis, we have one set of possible dates. If the sighting occurred in Thebes, we have a separate set of possible dates. The Memphis dates fall earlier than the Theban dates. This leads to a split between advocates of a High Chronology (earlier dates with a Memphite sighting) and a Low Chronology (later dates with a Theban sighting.) Within each camp there is a range of possible dates for the sighting and within each camp there is a tendency to rally around a narrow range within the respective ranges.

For most of twentieth century Egyptology, the High Chronology was considered the standard chronology. In the late twentieth century to the present a consensus has shifted towards the Low Chronology. There is no smoking gun in either camp that can resolve this issue. However, in this study, I have showed that the Patriarchal Chronology consistently aligns with the high end of the High Chronology. If my thesis is correct, then the Patriarchal Chronology provides an independent source that demonstrates the validity of the High Chronology.

The second major chronological conflict concerns the nature of the cattle censuses in the Third through Sixth Dynasties. Numerous inscriptions show that events in a king's reign occurred in connection with a numbered cattle count. However, in some cases, we have inscriptions showing that an event occurred in the year after a cattle count and, in some cases, we have indications that cattle counts occurred in consecutive years. The question, therefore, is whether cattle counts were mostly done on an irregular basis, a biennial basis, or on an annual basis.

The traditional view has been that the cattle counts were done on a biennial basis but occasionally in a consecutive year. Some Egyptologists now argue that the cattle counts may have occurred on an annual basis but occasionally skipped a year. This leads to two conflicting approaches to determining in what year of a king's reign a cattle count occurred. Again, we have a dispute between advocates of a High Chronology, who favor biennial counts as the norm, unless there is evidence suggesting an occasional cattle count might have occurred in consecutive years, and advocates of a Low Chronology, who favor annual cattle counts unless there is evidence that an occasional cattle count may have skipped a year. The longer a king ruled, the greater the chronological distance between the two camps.

Unless a cattle count references a king's death, the cattle counts only reflect a minimum length of reign. Therefore, I have referred to the High Chronology view as the Maximum Minimum length of reign and the Low Chronology as the Minimum Minimum length of reign. During this study, the Patriarchal Chronology consistently aligned with the Maximum Minimum lengths of reign, a strong independent indication that biennial cattle counts were the normal practice.

The one major area where I have departed from mainstream Egyptology, concerns my reconstructions of Manetho's original chronology. The fact of the matter is that Egyptological work on Manetho has been appalling. While the professionals acknowledge that the Manetho data seems to have roots in ancient sources, outside of my own work (and to the best of my knowledge) no Egyptologist has engaged in a systemic analysis of the Manetho sources to see if they can reconstruct Manetho's original chronology, in whole or part. Instead, they simply cherry-pick Manetho's data to fill in a gap here and there when they think such will enhance their own chronological theories.

In this study, I used Manetho's many overlong lengths of reign and dynastic durations as clues to indicate some sort of double-counting was going on in the transmission of sources. Wherever possible, I used the known archaeological data as a control process on my reconstructions and used simple logical numerical pattern analysis to do the reconstruction. I suspect that most Egyptologists, like most scholars in most non-STEM fields, tend to be uncomfortable around non-simple arithmetic.

My approach frequently assumed, as a starting point, that excessive lengths of reign or dynastic durations must have been due to scribal confusion in the transmission of summary data, either summation lines in the text or marginal summary notations made by earlier scribes during transmission. The confusion frequently involved equating partial summations for group kings with the length of reign for a particular king in the group or as a reference to an additional king with an additional length of reign. I corroborated this approach by showing that very often the proposed original data for Manetho frequently, if not perfectly, aligned with the other Egyptian king-lists and/or archaeological data.

More remarkable, in several instances, when simple logical analysis showed how the Manetho data was corrupted, the reconstructed chronology wound up in virtually perfect agreement with the Patriarchal Chronology as to the durations of several dynasties, and such data reconstructions were consistent with the Turin Canon and other king-lists.

Admittedly, this study depends in large part on my analysis and reconstruction of Manetho's data. But, even before we got to the Manetho material, when we looked at an outline of the proposed Patriarchal Chronology dynastic dates and durations and compared them with corresponding proposal outlines from various mainstream experts on Egyptian chronology, we could already see that the Patriarchal Chronology data shared a similar chronological pattern with the averages of the dates and durations proposed by the experts.

I should acknowledge that I made one important correction to one portion of the Genesis chronology. For all the Patriarchal Chronology dates falling in the Middle Kingdom (Eleventh and Twelfth Dynasties), other than Eber's birth date, I uniformly moved each birth date later by 15 years. When this was done, we saw that five out of six birth dates aligned almost perfectly with the standard High Chronology dates for five kings in the Twelfth Dynasty. Since this 15-year correction was applied uniformly over the entire group of dates, I think it appropriate to call it a correction rather than an example of cherry-picking or data manipulation.

As to Eber, we saw that his birth and death dates (2040, 1576) corresponded to High Chronology dates for the unification of Thebes in the Middle and New Kingdoms. I didn't add 15 years to his birth date because I assumed that it was obtained independently, the product of one of the most celebrated events among the ancient Egyptians. I wouldn't be surprised to learn that independent Sothic dates had been recorded for both unifications, although no such discovery has yet been made. I suspect the error came about because of the large number of coregencies in the Twelfth Dynasty, approximately 15 years' worth depending on how you round off the partial years, and that the Genesis author (or perhaps the author's source) mistakenly treated the coregency time as an extension of the dynasty's duration.

As to Enoch, we saw that his 365-year life span pointed precisely to the start of a Sothic Cycle, an Egyptian system for dealing with the lack of a leap-year in their 365-day solar calendar.

That left Only Methuselah's birth year as the possible starting for the First Dynasty. In this study, Methuselah's life span represented the duration of the Memphite Kingdom. Methuselah lived for 969 years. As noted in our study, Gardiner indicated that the Turin Canon assigned about 955 years to the first six dynasties, the same duration encompassed by Methuselah's life span, but the Turin Canon omitted about 9 or 10 kings with brief reigns from its Sixth Dynasty roster whereas the Methuselah span included that additional group of kings, bringing the Patriarchal Chronology into approximate agreement with the Turin Canon.

I mention these additional items here under methodology, to show that even without Manetho we have several important clues to the Egyptian origins of the Patriarchal Chronology. To quickly summarize:

- The outline of the Patriarchal Chronology dynastic dates and durations has the same general (if not precise) pattern as the averages for the various expert proposals for these same dynasties and durations;
- Enoch's 365-year life span pointed to the exact date thought by many Egyptologists to be the start of a Sothic Cycle;
- Methuselah's birth date plausibly coincided with the the start of the First Dynasty, and was the only date (other than Enoch's) in the Patriarchal Chronology that could be considered consistent with that starting date;
- Methuselah's life span of 969 years, as a proposed duration for the first six dynasties coincides very closely with the 955 years indicated by the Turin Canon, but the Methuselah figure includes a few extra kings with short reigns that were omitted by the Turin Canon.
- Eber's birth and death dates align with High Chronology dates for the first and second Theban unifications of Egypt;
- Without Manetho's input, subject to a 15-year uniform correction of the Patriarchal Chronology birth dates for Eber's Genesis 11

descendants, we had five dates in near perfect alignment with the standard High Chronology dates for 5 kings in the Twelfth Dynasty;

- With the same 15-year correction for Eber's father, we had the High Chronology date for the start of Menthotpe II's reign, the Theban king who unified Egypt during the Eleventh Dynasty.

The Manetho data greatly enhances our conclusion, but as the above shows, even without Manetho, we have substantial evidence pointing to a relationship between the Patriarchal Chronology and the Egyptian king-lists.

The Dynastic Correspondences

The Genesis 5 and 11 chronologies encompass 20 generations of Patriarchs and provide 38 birth and death dates. (The death dates for Noah and Abram fall outside of Genesis 5 and 11.) If we go outside of the Genesis 5 and 11 passages, we add three more generations, and have a grand total of 46 dates. The time frame covered ends in the early 18th Dynasty, so not all Patriarchal Chronology dates can define dynastic starting dates, and, as we saw, several Patriarchal Chronology dates coincide with the staring dates for several kings within the dynasties. Unfortunately, due to a lack of sufficient Egyptological data, some Patriarchal Chronology dates could not be associated with important Egyptian political events.

In addition to the collection of dates, we also have some patterns for how the dynastic dates are distributed. Table 9.1, *Egypt's Dynastic Chronology as Depicted in the Patriarchal Chronology*, provides a summary of the dynastic information gleaned from my analysis. Let me begin with some observations about the distribution of the dynastic data as it aligns with the Egyptian political divisions.

The Methuselah Grouping

Methuselah stands as a dividing line between the mythological chronology and the First Dynasty. His birth simultaneously represents the end of the mythic period and the start of the historic period. His life span encompasses the duration and dynastic breakdown for the Memphite Kingdom.

Table 9.1. Egypt's Dynastic Chronology as Depicted in the Patriarchal Chronology

Dynasty	Patriarch	Starting Dates	Years
Memphite Dynasties/Old Kingdom			
1/Unity, Start	**Methuselah**	**b. 3074**	**243**
2	Adam	d. 2831	112
3	Seth	d. 2719	98
4a	Enosh	d. 2621	95
4b	Kenan	d. 2526	55
Sum 4a+4b			150
5	Mahalalel	d. 2471	132
6-8	Jared	d. 2339	234
End of Kingdom	**Methuselah**	**d. 2105**	**969**
First Intermediate Period/Heracleopolitan Rivals			
9/10	Genesis 6:1-3	225	185
Middle Kingdom/Thebes *Except for Eber, I have subtracted 15 years for each of the Genesis Middle Kingdom birth dates.*			
11/start **Menthotpe II**	Shelah	**b. 2070 / 2055**	
11/unity **Menthotpe II**	**Eber**	**b. 2040**	
12/ Start Amenemhe I	Peleg	b. 2006 / 1991	
Senwosre I	Reu	b. 1976 / 1961	
Amenemhe II	Serug	b. 1944 / 1929	
Senwosre II	Nahor	b. 1914 / 1899	
Senwosre III	Terah	b. 1885 / 1870	
Amenemhe III	-		
Amenemhe IV	Abram	b. 1815 / 1800	
Sebeknofru	-		
13/early unity	-		
Second Intermediate Period/Theban and Hyksos Rulers			
13 Thebes/split	Peleg	**d. 1767**	190
14 Hyksos	Nahor	d. 1766	86
15 Hyksos	Terah	d. 1680	108
16 ?			
17 Thebes end	Eber	d. 1576	
New Kingdom			
18/Start	**Eber**	**d. 1576**	

Methuselah has seven ancestors, including his father Enoch. If we remove Enoch from the list, since he serves as a pointer to the Sothic Cycle, the six remaining birth dates for his ancestors fall into the predynastic period.

The death dates for these same six ancestors form the sequence of Memphite Kingdom starting dates from Dynasty 2 through 6. (Dynasty 4 was separated into two parts.) Methuselah's birth date signifies the start of the First Dynasty and his death marks the end of the Sixth Dynasty. This means we have a pattern relationship between Methuselah's ancestors, with births forming one chronological period and deaths forming the next chronological period.

Of Egypt's first 18 dynasties, starting dates for the first six fall into the Methuselah time frame. The existence of a Dynasty 7 and/or 8 is questionable. The problem is that the king-lists disagree on how many kings ruled during the Sixth Dynasty. The Table of Sakkara lists four kings, the Turin Canon 12 kings, the table of Abydos 22 kings. The standard Egyptological practice is to assign the extra 10 kings in the Abydos list to some arrangement of the Seventh and/or Eighth Dynasties.

Manetho, in its present form, is the only king-list to list these two dynasties, and, as I showed, Manetho's original king-list had no such listing. I also showed that Manetho originally had 21 kings in the Sixth Dynasty, agreeing with the Table of Sakkara in omitting one king in the Abydos list but otherwise acknowledging the other 21 kings in the latter's listing. This means that no king-list recognized any break in the Memphite king-list for a Dynasty 7 and/or 8.

The Patriarchal Chronology appears to have followed both the Table of Abydos and the original version of Manetho by incorporating 21 or 22 kings into the Sixth Dynasty and omitting any breaks for a Seventh and/or Eighth Dynasty. The Methuselah frame, therefore, coincides with the full dynastic chronology of the Memphite kingdom.

My own explanation for the disparity among the king-lists regarding the number of kings within the Sixth Dynasty was that the king-lists presented different claims by different political centers as to when the Memphite kings ceased being legitimate, Abydos being the most favorable to Memphis and Sakkara the least.

The Eber Grouping

I'm going to skip over the Heracleopolitan Ninth and/or Tenth Dynasties for now, as the evidence lies outside of Genesis 5 and 11. I'll come back to it later. I continue with the second major Patriarchal Chronology grouping, the Eber sequence.

Eber was born in 2040 and died in 1576. These are High Chronology dates for the two unifications of Egypt under Theban rule. Eber has six descendants. The birth dates for all six descendants fall into the timeframe of the Middle Kingdom and the death dates all fall into the timeframe for the Second Intermediate Period, when Thebes had lost control over portions of Egypt. Eber's death date corresponds to the start of the Eighteenth Dynasty and the end of the Seventeenth Dynasty.

As with Methuselah, the birth dates define one political era and the death dates define the next political era. In Methuselah's case, the frame was based on his ancestors. In Eber's case, the frame is based on his descendants. Between Methuselah's death and Eber's birth we have several Patriarchal Chronology dates, but, with one exception, we cannot confidentially connect the dates to Egyptian events. There may also have been a lot of tampering with the dates in this intermediate grouping by a later Genesis redactor. I'll discuss that issue later.

The Eber frame includes six birth dates and five death dates. (The missing death date is for Abram, the last Patriarch in the Genesis 11 sequence. His death date falls outside of the Genesis 11 passages.) Since Eber's frame begins in the middle of the Eleventh Dynasty, there are more birth and death dates than there are dynasties in the Middle Kingdom.

Eber's birthdate, in the High Chronology, is taken as the date of Egypt's unification under Menthotpe II, an event that occurred in the middle of that king's reign. The dynasty, however, began with an earlier king. As with the Tables of Abydos and Sakkara, the Patriarchal Chronology appears to jump from the end of the Memphite Dynasty and resume with this king's reign. I'll come back to the start of that king's reign shortly.

I'll turn first to the Twelfth Dynasty. In my analysis of the Patriarchal Chronology births for the Eber sequence, I made a uniform adjustment that moved all the birth dates fifteen years later. This resulted in an extraordinary discovery.

After this adjustment, five of Eber's six descendants had birth dates that corresponded almost perfectly with the Standard High Chronology starting dates (in some cases dealing with independent portions of reigns versus coregencies) for five kings in that dynasty, including the first king, Amenemhe 1. The sixth birth date, presumably intended to separate Senwosre II from Senwosre III, fell at the wrong break point. Interestingly, the Manetho sources also seem to have been confused about the relationship between these two kings, merging then together as a single entity.

If we make the same 15-year adjustment for Eber's ancestors in Genesis 11, we find that his father's adjusted date corresponds to the starting date for Menthotpe II. However, the unification of Egypt is the main event that defines the Eleventh Dynasty. The Patriarchal Chronology jumps from the death of Methuselah and the end of the Memphite Kingdom to the unification of Egypt under Thebes but does throw in the staring date for the king who unified Egypt.

In substance, then, we have the Eleventh Dynasty's High Chronology date for the unification of Egypt, the semi-official marker for when legitimacy attached to Theban rule, and the starting date for the Twelfth Dynasty. All six birth dates following Eber were applied to individual king's in the Twelfth Dynasty, but, sadly, one was erroneous. Nevertheless, the overall correlation was astounding.

Turning now to the Second Intermediate Period, Genesis 11 includes five death dates for Eber's descendants. This period encompasses Dynasties 13 through 17. Dynasties 14 and 15 are Hyksos dynasties. Dynasties 13 and 17 are Theban dynasties. Dynasty 16 is problematic. One Manetho source says it is Hyksos, the other says Theban. Some Egyptologists think the Sixteenth Dynasty never existed.

While the Tables of Abydos and Sakkara skip over the Second Intermediate Period, the Turin Canon does not. It begins with a Theban Thirteenth Dynasty followed by two Hyksos dynasties (the Fourteenth and Fifteenth) and concludes with a second list of Theban kings that includes a summation line for the last five kings. One common solution is to divide this second Theban list into a Sixteenth and Seventeenth Dynasty, with no clear understanding of where the division lies.

Since we lack convincing archaeological data for dating the start of the Sixteenth and Seventeenth Dynasties, I cannot determine whether certain Patriarchal Chronology death dates correspond to those dynasties. I did however identify when the Hyksos Fourteenth Dynasty split off from the Theban Thirteenth Dynasty and when the Hyksos Fifteenth Dynasty succeeded the Fourteenth.

In this study, through a reconstruction of Manetho's chronology and corroborated by archaeological data, I identified the death dates of Peleg ("In his day the earth was divided"), 1767, and Nahor, 1766, as the occasion of the initial Hyksos-Thebes split, dating the start of the Hyksos Fourteenth Dynasty to 1766. The death date for Nahor's son, Terah, in 1680, provided a perfect High Chronology date for the start of the Fifteenth Dynasty.

The 1767 date for Thebes falls slightly after the start of the Thirteenth Dynasty. The Thirteenth Dynasty started off peacefully, without conflict, and, for all practical purposes, was a continuation of the Twelfth Dynasty. But a few years after it started, it fell into a period of kinglessness and that time frame coincided closely to the 1767 date for the break with the Hyksos. The reconstruction of Manetho's original chronology for the Second Intermediate Period, confirmed our use of 1767/1766 as the year in which the Hyksos-Thebes split occurred and corroborated the duration of the Fourteenth Dynasty.

What we have, therefore, are solid High Chronology dates for that part of the Thirteenth Dynasty that coincides with the break with the Hyksos start of the Fourteenth Dynasty and an excellent High Chronology date for the Fifteenth Dynasty. What we are missing is the date for the start of the Sixteenth and Seventeenth Dynasties, which dates also elude Egyptologists. This leaves us with unassigned Patriarchal Chronology dates that may reflect Sixteenth and/or Seventeenth Dynasty starting dates but which we cannot confidently assign.

It is my suggestion that the Genesis author, writing from a Theban perspective, skipped over Dynasties 16 and 17, and treated all the Theban kings during the Second Intermediate Period as a single legitimate dynasty, and included the pre-split portion of the Thirteenth Dynasty as a continuation of the Twelfth Dynasty.

An Additional Frame Pattern

The Patriarchal Chronology uses births and deaths to frame and divide important political eras. The Methuselah frame used the birth dates of his ancestors to define the mythical era and used death dates of his ancestors to define the first historical era, running from the unification of Egypt under Memphite rule to the end of the Memphite era.

The Eber frame placed the births of his descendants into the Middle Kingdom of Dynasties 11 and 12 and placed their death dates into the Second Intermediate Period. Eber's birth and death dates corresponded to the two High Chronology dates for the unifications of Egypt under Theban rule.

There is also a second pattern within these two frames that helps the reader know where to make the chronological breaks. In each case, the Patriarch defining the dynastic period covered by the list has the latest death date within the chronology. In Genesis 5, Methuselah has the latest death date; in Genesis 11, Eber has the latest death date. Therefore, in each listing, the birth dates of Methuselah and Eber define the time frames under consideration. The final death date in each of the Genesis chronologies points to which Patriarch's birth date begins the dynastic frame.

Between Methuselah and Eber

Between the death of Methuselah and the birth of Eber we have several Patriarchal dates in Genesis 5 and 11. These fall into the chaotic and problematic First Intermediate Period. There is also some evidence that the dates for these patriarchs may have been altered in order to accommodate the Flood story.

As you may recall, Genesis attributed the Flood to God as a punishment for the "sons of God" marrying the "daughters of man," a claim that has always puzzled scholars, who have yet to provide a satisfactory explanation for what this marriage story signifies. More importantly, Genesis 6:3 said that God determined that he would destroy the human race 120 years after the marriages. When we counted back 120 years from the date of the Flood (the same year as Methuselah's death), we arrived at the date of 2225.

That date was 185 years before the unification of Egypt on Eber's birth date. That was also the same numbers years that Manetho assigned to the Heracleopolitan Tenth Dynasty, which dynasty also ended on the date of Eber's birth. Among Egyptologists, there is a debate as to whether the Heracleopolitan dynasties lasted about one century or two centuries. The Genesis chronology, therefore, is consistent with both the two-century viewpoint and Manetho's Tenth Dynasty.

There is a question as to whether the Ninth Dynasty ever existed. The Turin Canon has a damaged list of what once contained 18 Heracleopolitan kings. We don't know if there was a dynastic division within the list. Manetho has two Heracleopolitan dynasties, each with 19 kings. It is widely assumed that Manetho's two dynasties may be duplicates. However long the Heracleopolitans ruled, Egyptologists try to carve two dynasties out of the group, attempting to conform to Manetho's indication of a Ninth and Tenth Dynasty, but any dividing line is arbitrary and unsupported in the historical record. The Genesis correlation to Manetho's Heracleopolitan Tenth Dynasty, as with Manetho's Tenth Dynasty, should be understood as incorporating the full duration of the Heracleopolitan kings. Whether the 185-year duration encompasses one or two dynasties is speculation. In any event, the Genesis chronology, incorporates the main-stream view that the Heracleopolitans ruled for about two-centuries.

These coincidences suggest that the Flood story was overlaid onto the story of the rivalry between Memphis (the sons of God, i.e., the king who was equated with the god Horus) and Heracleopolis (the daughters of man, i.e., the non-god king of Heracleopolis.) If this is the case, then it is likely that the entire Flood cycle, was moved into its present location and intruded on the already existing Patriarchal Chronology. Several biblical scholars believe that the Flood story was originally a Creation myth and we will see, in Volume III of this study, that this is the case.

Because of the theological need to separate Pre-Flood humanity from post-Flood humanity, it is possible that at a later stage of the development of Genesis, several Patriarchal dates surrounding the Flood story, i.e., those between the death of Methuselah and the birth of Eber, may have been altered. Let's review some of the evidence.

Genesis 5 has three Patriarchs born after Methuselah, placing them outside of the frame based on Methuselah's ancestors. They are Lamech, Noah, and Shem. Death dates for the latter two, both of whom survived the Flood, do not appear in the pre-Flood listing of Genesis 5. Since both appear in the Flood story, which appears to have been moved into its present location from some other setting, we can't be sure that either Patriarch was originally part of the Patriarchal chronology. Shem's death date appears in Genesis 11 and Noah's death date appears outside of the Genesis 5 and 11 lists.

This leaves, in Genesis 5, just Lamech (son of Methuselah) unaccounted for. As the father of Noah, we should be somewhat suspicious to start with. More curious, though, is the problem of his death date. He is the only Genesis 5 Patriarch (other than Enoch, who serves a special symbolic role) to die before his father. This seems inconsistent with the design of the Genesis 5 birth-death chronology, with the earlier fathers dying before their sons. Furthermore, there are several inconsistencies in other biblical sources, such as the Septuagint and Josephus, concerning how long this Patriarch lived.

It is possible therefore, that Lamech's life span may have been cut short so that he dies before the Flood appears, which occurs on the death of his father. Or he may have only been a transitional character designed to incorporate the Noah story into the Genesis chronology.

On the other side of the Flood, in Genesis 11, Shem reappears, and we have the following Patriarchal sequence leading up to Eber's birth: Shem, Arphaxad, Shelah and Eber. As I showed in Chapter Six, there was some chronological inconsistencies surrounding the birth year of Arphaxad, which placed his birth date in the same year that

Methuselah died. I suggested that Arphaxad's birth year may have been cut short, so that his birth occurred after the Flood.

The birth date of Eber's father, Shelah, introduced a different sort of clue. If we placed his birth date 15 years later, like we did for the sequence of birth dates in the Eber frame, his birth date corresponded to the year on which Menthotpe II came to the throne. He was the king who reunited Egypt in the year of Eber's birth. So, we have at least one interesting Patriarchal Chronology correlation before Eber's birth to a key Egyptian date. But that is the only legitimate date we can establish in the post-Methuselah pre-Eber chronological period.

It is my suspicion, and we lack sufficient data to verify it, that there may have been a small chronological frame between Methuselah and Eber that provided some corresponding birth dates for the Eleventh Dynasty Theban kings that preceded Menthotpe II and perhaps some death dates corresponding to the Theban kings between the end of the Twelfth Dynasty and the occasion of the Hyksos-Theban split, but that this Patriarchal Chronology frame was disrupted by the insertion of the Flood story in between the Methuselah and Eber frames.

Unfortunately, we can only speculate as to the existence of this intervening frame. For now, we can only say, like much of the First Intermediate Period, the corresponding Genesis chronology remains lost. For this group of intervening Patriarchs, not only must we remain skeptical about those births and deaths falling within the First Intermediate Period, we must remain uncertain about their respective birth and death dates that fall outside of the First Intermediate Period. For example, I pointed out the possibility that Noah's birth date corresponds to the start of the reign of Djoser in the Third Dynasty, but we lack a good pattern analysis that places this match in a chronological context.

The Joseph Chronology

Outside of the Genesis 5 and 11 contexts, we saw evidence that the chronology of the Patriarch Joseph provides some indications that it is aligned with the earlier portion of the Eighteenth Dynasty. Joseph is the last of the Patriarchs in Genesis and his death brings the first book of the bible to a close. But his chronological pattern is different from that of the earlier lists.

While Eber's death date of 1576 corresponded to High Chronology date for the start of Ahmose I's reign, the pharaoh who is considered the founder of the Eighteenth Dynasty and the one who reunified Egypt, the unification didn't take place until later in his reign. His conquest over the Hyksos had two key stages. Hyksos forces were driven out of Egypt during the fourth year of his reign, but they remained a force to contend with. The final defeat of the Hyksos came in the eleventh year of his reign, coinciding with the birth year of Joseph.

Joseph's death year, 1454 coincides with what appears to be the start of a brief coregency between Thutmose III and his successor Amenhotep II. In between those two dates we have some data having to do with the rise of Joseph to the office of Prime Minister of Egypt. The data is both chronological and has some historical correlations. Joseph's rise to power came about because of his interpretation of the Pharaoh's dreams, in which he predicted seven good years and seven lean years, and then provided advice as to how Pharaoh should prepare for the seven lean years.

Under Joseph's guidance, the Pharaoh reached unprecedented heights of wealth and power. During this same chronological period in Egyptian history, Thutmose I, II, and II also achieved unprecedented power and wealth for an Egyptian pharaoh. Thutmose III is often thought of as the greatest pharaoh in Egyptian history.

On a chronological level, we could also date the seven good years and the seven lean years. The good years ended at about 1527/28 and the bad years ended at about 1520/21. The 1527/28 date coincided with the High Chronology date for the start of the reign of Thutmose I. Unfortunately, the archaeological record does not allow Egyptologists to confidently establish the true length of this king's reign and there is a considerable amount of debate. Within the parameters of this debate, the 1520/21 date for the end of the lean years is consistent with the evidence, but not conclusively so.

The Joseph chronology overlaps the era of Thutmose I, II, and III, when Egypt reached the height of its power. The Book of Genesis ends with the death of Joseph. Interestingly, the next book of the bible, Exodus, depicts Egypt's downfall when challenging the authority of Israel's God. The literary arc may have been intentional.

Chronological Highlights

The list below summarizes some of the major findings in this study. As we review the data, keep in mind that for the period coinciding with the Memphite kingdom (Dynasties 1-8) we had no reliable anchor dates and a wide range of differences among Egyptologists as to the starting dates of various dynasties. Therefore, we relied on relative chronology, comparing the durations of each dynasty in the Egyptological-archaeological framework with the indicated durations in the Patriarchal Chronology. The data in the Patriarchal Chronology was highly consistent with mainstream Egyptological opinions.

- In all relevant instances, the Patriarchal Chronology remained consistent with the high end of the High Chronology.
- In all relevant instances, the Patriarchal Chronology remained consistent with the Maximum Minimum biennial cattle counts.
- Enoch's lifespan of 365 years ends in 2774. the same year that a 1460-year Sothic Cycle, based on the solar calendar, started. By itself that would be a coincidence. In the context of the other Patriarchal Chronology data, Enoch's death date strongly suggests that the Genesis author intended it to point to the start of the Sothic Cycle, providing a chronological anchor date for all the other births and deaths in the Patriarchal Chronology.
- The Patriarchal Chronology distributes birth and death dates according to political eras. The Genesis 5 births of Methuselah's ancestors fell into the mythical era. The death dates of these same ancestors fell into the era of the Memphite kingdom. The birth dates of the Eber's Genesis 11 descendants fell into the Middle Kingdom (Dynasties 11 and 12) and the death dates of these same descendants fell into the Second Intermediate Period.

- Egyptologists date the start of Dynasty 1 to 3100 BCE, give or take 150 years. Other than Enoch, Methuselah is the only Patriarch with a birth or death date falling into that range. We used Methuselah's birth year (3074) as the starting date for Dynasty 1.
- The Turin Canon appears to indicate a 955-year duration for the Memphite Kingdom (Dynasties 1-6) but omits the last 10 Memphite kings from its total. Methuselah's 969-year lifespan covers the same period but includes the additional 10 kings. Even if we acknowledge some occasional errors in the Turin Canon data, the near perfect millennium-long parallel durations in the Turin Canon and the Patriarchal Chronology for Dynasties 1-6 seems remarkable.
- For Dynasties 1, 2, and 3 the Patriarchal Chronology provides respective durations of 243 years, 112 years and 98 years. Our reconstruction of Manetho's chronology showed durations of 243 years, 112 years, and 98 years. For the first two dynasties we have almost no chronological data outside of Manetho. For the Third Dynasty, the Turin Canon shows 74 years, but several Egyptologists believe the dynasty should have lasted for a century.
- For Memphite Dynasties 6, 7 and 8, the king-lists disagree with each other as to how many kings ruled in Memphis after the start of the Sixth Dynasty. The Table of Sakkara had four, the present version of Manetho had six, the Turin Canon had twelve and the Table of Abydos had twenty-two. Other than Manetho, none of the lists show any break for a Seventh and Eighth Dynasty. Manetho lists Dynasties 7 and 8 after his list of six kings but I showed that the numbers were corrupted summation lines and that originally Manetho closely agreed with the Table of Abydos, indicating that there were twenty-one kings in the final Memphite sequence. Once our reconstruction of Manetho's original chronology was complete, we saw that the Patriarchal Chronology and Manetho closely agreed on the duration of the 21 kings in the Sixth Dynasty. The Patriarchal Chronology had 239 years, Manetho 241, a difference that can be explained by rounding errors.
- Eber's birth year (2040) corresponds to the High Chronology date for the unification of Egypt by the Eleventh Dynasty Theban King

Menthotpe II. Both the Table of Abydos and the Table of Sakkara identify this king as the first legitimate ruler of Egypt after the collapse of the Memphite kingdom.

- A uniform correction of 15 years for all Genesis 11 birth dates following Eber's showed an almost perfect chronological correspondence to the starting dates of 5 kings in the Twelfth Dynasty.
- Applying the same 15-year correction to the birth date of Eber's father gave us the starting date for the year Menthotpe II became king.
- For the Second Intermediate Period we saw that the Turin Canon follows the Twelfth Dynasty with two Theban kings followed, in turn, by a short period of kinglessness. This period ended at just about 1767, exactly where the Patriarchal Chronology showed a split between the Theban Thirteenth Dynasty and the Hyksos Fourteenth Dynasty. The reconstruction of Manetho's Second Intermediate Period chronology corroborated the date of this split.
- The reconstruction of Manetho's Second Intermediate Period chronology showed that it was based on almost the identical data behind the Turin Canon of Kings.
- Terah's death date of 1680 corresponds precisely to the high end of the High Chronology date for the start of the Hyksos Fifteenth Dynasty.
- Eber's death year (1576) coincides with the high end of the High Chronology for the year that King Ahmose founded the Eighteenth Dynasty. The Table of Abydos and the Table of Sakkara identify this king as the first legitimate ruler of Egypt after the end of the Twelfth Dynasty. Four years later, he drove the Hyksos out of Egypt.
- Joseph's birth year (1565) corresponds to the high end of the High Chronology for the year in which King Ahmose delivered the final military defeat of the Hyksos in their non-Egyptian base.
- Joseph's death year (1454) corresponds to the High Chronology date for the end of the independent reign of Thutmose III, on the assumption that there was a short coregency with his successor, as some Egyptologists theorize. If there was no coregency, the date is only 3 years short of that king's full 54-year reign.
- The Genesis story of the Egyptian kings accumulating unprecedented wealth and power under Joseph's guidance, precisely

coincides chronologically with the rise of the Eighteenth Dynasty Thutmose kings who accumulated unprecedented wealth and power in Egypt.

- The start of the seven good years in the Joseph dream interpretation story, 1527/1528, coincides with the High Chronology starting date for Thutmose I's reign.

- The start of the seven lean years in the dream story, 1520/1521, provides a plausible date for the start of Thutmose II's reign and is consistent with the evidence, but we lack sufficient chronological data for this king to be sure that we have a precise chronological match.

- Genesis attributes the Flood to God's anger at the "sons of God" marrying the "daughters of man." A prophecy indicates that the Flood would occur 120 years after that event. Counting back 120 years from the Flood takes us to 2225. Counting forward to the reunification of Egypt in 2040, when Menthotpe II defeated the Heracleopolitan kingdom, gives us a period of 185 years. This is the same duration Manetho gives to the Heracleopolitan Tenth Dynasty, the rivals of Memphis and Thebes.

- All Egyptian kings, with just a few exceptions, were identified as the God Horus. The marriage conflict in Genesis may refer to the sons of the Theban king as the "sons of God" and the daughters of the (illegitimate) Heracleopolitan king as the "daughters of man." If such an event occurred, some later Egyptians may have considered this a traitorous and wicked act.

- The evidence suggests that a later Genesis author/redactor inserted the Flood story into Egypt's First Intermediate Period, possibly as a metaphor for the conflict between Memphis and Heracleopolis.

The above list outlines some of the many features which, when taken collectively, clearly show a close connection between the Patriarchal Chronology and the Egyptian king-lists. While one may quibble here and there as to a small inconsistency or an occasional lack of precision, when one looks at the pattern of evidence, there can be little doubt that the author of the Patriarchal Chronology worked from authentic Egyptian archival records.

As we have seen, even among the ancient scribes, there were occasional conflicts and disagreements about what the data showed about Egyptian kings.

As a final reminder, this study attempts to show how an ancient scribe looking at ancient Egyptian records would reconstruct an Egyptian king-list for the first eighteen dynasties of Egypt. In theory, the broad picture should exhibit a high degree of correlation with modern reconstructions of the same project. At both ends of the process, ancient and modern, some errors and disagreements arise. In this study, there is a consistent alignment between this ancient record in Genesis and the High Chronology, and a consistent alignment with the High Minimum cattle count censuses. That makes the Patriarchal Chronology as much of an important independent witness to ancient Egyptian chronology as the Turin Canon and Manetho. Neither of those are perfect sources and we shouldn't hold the Genesis chronographer to a higher standard.

The Patriarchal Chronology is an Egyptian king-list that testifies to the validity of the High Chronology, the widespread use of biennial cattle counts in the Old Kingdom, and when the Sothic Cycle started. It is the only ancient source that gives us a reasonable accurate guide to anchor dates for the Memphite dynasties, subject to very minor tweaking at most. When properly used it provides frequent confirmation of the Turin Canon and the reconstruction of Manetho's original chronology, which, in turn, also frequently aligns with the Turin Canon.

Appendix A
Transition to Volume II
The Mythic Period

IN THIS VOLUME WE LOOKED AT THAT PORTION OF THE PATRIARCHAL Chronology that began with the birth of Methuselah in 3074, which I identified as the starting date for the First Dynasty. In Volume II, I look at that portion of the Patriarchal Chronology that precedes the birth of Methuselah. Removing Enoch from the mix, as his life span points to the start of a Sothic Cycle, we have a list of six Patriarchal births: Adam, Seth, Enosh, Kenan, Mahalalel, Jared, and Methuselah.

Since Adam was born in 3761, presumably at the end of the Creation process, and Methuselah was born in 3074, this gives us a period of 687 years from Creation to the start of Egypt's First Dynasty. At first glance, when compared to the predynastic mythology in Manetho and the Turin Canon, we wouldn't think there could be any relationship between the Patriarchal Chronology and the Egyptian king-lists, with their significantly longer durations for many rulers. That would be a mistake. Volume II demonstrates the relationship, but that study will look nothing like this study.

In the present volume we were dealing with actual rulers and real king-lists. The predynastic Egyptian king-lists are something else, mythical accounts of various deities, demigods, spirits and humans that ruled over Egypt for thousands of years. As with the dynastic portions of Manetho, the various sources disagree with each other in many ways. But with these lists, we can see that the source authors were quite confused over what to make of these predynastic king-lists. They offered assorted commentaries to explain away long lives, arguing that in these very ancient times Egyptians used different definitions for months, seasons, and years, substituting terms in one calendar system for the same terms in another calendar system.

According to the Armenian version of Eusebius's version of Manetho, for example, "the year I take, however, to be a lunar one, consisting, that is, of 30 days: what we now call a month the Egyptians used formerly to style a year."[333] Syncellus, who preserved portions of both the Manetho and Africanus versions of Manetho, said, "the most ancient Egyptian kings, indeed, alleged that their years were lunar years consisting of thirty days, whereas the Demigods who succeeded them gave the name horoi [= seasons] to years which were three months long."[334] Independent of the Manetho sources, we have an observation by Diodorus Siculus, a Greek historian who visited Egypt for a short time in the first century B.C. and wrote extensively about the country's history and culture.

> "And, as their legends say, the most ancient of their gods ruled more than twelve hundred years, and the later ones not less than three hundred. But since this great number of years surpasses belief, some men would maintain that in early times, before the movement of the sun had as yet been recognized, it was customary to reckon the year by the lunar cycle. Consequently, since the year consisted of thirty days, it was not impossible that some men lived twelve hundred years; for in our own time, when the year consists of twelve months, not a few men live over one hundred years. A similar explanation they also give regarding those who are supposed to have reigned for three hundred years; for at their time, namely, the year was composed of the four months which comprise the seasons of the year, that is spring, summer, and winter; and it is for this reason that among the Greeks the years are called "seasons" (horoi) and that their yearly records are given the name "horographs."[335]

As you can see, there is a good deal of confusion among early non-Egyptian historians about how to understand what the Egyptians meant by various calendar terms. Egyptologists are adamant in rejecting such claims. There is no evidence, they argue, that the

Egyptians ever equated "months" or "seasons" with "years." [336] But such evidence is plainly before them.

The 1460-year Sothic Cycle is organized like a solar year calendar, with dates recorded in terms of specific Sothic days, Sothic months, and Sothic seasons. Four civil years equals one Sothic day; 120 civil years equals one Sothic month; 480 years equals one Sothic season (a four-month period); and, of course, 1461 civil years equals one Sothic year. If for example, a date on the Sothic calendar was entered as Day 3, Month 2, Season 1, it would indicate the passage of one month and three days, which in the Sothic calendar would be a period of 132 years (= 33 X 4 years.)

In addition to a Sothic Cycle, the Egyptians also had a 25-year Lunar Cycle calendar. That was the number of years it would take for the annual lunar calendar New Year to coincide with the civil calendar New Year. This 25-year cycle, considered a lunar-solar calendar, was separate and apart from the basic twelve-month lunar calendar of 354 days (with an occasional thirteenth month interpolated into the annual calendar), affording other possibilities of cross-calendar equations for time periods.

Another feature we will discover when looking at the commentaries in the ancient sources is that the source authors didn't fully understand the Egyptian calendar systems. They also made several arithmetic errors in calculations. We know they made errors because we know what they were calculating. So, there is some evidence that Egyptians had some practices which equated some civil calendar terms with parallel terms in another calendar system.

What we will discover in Volume II is that the predynastic king-lists were a sophisticated theological document that integrated various Egyptian creation theories into a single source consistent with Theban theology and that numerous kings (deities, etc.) ruled over time frames that were associated with various time elements within Sothic, solar and lunar calendars.

Once we understand the organizational structure of Egypt's calendar-based predynastic king-lists and what sort of conversions they made, we will then be able to analyze the Patriarchal Chronology.

When we do, we will see that it follows the same organizational prin-
ciples as the Egyptian predynastic king-list, and that Genesis creation
chronology is intimately connected to Egyptian Creation theology.

Appendix B
Transition to
The Moses Mystery

IN 1996 I PUBLISHED *THE MOSES MYSTERY: THE AFRICAN ORIGINS OF THE Jewish People*, (since republished in several editions under different titles and/or subtitles,) which offered a new theory on the origins of Israel's exodus from Egypt. Some ancient Egyptian sources traced the story of Moses to events surrounding the reign of the monotheistic pharaoh Akhenaten and the political conflicts that followed his death. I wondered if I could validate that thesis.

Egyptologists and some biblical scholars knew about these sources, primarily in the writings of Manetho as preserved by Josephus in the first century, but they uniformly dismissed these claims because the thesis didn't agree with their personal academic agendas. Both Egyptologists and biblical scholars try to keep their respective fields independent of each other except in the most trivial of cases. They all had preferred alternative theories as to when the Exodus happened, if, in fact, they even believed there was an Exodus.

The orthodox Jewish view is that the Exodus occurred in the year 1311. Based on my own analysis, in large part dependent on the validity of the Patriarchal Chronology as an Egyptian source, I placed it in 1315. Although the dates are close, they were arrived at by very different methodologies derived from different interpretations of biblical passages. Nevertheless, both claims fall into the same historical context. Both conclusions, based on the High Chronology, make Moses and Akhenaten contemporaries during the period Moses was in Egypt. Despite the historical context of the orthodox date, any connection between Moses and Akhenaten has been studiously ignored. As I demonstrate in *The Moses Mystery*, my analysis has the further advantage of aligning several biblical claims with historical facts, including parallel sequences about when pharaonic reigns ended.

My argument in *The Moses Mystery* noted that after Akhenaten's death, his politically unpopular monotheistic reforms led to a counterrevolution by the Theban priests. The followers of Akhenaten were subsequently persecuted. When the Akhenaten bloodline came to an end, military leaders became the rulers of Egypt. Moses, adopted as a member of the royal family by Akhenaten's father, had a legitimate claim to the throne and when the current ruling general died, Moses rallied the Akhenaten forces to take back the throne, but the revolution failed. Moses and pharaoh reached an agreement to allow Moses and his flowerers safe passage out of Egypt, and that withdrawal was the Exodus. I'm not going to review the arguments here. You'll need to read *The Moses Mystery* if you are interested.

To prove my thesis, I relied heavily on the underlying study behind the present volume, showing that Genesis chronology was based on the High Egyptian chronology. *The Moses Mystery* also extended the analysis of the High Chronology into the Eighteenth and Nineteenth Dynasties in order to put the events of the Exodus into historical context. But, as you can see from this study and the fact that there are two more volumes to go, such a lengthy analysis would be way too long for an ordinary commercial book. My original manuscript was well over a thousand pages.

After some negotiations with my editor, we reached a compromise. I could include enough information to show a connection between the Patriarchal Chronology and the High Chronology, but I had to keep it brief and mostly reduced to summaries. Since most of the chronological study didn't appear in the book, the text included a notice that I would separately publish the full independent chronological study that stood behind my analysis.

Few things often go as planned. Over the years, I wound up with several contracts for books on different topics and moved into other areas of study. Now, over 20 years later, and hopefully not too late, I have gone back to my original work, updated the scholarship to include present Egyptological points of view, and have committed to putting this study in print. I hope to publish each of the next two volumes within a year or two of this one. I may be too optimistic.

Notes

[1] (Pritrchard, 1969), 265.

[2] (Waddell, 1940; reprint 1980), 13.

[3] (Waddell, 1940; reprint 1980), 229.

[4] (Greenberg, Manetho's 7th and 8th Dynasties: A Puzzle Solved, 1995)

[5] Genesis 9:29.

[6] Genesis 11:26, 32.

[7] Genesis 12:1.

[8] Genesis 25:7.

[9] Genesis 10:25.

[10] Genesis 21:5.

[11] Genesis 35:28.

[12] Genesis 25:26.

[13] Genesis 47:28.

[14] Genesis 41:46.

[15] Genesis 47:28.

[16] Genesis 45:6.

[17] Genesis 50:26.

[18] Genesis 6:1–3.

[19] (Gardiner, 1961), 53.

[20] Gardiner, 51.

[21] (Kitchen K. , 1996), 3

[22] (Greenberg, Manetho, a Study in Egyptyian Chronology: How ancient scribes garbled an accurate chronology of dynastic Egypt, 2003)

[23] (Waddell, 1940; reprint 1980), 85.

[24] (Waddell, 1940; reprint 1980), 87, 101. The first citation identifies the king as Misphragmuthosis, the second as Tethmosis.

[25] (Waddell, 1940; reprint 1980), 125, 131.

[26] (Waddell, 1940; reprint 1980), xvii.

[27] (Waddell, 1940; reprint 1980), xix–xx.

[28] (Waddell, 1940; reprint 1980), 234, n 1.

[29] (Waddell, 1940; reprint 1980), 227.

[30] (Gardiner, 1961),430.

[31] (Waddell, 1940; reprint 1980), xxi.

[32] (Waddell, 1940; reprint 1980), xxi.

[33] (Gardiner, 1961), 440.

[34] (Gardiner, 1961), 108.

[35] (Waddell, 1940; reprint 1980), xxi.

[36] (Gardiner, 1961), 50.

[37] (Waddell, 1940; reprint 1980), xxi.

[38] Gardiner, 50.

[39] (Gardiner, 1961), 50.

[40] (Gardiner, 1961), 63.

[41] Waddell, xxi.

[42] (Waddell, 1940; reprint 1980), xxi.

[43] (Gardiner, 1961), 48.

[44] (Gardiner, 1961), 149.

[45] (Gardiner, 1961), 437–38.

[46] (Gardiner, 1961), 436.

[47]   (Redford, Pharaohnic King-lists, Annals and Day-books: A Contribution to the Study of the Egyptian Sense of History, 1986), 5.

[48] (Gardiner, 1961), 64.

[49] (Parker, The Sothic Dating of the Twelfth and Eighteenth Dynasties, 1977), 182.

[50] The year immediately before 1 AD is 1 BC. There is no Year 0.

[51] (Parker, The Sothic Dating of the Twelfth and Eighteenth Dynasties, 1977), 182, n.17, citing M. F. Ingham, "The Length of the Sothic Cycle", JEA 55 (1969) 36–40.

[52] (Parker, The Sothic Dating of the Twelfth and Eighteenth Dynasties, 1977), 182.

[53] (Gardiner, 1961), 65.

[54] (Parker, The Sothic Dating of the Twelfth and Eighteenth Dynasties, 1977), 183.

[55] (Wente & Van Siclen III, 1977), 233.

[56] (Parker, The Sothic Dating of the Twelfth and Eighteenth Dynasties, 1977), 186, citing the work of Erik Hornung, *Untersuchungen zur Chronologie und Gesichte des Neuen Reiches* ("Ägyptologische Abhandlulungen," Vol. 11 [Wiesbaden, 1964]) pp 20–21.

[57] (Parker, The Sothic Dating of the Twelfth and Eighteenth Dynasties, 1977), 186, citing the work of Erik Hornung, *Untersuchungen zur Chronologie und Gesichte des Neuen Reiches* ("Ägyptologische Abhandlulungen," Vol. 11 [Wiesbaden, 1964]) pp 20–21.

[58] (Edgerten, 1942), 309.

[59] (Parker, The Calendars of Ancient Egypt, 1950), 63–69.

[60] (Beckerath, 1997), 132–34.

[61] (Gardiner, 1961), 66.

[62] (Hayes, 1970), 175. Hayes cites several studies ranging from as few as 295 years to as much as 545 years.

[63] (Gardiner, 1961), 420.

[64] (Gardiner, 1961), 433.

[65] (Gardiner, 1961), 67.

[66] (Clagett, 1995), 45.

[67] (Freedman, 1992), Vol. 2, 508.

[68] (Gardiner, 1961), 109.

[69] (Gardiner, 1961), 430.

[70] (Strong, 2001), 4968.

[71] (Freedman, 1992), Vol 4, p 801.

[72] (Gardiner, 1961), 406.

[73] (Gardiner, 1961), 67.

[74] (Krauss & Warburton, 2006), 486.

[75] (Gardiner, 1961), 420.

[76] (Gardiner, 1961), 420.

[77] (Hayes, 1970), 175.

[78] (Hayes, 1970), 175.

[79] (Gardiner, 1961), 430–431. It is unclear from Gardiner's descriptions if Turin Canon II:13 and II:14 contain king names.

[80] (Gardiner, 1961), 430–31.

[81] (Gardiner, 1961), 430–31.

[82] (Gardiner, 1961), 430–31.

[83] (Emery, 1987), 22.

[84] (Gardiner, 1961), 430–31.

[85] (Gardiner, 1961), 432.

[86] (Gardiner, 1961), 431.

[87] (Verner, Dynasties 4 to 5, 2006), 147.

[88] (Verner, Archaeological Remarks on the 4th and 5th Dynasty Chronology, 2001), 364.

[89] (Hayes, 1970), 178.

[90] (Verner, Dynasties 4 to 5, 2006), 124.

[91] (Smith, 1971), 147.

[92] (Verner, Dynasties 4 to 5, 2006), 147.

[93] (Verner, Dynasties 4 to 5, 2006), 124.

[94] (Verner, Dynasties 4 to 5, 2006), 127.

[95] (Verner, Dynasties 4 to 5, 2006), 124.

[96] (Smith, 1971), 149.

[97] (Gardiner, 1961), 433.

[98] (Gardiner, 1961), 431, 433.

[99] (Gardiner, 1961), 72.

[100] (Gardiner, 1961), 75.

[101] (Gardiner, 1961), 433.

[102] (Gardiner, 1961), 433.

[103] (Gardiner, 1961), 431, 433.

[104] (Gardiner, 1961), 75, 433–434. Gardiner gives little information here. His primary objection is to the Turin Canon's 19 years for Djoser. He gives conjectured dates of 2700 for the Third Dynasty and 2620 for the Fourth Dynasty, a period of 80 years, excluding Nebka, and doesn't challenge any of the Turin Canon figures for the Third Dynasty. This implies that he adds approximately 25 additional years to the Turin Canon's 19 years for Djoser.

[105] (Krauss & Warburton, 2006), 490.

[106] (Krauss & Warburton, 2006), 490.

[107] (Gardiner, 1961), 433.

[108] (Gardiner, 1961), 433.

[109] (Gardiner, 1961), 433.

[110] (Seidlmayer, Dynasty 3, 2006), 118.

[111] (Gardiner, 1961), 74–75.

[112] (Shaw, 2000), 482.

[113] (Seidlmayer, Dynasty 3, 2006), 118.

[114] (Hornung, Krauss, & Warburton, Ancient Egyptian Chronology, 2006), 21.

[115] (Gardiner, 1961),432.

[116] (Gardiner, 1961), 433, n1.

[117] (Hornung, Krauss, & Warburton, Ancient Egyptian Chronology, 2006), 491.

[118] (Gardiner, 1961), 419–20.

[119] (Gardiner, 1961), 416–19.

[120] (Gardiner, 1961), 420.

[121] (Smith, 1971), 146.

[122] (Smith, 1971), 147.

[123] (Smith, 1971), 147.

[124] (Smith, 1971), 147.

[125] The Turin Canon from Djoser's 19 years on, had a duration of 55-years. If we subtract that from 80, we get 25 years. Adding that to the 19 years already assigned to Djoser gives us a total of 44 years for Djoser.

[126] (Gardiner, 1961), 89.

[127] (Verner, Dynasties 4 to 5, 2006), 132.

[128] (Verner, Archaeological Remarks on the 4th and 5th Dynasty Chronology, 2001), 135. (Smith, 1971), 173.

[129] (Beckerath, 1997), 188.

[130] (Krauss & Warburton, 2006),491.

[131] (Cambridge Ancient History, 1971), Vol 1. Part 2B, 995.

[132] (Gardiner, 1961), 434.

[133] (Gardiner, 1961), 434.

[134] (Gardiner, 1961), 434.

[135] (Verner, Dynasties 4 to 5, 2006), 134. See also (Smith, 1971), 174.

[136] (Verner, Archaeological Remarks on the 4th and 5th Dynasty Chronology, 2001)

[137] (Verner, Dynasties 4 to 5, 2006), 125.

[138] (Hornung, Krauss, & Warburton, Ancient Egyptian Chronology, 2006), 45–46.

[139] A 24th Occasion of the Count would be 47 years, but the presence of one consecutive count reduces the total by one year to 46 years.

[140] (Verner, Dynasties 4 to 5, 2006), 127.

[141] (Verner, Dynasties 4 to 5, 2006), 125.

[142] (Gardiner, 1961), 434.

[143] (Gardiner, 1961), 434.

[144] (Gardiner, 1961), 83.

[145] (Gardiner, 1961), 83.

[146] (Gardiner, 1961), 434.

[147] (Smith, 1971), 172.

[148] (Hayes, 1970), 177.

[149] (Smith, 1971), 172.

[150] (Smith, 1971), 172.

[151] (Smith, 1971), 145

[152] See, for example, (Gardiner, 1961), 434.

[153] (Redford, Pharaohnic King-lists, Annals and Day-books: A Contribution to the Study of the Egyptian Sense of History, 1986), 237.

[154] (Redford, Pharaohnic King-lists, Annals and Day-books: A Contribution to the Study of the Egyptian Sense of History, 1986), 237.

[155] (Herodotus, 1972, reprinted 1978, 1980), 174–83.

[156] (Herodotus, 1972, reprinted 1978, 1980), 178.

[157] (Herodotus, 1972, reprinted 1978, 1980), 179.

[158] (Herodotus, 1972, reprinted 1978, 1980), 179.

[159] (Herodotus, 1972, reprinted 1978, 1980), 179.

[160] (Herodotus, 1972, reprinted 1978, 1980), 180.

[161] (Herodotus, 1972, reprinted 1978, 1980), 180.

[162] (Herodotus, 1972, reprinted 1978, 1980), 180.

[163] (Herodotus, 1972, reprinted 1978, 1980), 180.

[164] (Smith, 1971), 175.

[165] (Waddell, 1940; reprint 1980), 88.

[166] (Krauss & Warburton, 2006), 484–85.

[167] (Krauss & Warburton, 2006), 484–85.

[168] (Verner, Archaeological Remarks on the 4th and 5th Dynasty Chronology, 2001), 402.

[169] (Smith, 1971), 185.

[170] (Smith, 1971), 185. See also (Verner, Dynasties 4 to 5, 2006), 127.

[171] (Smith, 1971), 185.

[172] (Smith, 1971), 185.

[173] (Gardiner, 1961), 435.

[174] (Verner, Archaeological Remarks on the 4th and 5th Dynasty Chronology, 2001), 408.

[175] (Verner, Archaeological Remarks on the 4th and 5th Dynasty Chronology, 2001), 410.

[176] (Verner, Dynasties 4 to 5, 2006), 137, n. 123.

[177] (Smith, 1971), 183.

[178] (Verner, Archaeological Remarks on the 4th and 5th Dynasty Chronology, 2001), 400.

[179] (Hayes, 1970), 178.

[180] (Verner, Dynasties 4 to 5, 2006), 137.

[181] (Gardiner, 1961), 436.

[182] (Gardiner, 1961), 438.

[183] (Gardiner, 1961), 436–438.

[184] (Gardiner, 1961), 438.

[185] (Gardiner, 1961), 435. See Turin Canon entry T.3:26.

[186] (Gardiner, 1961), 436.

[187] (Beckerath, 1997), 149.

[188] (Gardiner, 1961), 93.

[189] (Gardiner, 1961), 436.

[190] (Baud, 2006), 158.

[191] (Baud, 2006), 158.

[192] (Gardiner, 1961), 93.

[193] (Baud, 2006), 156.

[194] (Gardiner, 1961), 436.

[195] (Smith, 1971), 193.

[196] (Beckerath, 1997), 188.

[197] (Krauss & Warburton, 2006), 491.

[198] (Shaw, 2000), 483.

[199] (Smith, 1971), 91.

[200] (Baud, 2006), 156.

[201] (Baud, 2006), 156.

[202] (Smith, 1971), 192.

[203] (Baud, 2006), 156.

[204] *Manetho*, 53–5.

[205] (Seidlmayer, The Relative Chronology of the First Intermediate Period, 2006), 165.

[206] (Gardiner, 1961), 438.

[207] (Gardiner, 1961), 438.

[208] (Seidlmayer, The Relative Chronology of the First Intermediate Period, 2006), 162.

[209] (Seidlmayer, The Relative Chronology of the First Intermediate Period, 2006), 165.

[210] (Seidlmayer, The Relative Chronology of the First Intermediate Period, 2006), 166.

[211] (Gardiner, 1961), 67.

[212] (Seidlmayer, The Relative Chronology of the First Intermediate Period, 2006), 167.

[213] (Seidlmayer, The Relative Chronology of the First Intermediate Period, 2006), 167.

[214] (Hayes, 1970), 181.

[215] (Gardiner, 1961), 112.

[216] (Seidlmayer, The Relative Chronology of the First Intermediate Period, 2006), 165.

[217] (Gardiner, 1961), 438.

[218] (Gardiner, 1961), 438.

[219] (Gardiner, 1961), 438.

[220] Genesis 6:1–3.

[221] (Gardiner, 1961), 438.

[222] (Gardiner, 1961), 438; (Cambridge Ancient History, 1971), Vol I Part 2B, 996.

[223] (Baud, 2006), 75.

[224] (Krauss & Warburton, 2006), 482.

[225] (Gardiner, 1961), 109.

[226] Although the Hebrew and Greek texts agree on those life spans, they disagree as to how old several of the patriarchs were when the next patriarch was born. In several instances, the Septuagint adds an additional hundred years before the birth of the next patriarch. As a result, the Septuagint has a much earlier date for Creation than the Hebrew text.

[227] (Josephus, Jewish Antiquities, 1930, reprinted 1991) I.82–88. The traditional Whitson translation appears to insert 777 years, apparently correcting the Josephus text. This citation is to the Loeb Classical Library edition, which provides the underlying Greek text along with the more accurate English translation of 707 years.

[228] By source documents, I don't mean the original biblical text, which was obviously written before both the Septuagint and Josephus, but rather the specific documents that are the source of the current text used in our modern bibles.

[229] Genesis 5:29.

[230] Genesis 4:24.

[231] (Kitchen K. A., 1999), 245.

[232] (Gardiner, 1961), 439, n 7.

[233] (Parker, The Sothic Dating of the Twelfth and Eighteenth Dynasties, 1977), 188-89.

[234] (Gardiner, 1961), 419, but Gardiner wrote before the discovery of the 13-year reign for Amenemhe IV, so I have extended his end date by four years.

[235] (Gardiner, 1961), 438.

[236] (Shaw, 2000), 139.

[237] (Hayes, 1970), 181.

[238] (Parker, The Sothic Dating of the Twelfth and Eighteenth Dynasties, 1977), 186.

[239] (Gardiner, 1961), 75.

[240] (Waddell, 1940; reprint 1980), 109, 115.

[241] See, for example, (Shaw, 2000), 484; (Gardiner, 1961), 443; (Hornung, The New Kingdom, 2006), 198; (Beckerath, 1997), 189.

[242] (Hornung, The New Kingdom, 2006), 199.

[243] (Gardiner, 1961), 443.

[244] (Wente & Van Siclen III, 1977), 225

[245] (Gardiner, 1961), 136.

[246] (Hayes, 1970), 479.

[247] (Shaw, 2000), 139.

[248] (Kitchen K. A., 1999), 245.

[249] Some Egyptologists would date the start of the Second Intermediate Period to that point in the Thirteenth Dynasty when Egyptian hegemony over the country ended. The earlier portion of the dynasty would then be considered a direct continuation of the Middle Kingdom.

[250] (Waddell, 1940; reprint 1980), 85. Josephus says that one copy of Manetho translates Hyksos as "Shepherd-kings" while another copy says it means "captive-kings." Josephus adopts the "Shepherd-Kings" translation and his usage has influenced many subsequent discussions of the Hyksos period.

[251] (Gardiner, 1961), 156.

[252] (O' Connor, 1997), 48.

[253] (Hayes, 1970), 186.

[254] (Gardiner, 1961), 440.

[255] (Gardiner, 1961), 440.

[256] (Ryholt, 1997), 294. Ryholt contends that Amenemhe IV was not of royal blood and may have imposed himself on Amenemhe III as coregent. Sebeknofru, however, was a descendant of Amenemhe III. But Sebeknofru's two immediate successors, he says, were sons of Amenemhe IV. Thus, there appears to have been political rivalries between the families of Amenemhe III and Amenemhe IV, with Sobeknofru temporarily seizing the throne back for Amenemhe III's family but losing the throne to Amenemhe IV's family after her death.

[257] (Ryholt, 1997), 294.

[258] (Gardiner, 1961), 148.

[259] (Gardiner, 1961), 148.

[260] (Gardiner, 1961), 148.

[261] (Gardiner, 1961), 148.

[262] (Gardiner, 1961), 148.

[263] (Gardiner, 1961), 442.

[264] (Gardiner, 1961), 442.

[265] (Redford, Pharaohnic King-lists, Annals and Day-books: A Contribution to the Study of the Egyptian Sense of History, 1986), 106–107.

[266] Redford, Egypt, Canaan, and Israel in Ancient Times, 106.

[267] (Hayes, 1970), 44.

[268] (Hayes, 1970), 44.

[269] (Hayes, 1970), 44.

[270] (Kitchen K. A., 1999), 85.

[271] (O' Connor, 1997), 48.

[272] (Kitchen K. , 1996), 7.

[273] Since the Twelfth Dynasty, ironically, ends earlier in the low chronology (1795) than in the high chronology (1782), the low chronology dates the break to an earlier date.

[274] (Gardiner, 1961), 166–67.

[275] (James, 1973), 292.

[276] (Gardiner, 1961), 158.

[277] (Gardiner, 1961), 158.

[278] (Hayes, 1970), 60.

[279] (Gardiner, 1961), 258.

[280] (Gardiner, 1961), 165.

[281] (Gardiner, 1961), 165.

[282] (Hayes, 1970), 52.

[283] Sharuhen is often referred to as Sile, an alternative spelling preferred by some scholars.

[284] See, for example, (Goedicke, 1986).

[285] (Gardiner, 1961), 168–69.

[286] (O' Connor, 1997), 45.

[287] (Gardiner, 1961), 168–69.

[288] (Hayes, 1970), 63.

[289] (Waddell, 1940; reprint 1980), 83.

[290] Genesis 10:25.

[291] (Speiser, 1962), 70, n. 25.

[292] (Gardiner, 1961), 151, 440.

[293] (Gardiner, 1961), 151, 440.

[294] (Beckerath, 1997), 189.

[295] (Kitchen K. A., 1999), 85.

[296] (Hayes, 1970), 187; (Wente & Van Siclen III, 1977), 223.

[297] (Wente & Van Siclen III, 1977), 223.

[298] (Wente & Van Siclen III, 1977), 223.

[299] (Wente & Van Siclen III, 1977), 223.

[300] (Wente & Van Siclen III, 1977), 223.

[301] (Wente & Van Siclen III, 1977), 223.

[302] (Wente & Van Siclen III, 1977), 225; (Gardiner, 1961), 443; (Hornung, The New Kingdom, 2006), 200.

[303] (Gardiner, 1961), 443.

[304] (Wente & Van Siclen III, 1977), 218.

[305] (Wente & Van Siclen III, 1977), 227.

[306] (Wente & Van Siclen III, 1977), 227.

[307] (Hornung, The New Kingdom, 2006), 200.

[308] (Gardiner, 1961), 443.

[309] (Gardiner, 1961), 443.

[310] (Hornung, The New Kingdom, 2006), 203.

[311] (Hornung, The New Kingdom, 2006),203

[312] (Hayes, 1970). 313.

[313] (Hayes, 1970). 313.

[314] (Redford, Akhenaten, the Heretic King, 1984), 17.

[315] (Redford, Akhenaten, the Heretic King, 1984), 17.

[316] (Gardiner, 1961), 179.

[317] (Hayes, 1970). 313.

[318] (Gardiner, 1961), 180.

[319] (Hayes, 1970), 319.

[320] (Hayes, 1970), 319.

[321] (Hayes, 1970), 319.

[322] (Hayes, 1970), 313.

[323] (Hayes, 1970), 313–14.

[324] (Hayes, 1970), 314.

[325] Genesis 41:1–4.

[326] Genesis 41:5–7.

[327] Genesis 41:34–36.

[328] Genesis 41:46.

[329] Genesis 47:13–26.

[330] (Hornung, The New Kingdom, 2006), 203.

[331] (Wente & Van Siclen III, 1977), 225; (Gardiner, 1961), 443; (Hornung, The New Kingdom, 2006), 200.

[332] (Wente & Van Siclen III, 1977), 218.

[333] (Waddell, 1940; reprint 1980), 5.

[334] (Waddell, 1940; reprint 1980), 11.

[335] (Siculus, 1948, reprinted 1968), I:26,1-5.

[336] (Waddell, 1940; reprint 1980), 4, n. 2

Bibliography

Baud, M. (2006). The Relative Chronology in Dynasties 6 and 8. In E. Hornung, R. Krauss, & D. Warburton, *Ancient Egyptian Chronology* (pp. 148-158). Leiden;Boston: Brill.

Beckerath, J. v. (1997). *Chronolgie Des Pharaonischen Aegypten*. Mainzam Rhein: von Zabern.

Cambridge Ancient History. (1971). Cambridge: Cambridge University Press.

Clagett, M. (1995). *Ancient Egyptian Science, Volume II: Calendars, Clocks, and Astronomy*. Philadelphia: American Philosophical Society.

Edgerten, W. F. (1942). Chronology of the Twelfth Dynasty. *JNES*.

Emery, W. B. (1987). *Archaic Egypt*. Harmondsworth: Penguin.

Freedman, D. N. (Ed.). (1992). *Anchor Bible Dictionary*. New York: Doubleday.

Gardiner, S. A. (1961). *Egypt of the Pharaohs*. Oxford: Oxford University Press.

Goedicke, H. (1986). The End of the Hyksos in Egypt. In L. H. Lesko (Ed.), *Egyptological Studies in Honor of Richard A. Parker* (pp. 37-48). Hanover; London: Brown University Press.

Greenberg, G. (1995). Manetho's 7th and 8th Dynasties: A Puzzle Solved. *The SSEA Journal, XXV*, 50-55.

Greenberg, G. (2003). *Manetho, a Study in Egyptyian Chronology: How ancient scribes garbled an accurate chronology of dynastic Egypt*. Warren Center: Shangri-la Publications.

Hayes, W. C. (1970). Chronology 1. Egypt--To the End of the Twelfth Dynasty. In *Cambridge Ancient History 1:1*. Cambridge: University of Cambridge Press.

Herodotus. (1972, reprinted 1978, 1980). *Herodotus*. (A. de Selincourt, Trans.) New York: Penguin Classics Edituion.

Hornung, E. (2006). The New Kingdom. In E. Hornung, R. Krause, & D. A. Warburton, *Ancient Egyptian Chronology* (pp. 197-217). Leiden; Boston: Brill.

Hornung, E., Krauss, R., & Warburton, D. A. (Eds.). (2006). *Ancient Egyptian Chronology*. Leiden; Boston: Brill.

James, T. G. (1973). Egypt from the Expulsion of the Hyksos to Amenophis I. In *Cambridge Ancient History* (Vol. II:1, pp. 289-312). Cambridge: Cambridge University Press.

Josephus. (1930, reprinted 1991). *Jewish Antiquities* (Vols. Books I-IV). (H. S. Thackeray, Trans.) Cambridge, Massachusetts: Harvard University.

Josephus. (1987). *The works of Josephus: complete and unabridged.* (W. Whitson, Ed., & W. Whitson, Trans.) Peabody: Hendrickson.

Kitchen, K. (1996). The Historical Chronology of Ancient Egypt, a current assesment. In K. Randsborg (Ed.), *Absolute Chronology, Archaeological Europe 2500-500BC, Acta Archaeological Supplemta I, (appearing simultaneously as Acta Archaologica 67 (1996/1997))*. Copenhagen.

Kitchen, K. A. (1999). Book Review of Chronologie des PharaonischenAegypten by J. Beckareth. *Journal of Egyptian Archaeology, 85*, 245.

Krauss, R., & Warburton, D. A. (2006). Conclusions. In E. Hornung, R. Krauss, Warburton, & David (Eds.), *Ancient Egyptian Chronology* (pp. 473-489). Ledien; Boston: Brill.

O' Connor, D. (1997). The Hyksos. In E. D. Oren, & E. D. Oren (Ed.), *The Hyksos: New Historical and Archaeological Evidence* (p. 48). University Museum, University of Pennsylyvania.

Parker, R. A. (1950). The Calendars of Ancient Egypt. *Studies in Ancient Oriental Civilization*(26).

Parker, R. A. (1977, January 12th). The Sothic Dating of the Twelfth and Eighteenth Dynasties. *Studies in Ancient Oriental Civilization*(39), 177-189.

Pritrchard, J. B. (1969). *Ancient Near Eastern Texts relating to the Old Testament* (Third Edition with Supplement ed.). Princeton: Prinston University Press.

Redford, D. B. (1984). *Akhenaten, the Heretic King.* Princeton: Princeton University Press.

Redford, D. B. (1986). *Pharaohnic King-lists, Annals and Day-books: A Contribution to the Study of the Egyptian Sense of History.* Mississauga: BenBen Publications.

Ryholt, K. S. (1997). *The Political Situation in Egypt During the Second Intermediate Period.* Copenhagen: Museum Tusculanum Press.

Ryken, L. W. (2000). *Dictionary of Biblical Imagery* (electronic ed. ed.). Downers Grove, IL: InterVarsity Press.

Seidlmayer, S. J. (2006). Dynasty 3. In E. Hornung, R. Krauss, D. A. Warburton, E. Hornung, R. Krauss, & D. Warburton (Eds.), *Ancient Egyptian Chronology* (pp. 116-123). Leiden; Boston: Brill.

Seidlmayer, S. J. (2006). The Relative Chronology of the First Intermediate Period. In E. Hornung, R. Krauss, & D. A. Warburton, *Ancinet Egyptian Chronology* (pp. 159-167). Leiden;Boston: Brill.

Shaw, I. (2000). *Oxford History of Ancient Egypt.* New York: Oxford University Press.

Siculus, D. (1948, reprinted 1968). *Diodorus of Sicily* (Vol. I). (C. H. Oldfather, Trans.) Cambridge: Loeb Classical Libraray.

Smith, W. S. (1971). The Old KIngdom in Egypt and the Beginning of the First Intermediate Period. In I. E. Edwards (Ed.), *The Cambridge Ancient History, I:2A* (pp. 145-207). Cambridge: Cambridge University Press.

Speiser, E. A. (1962). *Genesis: a new translation with introduction and commentary.* New York;London: Doubleday.

Strong, J. (2001). *Enhanced Strong's Lexicon.* Bellingham, WA: Logos Bible Software.

The Holy Bible: New Revised Standard Version. (1989). Nashville: Thomas Nelson Publishers.

Verner, M. (2001, August). Archaeological Remarks on the 4th and 5th Dynasty Chronology. *Archiv Orientalni, 69*(3), 363-418.

Verner, M. (2001, August). Archaeological Remarks on the 4th and 5th Dynasty Chronology. *Archiv Orientalni, 69*(3).

Verner, M. (2006). Dynasties 4 to 5. In E. Hornung, R. Krauss, & D. Warburton (Eds.), *Ancient Egyptian Chronology*. Leiden, Boston: Brill.

Waddell, W. G. (1940; reprint 1980). *Manetho*. (W. G. Waddell, Ed., & W. G. Waddell, Trans.) Cambridge: Harvard University Press, Loeb Classical Library.

Wente, E. F., & Van Siclen III, C. C. (1977, January 12). A Chronology of the New Kingdom. *Studies in Ancient Oriental Civilization*(39), 217-261.

About the Author

Gary Greenberg has authored several books on biblical and Egyptological matters, including the popular biblical classic, *101 Myths of the Bible* (Sourcebooks, 2000), translated into several foreign editions. Other books include *Proving Jesus' Authority in Mark and John* (Cambridge Scholars Publishing, 2018), a highly-praised academic study on the literary relationship between these two gospels; *The Judas Brief* (Continuum, 2007), a scholarly critique of the historical accuracy of the gospel Passion accounts; *The Moses Mystery: the African Origins of the Jewish People* (Birch Lane, 1996, republished in several editions and different titles, including foreign translations); *King David, a new history* (Sourcebooks, 2002); and *Manetho, a study in Egyptian Chronology* (Shangri-la, 2003), the only systematic reconstruction of Manetho's historically important third century BCE account of Egyptian dynastic chronology. He was a co-contributor with Richard Dawkins and others to *Everything You Know about God is Wrong* (Disinformation, 2007).

In addition to his several books, Greenberg has published articles in academic journals, including peer-reviewed articles on Manetho's chronology in the *Journal of the Society for the Study of Egyptian Antiquities*. and he presented papers at several distinguished conferences, including those of the International Society of Biblical Literature, regional meetings of the Society for Biblical Literature, the annual American Research Center in Egypt, and the triennial International Congress of Egyptologists. He was President of the Biblical Archaeology Society of New York for over fifteen years and lectured there and in other forums on a regular basis. He served as a consultant to the National Geographic Television Series *Science of the Bible*. He maintains a web site at **www.biblemyth.com**, where you can find a more extensive account of his books, articles and academic papers. He also blogs on biblical matters at **www.biblemythhistory.com.**

Academic Praise for Greenberg's Books

David Noel Freeman, a leading biblical scholar and former editor of the *Anchor Bible* and the *Anchor Bible Dictionary*, described Greenberg's biography of King David as "a worthy addition to the library of first-rate and challenging books on King David." *Catholic Biblical Quarterly*, in a review of *The Judas* Brief, says that Greenberg has "a keen eye for the ways religious and political motives have shaped the story of Jesus' arrest and execution. . . Greenberg presses important historical questions and rightly insists on fresh consideration of the evidence." The prominent Egyptologist, **Frank Yurco**, referring to Greenberg's book on Manetho, wrote, **"An excellent and well-written analysis that makes a valuable contribution to** the study of Egyptian chronology and king-lists." **Aidan Dodson**, another prominent Egyptologist, called Greenberg's Manetho study "An intriguing approach to a long-debated problem." **Paul Anderson**, a leading Johannine scholar, described Greenberg's *Proving Jesus's Authority in Mark and John* as an "engaging new approach." Markan scholar **Adam Winn**, wrote about the same book, "This careful and erudite comparison of Mark and John should be read by any engaged in the field of comparative gospel studies." **James Tabor**, the well-known biblical scholar described *Proving Jesus' Authority* as a "fascinating new book." **Barrie Wilson**, a scholar of early Christianity, called Greenberg "a superb literary detective, following up on tantalizing clues in ancient texts to uncover sources and insights that others have missed."

Excerpts from various book reviews

- "[Greenberg has] a keen eye for the ways religious and political motives have shaped the story of Jesus' arrest and execution, and acceptance of certain historical elements of canonical accounts . . . Greenberg presses important historical questions and rightly insists on fresh consideration of the evidence." (*Catholic Biblical Quarterly*)

- "seems to delight in a game of scholarly 'gotcha." (*NY Times*)
- "Placing these texts into their historical, political, and geographical setting, Greenberg is able to separate much historical fact from biblical fiction." (Library Journal)
- "fascinating and thought provoking" (*Today's Librarian*)
- "guaranteed to raise hackles and lively debate" (*Denver Post*)
- "ingenious" (*St. Louis Post-Dispatch*)
- "intriguing and controversial" *Multi-cultural Review*"
- "a riveting read" (*Florence SC News*)
- "a must read" (*The Tennessee Tribune*)
- "will make for lively dinner table discussions" (*Spokesman-Review*)
- "will make you think" (*Green Bay Press-Gazette*).
- "insightful and valuable" (*KMT Magazine*)
- "offers compelling new evidence that changes our perceptions— turns David, in essence, from a mythological figure into a living breathing human being." (*Book Loons*)
- "offers a carefully researched survey of the landmark events of Egyptian history. Straightforward writing adds life to the trek through years and centuries, in this fascinating study of dynasties, war, achievements, and lasting cultural legacy." (*Midwest Book Review*)
- In this controversial new book, author Gary Greenberg offers insight into the meaning, origin and accuracy of stories from the Old Testament. (*The Jewish Transcript*)
- Rated "Must Read." (*Today's Books*)

Greenberg holds a Juris Doctor degree in Law from Seton Hall University and a B.A. Degree in Mathematics from Brooklyn College. He practiced Criminal Defense law in New York City for the Legal Aid Society. In 2003 he received the Freedom Award from the Korean Immigrant Services of New York in recognition of his trial work. In 1973 he was a candidate for District Attorney of New York County. He has also published several articles on law and public policy issues and authored a book on computer programming.

Over the years Mr. Greenberg has been a well-received guest on many radio and television shows across the country, where he has been recognized as an articulate and engaging speaker on biblical issues, a highly-effective debater, and often ready with a quick quip. His appearances on radio call-in shows usually result in nonstop listener responses.

Index

PERESET PRESS

If you enjoyed this book, please consider submitting a review on the Amazon web site, even if it is just to give it a star rating. You might also enjoy some of my other books published by Pereset Press, so I placed a few book ads on the following pages.

I currently maintain a blog site at **www.biblemythhistory.com.** My primary (but not exclusive) focus there will be on problem **areas** in biblical studies, both Jewish and Christian, that either remain unresolved in academic circles or that I believe need to be reconsidered from a new perspective. My main areas of concern are source criticism, outside influences, historical credibility of scriptures, and chronological issues.

I also have a website at **www.biblemyth.com** that contains more information on my writings and ideas, including several articles and papers presented at conferences.

THE MOSES MYSTERY
The Egyptian Origins of the Jewish People

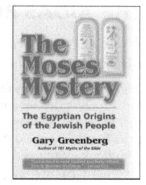

What do history and archaeology really say about the origins of ancient Israel?

The Egyptian Origins of the Jewish People

Gary Greenberg
Author of *101 Myths of the Bible*

   Although the bible says that Israel's formative history took place in ancient Egypt, biblical scholars and Egyptologists have steadfastly refused to explore the role of Egyptian history and literature on the origins of Jewish religion. *The Moses Mystery* attempts to set the record straight. Based on extensive research into biblical and Egyptian history, archaeology, literature and mythology Greenberg argues that the first Israelites were Egyptians, followers of the monotheistic teachings of Pharaoh Akhenaten.

Some of the many intriguing revelations in *The Moses Mystery* include:

- Ancient Egyptian records specifically identify Moses as Akhenaten's chief priest and describe the Exodus as the result of a civil war for control over the Egyptian throne

- Abraham, Isaac, and Jacob were characters from Egyptian mythology

- The Twelve Tribes of Israel never existed

> *Mr. Greenberg seems to delight in a game of scholarly "gotcha."* —N.Y. TIMES

> *An ingenious comparison of Biblical and Egyptian history.* — ST. LOUIS POST-DISPATCH

> *A must read for those interested in biblical scholarship.* —TENNESSEE TRIBUNE

> *Insightful and valuable.* —KMT MAGAZINE

ISBN 978-0-9814966-0-3

PERESET PRESS

THE JUDAS BRIEF

Judas did not betray Jesus.
He tried to save his teacher's life.

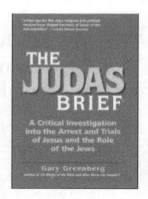

The Judas Brief offers the first full-scale
historically-based rebuttal to Gospel accusations
that Judas betrayed Jesus and that the Jewish
priesthood demanded that Pilate crucify him.
This book examines the roles of Judas, Pilate, and
Herod Antipas in the execution of Jesus as a threat
against Roman order.

Some astonishing revelations from The Judas Brief

- Pre-Gospel Christians did not believe that Judas betrayed Jesus.

- Pontius Pilate's contemporaries described him as a cruel corrupt
  murderer who tolerated no disagreement from Jewish leaders and
  brutally suppressed any protest against his rulings.

- The chief Jewish priests had no political leverage over Pilate and little
  political support from the Jewish population.

- The only major Jewish leader who felt threatened by Jesus was Herod
  Antipas, who had beheaded John the Baptist for speaking out against
  Herod's wickedness.

- The Gospel of John radically differs from and contradicts the other
  three Gospels regarding the events leading up to the arrest of Jesus.

> *"Presses important historical questions and rightly insists on a fresh
> consideration of the evidence."*—CATHOLIC BIBLICAL QUARTERLY"

> *"This well-documented work . . . presents some interesting history."*
> —LIBRARY JOURNAL

ISBN 978-0-9814966-4-1

PERESET PRESS

WHO WROTE THE GOSPELS?
Why New Testament Scholars Challenge Church Traditions

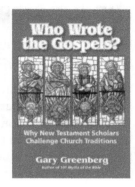

By Gary Greenberg

*Matthew, Mark, Luke and John
Did Not Write the Gospels . . .*

. . . at least, not according to modern New Testament scholarship. The evidence shows that all four Gospels were written anonymously, and for almost two centuries after they were completed early Christians had no idea who wrote them.

Some Of The Fascinating Topics Covered In Who Wrote The Gospels

- What is the Synoptic Problem and how do scholars resolve it?
- What is the mysterious Q source that influenced Matthew and Luke?
- Is there a literary relationship between the Gospels of Mark and John?
- Did the original Gospel of Mark depict the resurrection of Jesus?
- What manuscripts stand behind our modern Gospel texts and how accurate are they?
- When scholars encounter contradictory ancient Gospel manuscripts, how do they decide which text comes closest to the original?

"Who Wrote the Gospels?" is a fascinating study of early Christianity and the creation of the New Testament. —Midwest Book Review

ISBN 978-0-9814966-3-4

PERESET PRESS

THE JUDAS BRIEF

Judas did not betray Jesus.
He tried to save his teacher's life.

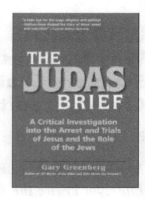

The Judas Brief offers the first full-scale historically-based rebuttal to Gospel accusations that Judas betrayed Jesus and that the Jewish priesthood demanded that Pilate crucify him. This book examines the roles of Judas, Pilate, and Herod Antipas in the execution of Jesus as a threat against Roman order.

Some astonishing revelations from The Judas Brief

- Pre-Gospel Christians did not believe that Judas betrayed Jesus.

- Pontius Pilate's contemporaries described him as a cruel corrupt murderer who tolerated no disagreement from Jewish leaders and brutally suppressed any protest against his rulings.

- The chief Jewish priests had no political leverage over Pilate and little political support from the Jewish population.

- The only major Jewish leader who felt threatened by Jesus was Herod Antipas, who had beheaded John the Baptist for speaking out against Herod's wickedness.

- The Gospel of John radically differs from and contradicts the other three Gospels regarding the events leading up to the arrest of Jesus.

"Presses important historical questions and rightly insists on a fresh consideration of the evidence."—CATHOLIC BIBLICAL QUARTERLY"

"This well-documented work . . . presents some interesting history."
—LIBRARY JOURNAL

ISBN 978-0-9814966-4-1

PERESET PRESS

CPSIA information can be obtained
at www.ICGtesting.com
Printed in the USA
LVHW010521200723
752659LV00010B/141